About the Editor

Bill Fawcett is the author and editor of more than a dozen books, including *You Did What?* and *How to Lose a Battle*. He is also the author and editor of three historical mystery series and two oral histories of the U.S. Navy SEALS. He lives in Illinois.

YOU SAID WHAT?

ALSO BY BILL FAWCETT

Hunters & Shooters

How to Lose a Battle

You Did What?

It Seemed Like a Good Idea

COMING SOON

Oval Office Oddities

YOU SAID WHAT?

LIES AND PROPAGANDA THROUGHOUT HISTORY

EDITED BY

BILL FAWCETT

HARPER

NEW YORK • LONDON • TORONTO • SYDNEY

HARPER

HarperCollins books may be purchased for educational, business, or sales promotional use. For information please write: Special Markets Department, HarperCollins Publishers, 10 East 53rd Street, New York, NY 10022.

FIRST EDITION

Library of Congress Cataloging-in-Publication Data is available upon request.

ISBN: 978-0-06-113050-2
ISBN-10: 0-06-113050-8

07 08 09 10 11 OV/RRD 10 9 8 7 6 5 4 3 2 1

Dedicated to the memory of
James Patrick Baen,
the most honest person I have known

CONTENTS

INTRODUCTION

So Many Lies, so Few Pages

So many lies, so few pages. When this book was proposed there was no shortage of lies, deceptions, and frauds great and small to use as examples. The fact is that the lies told in an era give us some real insights into history. So this book could be a deep study of the philosophical ramifications of deceptions on historical, um . . . okay, you got me. It isn't philosophical anything. We did this book because lies, when you are not the one caught telling them, anyhow, are both fascinating and fun. They do tell you a lot—mostly that some of the greatest leaders in history should be embarrassed. So we looked at all those uncounted thousands of lies that have been told to us and to those who came before us and came up with what follows, the story of some of the strangest, best known, and darkest lies. You are even likely to find a few lies here that you thought were truths. (Hint, I threw out my coonskin cap, and it wasn't to please the terrorists at PETA.) This selection of lies from history are fun and interesting—and a few will simply amaze you that anyone ever believed them. Their topics run the gamut from war and politics to medicine and crime. Oh, and it's safe to leave this book in the bathroom or take it to the office. We carefully did not cover the lies lovers and married couples tell each other and will leave to you all of those deceptions perpetrated by our current leaders.

Some of the lies we include caused great pain, others great embarrassment. Through the perspective of history it may seem strange that anyone, occasionally just about everyone who heard them, believed some of the whoppers in this book. Still they "made sense at the time." There are some lies people just want to believe. Other lies are accepted because no one knows better. Many lies are successful simply because the liar is so good at telling them.

This book is written in many small sections. It really is meant to be picked up, put down, read while commuting. It may make you think, it might even outrage you a few times, and it will occasionally elicit a chuckle or two. When editing this book, it has been tempting to draw conclusions about the nature of truth and the state of man from its contents, but I will leave that to those of you so inclined. That said, while the intent of this book is to entertain, no one who has contributed to it will be upset if you view the lies we are hearing and accepting today with a little more skepticism. That said, to get us off to a roaring start and because it just has to be in a book on lying somewhere, so needing no introduction here it is:

"I did not have sex with that woman" (President William Jefferson Clinton).

Bill Fawcett
Editor

POLITICS

How can you tell a politician is lying?
His mouth is moving . . .

A joke that likely first appeared sometime during the Sumerian Empire.

"I am not a crook" (Richard Nixon, 1956).

(He should have added "yet.")

Lesson one: If you are going to lie, don't record the truth.

WATERGATE

The Great American Scandal

Peter Archer

The biggest political scandal in American history began with a lie and contained so many different lies told by so many different people that it's almost impossible to keep track of who *wasn't* lying. Looking back on the affair, the curious thing is that Richard Nixon, hailed by many as the consummate American politician, made so many missteps—mistakes that ultimately led to his resignation in August 1974. Yet had Nixon been able to pull himself free of an almost pathological fear of the truth, he might have ended the scandal almost before it began.

The events that were to consume the national consciousness for two years began in the early morning hours of June 17, 1972, when a security guard at the Watergate hotel in Washington, D.C., noticed tape over the lock of an entry door. He removed the tape, but when, an hour or so later, he found it had been replaced, he called the police. An unmarked squad car responded, and the cops swiftly searched the building's offices. In the suite housing the national headquarters of the Democratic Party, they arrested five men wearing business suits and surgical gloves, carrying photographic equipment and walkie-talkies.

Clearly this was no ordinary burglary, but the D.C. police weren't sure what they had. One of the men, James McCord, identified himself as a "security consultant" who had just left government service.

"What service?" the judge later asked.

"CIA," McCord answered.

Later that day, it was revealed that McCord's security consulting had been done for the Nixon reelection campaign, then in full swing.

John Mitchell, former attorney general of the United States and chairman of the Committee to Reelect the President (CRP), announced, "We want to emphasize that this man and the other people involved were not operating on either our behalf or with our consent. There is no place in our campaign or in the electoral process for this type of activity, and we will not permit or condone it." The statement is notable for being the first major lie of Watergate.

On the surface, there seemed to be no reason for Mitchell not to be telling the truth. By June it was clear that the Democratic presidential candidate that fall would be George McGovern, considered by most analysts to be the weakest opponent Nixon could face. Nixon's campaign committee had already raised vast sums of money and had a highly efficient and ruthless campaign organization in place, ready for the post-convention season of campaigning.

What no one outside a small circle of White House officials knew was that Watergate was merely part of a larger program of dirty tricks, spying, and political sabotage organized by Nixon's aides. Nixon especially feared a Ted Kennedy candidacy, and he was willing to do anything to avoid it.

The spy campaign had first been organized around a plan proposed by a young Republican activist, Thomas Charles Huston. The

"Huston Plan," as it came to be known, was personally approved by Nixon and included spying on political opponents through illegal wiretaps, mail opening, and burglary, as well as drawing up plans to intern thousands of dissenters in the event of a national emergency. Shortly after approving the plan, though, Nixon rescinded his approval, and the Huston Plan was quietly put on the shelf.

The second plan of operation was code-named GEMSTONE and was drawn up by G. Gordon Liddy, a White House aide with a fascination for the world of spies and secret intelligence. Liddy's plan included "black bag jobs" (burglaries), bugging, and even less savory ideas. (Part of the plan suggested that leaders of the protests at the Republican National Convention should be kidnapped, drugged, and spirited over the border to Mexico.) Liddy and his backers presented the plan to John Mitchell. Though Mitchell later testified that he was "aghast" at the plan, he gave no indication of this at the time, and his underlings began to carry out elements of it.

At the same time, Nixon himself, furious at the leaking of the Pentagon Papers study of the war in Vietnam, raged against Daniel Ellsberg, a military analyst employed by the RAND Corporation, who had leaked the papers. With Nixon's knowledge, if not exactly his consent, operatives broke into the office of Ellsberg's psychiatrist, Dr. Lewis Fielding, hunting for information that could be used to discredit Ellsberg.

Nixon also grew increasingly paranoid about leaks from the administration to the press. Under the direction of Charles Colson, one of the president's advisers on domestic policy, Liddy and a compatriot, E. Howard Hunt, a former CIA operative, formed a unit within the White House to seek out and prevent leaks. When one of those affiliated with the unit told his mother-in-law about it, she joked that now they had a plumber in the family. From that remark, the unit was named the Plumbers.

Watergate, therefore, was simply part of a much larger plan designed to disconcert and upset Nixon's political opponents. Much of the plan came under the direction of Jeb Stuart Magruder. Typical of the young men working in the Nixon White House, Magruder was bright, fanatically devoted to Nixon, and beholden to the White House chief of staff H. R. Haldeman. It was Haldeman who had picked Magruder to be the first director of CRP, thus setting in motion the events that led to Watergate.

When Magruder was replaced by Mitchell, the younger man kept his new boss, Haldeman, in the loop, though Mitchell rarely knew the details of what was being done against "the opposition."

Liddy and Hunt recruited a group of Cuban anti-Castro activists and a mercenary named Frank Sturgis, who had trained Cubans for action in the Bay of Pigs invasion in 1961, as well as the ex-CIA man McCord, to carry out the burglary at the Democratic National Headquarters. When the burglars were caught, their handlers panicked. Liddy told his wife, "There was trouble. Some people got caught. I'll probably be going to jail." He began shredding documents and records having to do with the Plumbers and their secrets.

Hunt was caught when someone noticed that one of the Cubans arrested had an address book that contained the name and phone number of Howard E. Hunt and a notation: "W. House." Reporter Bob Woodward of the *Washington Post,* whose name, along with that of his colleague Carl Bernstein, would become forever linked to the Watergate story, called the phone number and confirmed that Hunt knew the burglars. Hunt was arrested, and he and Liddy would later both be indicted in connection with the burglary.

Woodward and Bernstein gained a second important lead when they discovered that a cashier's check to the order of Kenneth Dahlberg had made its way into the bank account of Bernard Barker, one of the burglars. Dahlberg, it turned out, was a major fund-raiser for Nixon. He claimed to have no idea how the check, money he'd raised for the campaign, had ended up in Barker's account, telling Woodward that he had turned the check over to CRP.

By now, within the White House itself, the cover-up of the burglars' connection to Nixon's campaign was in full swing. Those who were part of the crime justified their lies to themselves and to others by claiming there were bigger issues involved. Magruder later wrote, "We were not covering up a burglary; we were safeguarding world peace." Surely Nixon's work to establish a viable détente with the Soviet Union and China was more important than who broke in to see the Democrats' mail?

On August 29 at a news conference, Nixon himself said, "I can state categorically that no one in the White House staff, no one in this administration, presently employed, was involved in this very bizarre incident." In a prescient piece of irony, he went on to say, "What really hurts in matters of this sort is not the fact that they occur. . . . What really hurts is if you try to cover it up."

Nixon already knew the details of the emerging cover-up, though. As early as June 23, only six days after the burglary, Haldeman and Nixon had had a frank conversation about it in the Oval Office. Haldeman expressed concern that the FBI, under its new director, L. Patrick Gray, was "not under control . . . their investigation is now leading into some productive areas."

Nixon and Haldeman devised a plan whereby Vernon Walters, head of the CIA, would call Gray and warn him off, telling him that further investigation could expose CIA secrets. This was blatantly untrue, of course. At one point in the conversation, Nixon asked, "Did Mitchell know about this [the Watergate break-in]?" "I think so," Haldeman replied. "I don't think he knew the details, but he knew."

For aid in orchestrating the cover-up, Nixon and Haldeman turned to the White House Counsel, John Dean. Dean was put in charge of handing out hush money to Hunt, Liddy, and the other defendants, making sure they didn't talk about their other White House contacts. Nixon and Haldeman had several conversations about how to give clemency to the burglars, at one point suggesting that they could grant pardons to antiwar dissidents to pacify the Left.

Nixon's reelection by an overwhelming majority in November 1972 did not stop Watergate. The conspiracy was too big and involved too many people to work effectively. Dean ran from crisis to crisis, "putting your fingers in the dikes every time that leaks have sprung up here," as Nixon put it to him. On March 21, 1973, things came to a head. Dean met with the president and warned him that "these people are going to cost a million dollars over the next two years."

Calmly, Nixon discussed with his lawyer raising a million dollars to pay off the burglars and conspirators. Dean, in his own account, grew more and more uncomfortable with his role and warned the president of a "cancer that is gnawing away at the heart of the presidency." Then, the same month, McCord turned state's evidence, saying there had been political pressure applied to the defendants to plead guilty and keep silent. Dean resigned in April and began cooperating with the Ervin Committee, the committee empowered by the Senate to investigate Watergate. His testimony, giving details of how the cover-up had been orchestrated, held the country spellbound.

Throughout the spring of 1973 the committee hearings dragged on. Then, on July 13, Alexander Butterfield, who managed the paper flow in the Oval Office, testified that on Nixon's orders, the Oval Office and Cabinet Room had been bugged. The tapes, more than five thousand hours of conversation, were being held at the White House.

This was the beginning of the end. Everyone knew that the evidence of "what the president knew and when he knew it" as Senator Howard Baker put it, was on those tapes. Nixon engaged in a prolonged battle to keep the tapes confidential, a battle he lost before the Supreme Court a year after the tapes' existence had been revealed. The White House was forced to make public the June 23, 1972, tape in which Nixon and Haldeman conspired to use the CIA to limit the FBI investigation into Watergate. Most painfully, perhaps, Nixon had to admit to his own family on some level that he had lied to them, along with everyone else.

On August 4, 1974, facing certain impeachment by the House and conviction by the Senate, Richard Milhous Nixon became the first U.S. president to resign his office.

No one told more self-serving lies than Joseph Stalin. From "disappearing" commissars to rationalizing the destruction of entire ethnic groups, he justified his every action with lies repeated as THE TRUTH by a press he controlled.

STALIN'S BIG LIES

MOSCOW, 1936–1938

Peter Archer

To much of the world at the beginning of 1936, it must have appeared that Joseph Stalin had consolidated and stabilized his rule over the Soviet Union. His main enemy, Leon Trotsky, had been politically defeated and driven into exile seven years before. A coterie of fawning admirers and bureaucratic administrators surrounded the dictator, ruling the country and the Communist Party with an iron fist.

So, in August 1936, the world watched in amazement as Stalin launched a series of trials, through which he destroyed not only the leadership of the Party but also purged and destroyed the officer corps of the Red Army.

What was as surprising to many was the public aspect of the trials. They were not hidden away but were conducted in the full light of day, and the transcripts of their proceedings were made available on a daily basis to the world's press.

Still more astonishing were the statements made by the defendants. Men who had been among Lenin's closest associates, who had been members and leaders of the Communist Party for decades before its ascension to power, declared that they had in fact been working for foreign secret services. Some said they had attempted to assassinate Lenin, Stalin, and others, while some also said they had plotted with the exiled Trotsky to launch terrorist attacks within the country.

Finally, most astonishing of all—at least astonishing to us today—is that despite the obvious and provable falsehoods that were told during the trials, some by the defendants and others by the prosecution, many people, both in the USSR and in Communist Parties around the world, believed every word that came out of Stalin's mouth.

Four main purge trials were held. In August 1936, party leaders Gregory Zinoviev, Lev Kamenev, and fourteen others were tried as members of a "Trotskyite-Zinovievite terrorist center." In November and December of that year, seventeen more party officials were put on trial. In June 1937 the top officers of the Red Army were put on trial, accused of conspiracy, Trotskyism, and collaboration with Germany and Japan. Defendants in this trial included the Soviet chief of staff Michael Tukhachevsky. Finally, in March 1938, twenty-one party members were tried, including the well-known leader Nikolai Bukharin. The purge trials themselves precipitated a wider purge in the Party and in Soviet society, during which hundreds of thousands were imprisoned, tortured, exiled, and murdered.

The event that set the stage for the purge trials was the assassination in 1934 of Serge Kirov, a member of the Central Committee. Since his popularity was growing in the early 1930s, most historians now suspect that Stalin saw Kirov as a rival and ordered him killed. The murder was then blamed on a Trotskyite conspiracy, allowing Stalin to attack any other perceived threats to his eminence.

All the defendants were convicted, and most were executed. The purges destroyed virtually every member (save for Stalin) of Lenin's

Central Committee of the Party, the men and women who had led the 1917 revolution.

While on trial, the defendants confessed, often seeking to outdo each other in the fervor with which they denounced themselves. One said, "The facts revealed before this court show to the whole world that the organizer of this . . . counterrevolutionary terrorist bloc, its moving spirit, is Trotsky. . . . I am deeply oppressed by the thought that I became an obedient tool in [his] hands, an agent of the counterrevolution, and that I raised my arm against Stalin."

The prosecutor, Andrey Vyshinsky, accused representatives of Kamenev and Zinoviev of meeting Trotsky's son, Leon Sedov, at the Bristol Hotel in Copenhagen in 1932 to discuss in detail their plans to carry out terrorism in the Soviet Union. Unfortunately, a Danish newspaper pointed out that the hotel in question had been demolished long before 1932 and that on the day the meeting was alleged to have taken place, Sedov was taking a written exam at the Berlin Technical College.

Tukhachevsky was convicted largely on the basis of a letter he supposedly wrote to a German general in which he described plans to overthrow Stalin. It emerged later that the letter had been forged by Reinhardt Heydrich, leader of the Gestapo, who wanted to create dissension in the ranks of the Soviet army. He certainly succeeded.

Reading the transcripts of the trials today, it's easy to see that much of the "testimony" consisted either of Party members denouncing the defendants, or the defendants trying desperately to agree with every charge the prosecution hurled at them. The trials provided inspiration for later authors such as George Orwell in *1984* and Arthur Koestler in *Darkness at Noon.*

Curiously, though, there were many abroad who took the proceedings quite seriously. Within the Soviet Union, even such a prominent figure as the writer Maxim Gorky supported the government's tactics. The American ambassador, Joseph Davies, defended the trials in his book *Mission to Moscow,* later made into a film starring Walter Huston. A number of left-wing intellectuals in Europe declared that the trials were justified because the Soviet Union was fighting for its existence. Anyway, the claim ran, with so many defendants saying there had been a conspiracy, there probably had been one.

Trotsky, the only one of the defendants still at liberty, fought back. He was restrained by the conditions imposed on him by the government of Norway, where he was living in 1936, and could make no answers to the charges leveled against him in the first trial. The prosecutor, Vyshinsky, aware of Trotsky's situation, gleefully remarked that the charges against him must be true because if they weren't, Trotsky would have answered them.

The initial reply to the accusations came from Trotsky's son, Lyova, who published *The Red Book on the Moscow Trial* shortly after the first purge trial. After Trotsky moved from Norway to Mexico in January 1937, he was free to organize and publish his defense. His followers in the United States organized the American Committee for the Defense of Leon Trotsky, headed by the distinguished philosopher and educator John Dewey. The committee held hearings in Coyoacan, Mexico, in April 1937, at which Trotsky was allowed to testify and tell his own story, exposing a number of the falsehoods in the Moscow trials.

Trotsky's defense was attacked by Stalin's supporters, who accused him of giving aid and comfort to capitalist charges of Communist corruption. Many wrote that it was inadvisable to criticize the Soviet Union when it was under attack.

Stalin struck at Trotsky, his greatest enemy and one who had obsessed him for many decades, in 1940. In August of that year, an assassin entered Trotsky's study and drove an ice ax into the old revolutionary's head. His blood stained the manuscript pages of a biography of Stalin on which he was at work when he was struck down.

The broader purge of Soviet society carried out in the late 1930s was overseen by the People's Commissariat for Internal Affairs (NKVD). In the immediate wake of the Kirov assassination, half a million people were arrested. Many were deported without trial, and it was this period that saw the rise of what Alexander Solzhenitsyn would later call the Gulag Archipelago, the vast series of prison camps (GULAG is an acronym for the Russian term meaning Main Camp Administration) that spread, like a chain of islands, across the Soviet Union.

In the wake of the trials, Stalin and his henchmen began systematically to erase the existence of the defendants. Textbooks and histories of the Communist Party and the revolution were rewritten so as to downplay the role of figures such as Trotsky and Zinoviev and to improve the position of Stalin, who at the time of the 1917 revolution had been a comparatively minor figure in the Party's leadership. Photographs that showed disgraced leaders were retouched to remove the "unpersons."

In 1938, the Soviet government produced *History of the All-Union Communist Party: Short Course*. Stalin claimed authorship, though he probably wrote only part of it. The work was subsequently rewritten at intervals to remove the names of those who had fallen out of favor and to elevate the roles of those rising within the Party.

In the book, Stalin declared that he himself had stood by Lenin's side to lead the November 1917 revolution, not Trotsky, who was portrayed as resisting Lenin's call for a revolutionary uprising. This despite the fact that in November 1917, Trotsky had been head of the Military Revolutionary Committee that organized and led the uprising. In point of fact, in late 1917, Trotsky was probably better known to the Russian public than Lenin, as he was a far more dynamic speaker.

Trotsky had led the delegation that negotiated peace with Germany in 1918; Stalin's "history," however, accused Trotsky of sabotaging the peace talks, which then had to be rescued by Stalin's intervention. And so it went.

After Stalin's death in 1953, his successors engaged in their own struggle for power. Nikita Khrushchev emerged triumphant, and in a secret speech to a Party congress in 1956, he denounced some of Stalin's crimes and declared that the 1930s purge trials had been a "mistake." However, the Party history continued to be rewritten and rewritten to take account of the shifting sands of political fortune.

The Soviet government appears to have operated on the principle that He Who Holds the Guns Writes the History.

Ignorance or self-serving lies . . . you decide.

McKINLEY'S MISSIONARY POSITION

Joshua Spivak

"There was nothing left for us to do but to take them all, and to educate the Filipinos, and uplift and Christianize them. . . ."

—William McKinley

Never one to jump heedlessly out in front of an issue, William McKinley may have been one of the most indecisive American presidents. After taking the islands in the Spanish-American War, McKinley was in a bind as to whether the United States should keep the recently annexed colony of the Philippines or allow it to declare full independence. The United States, looking to assert its newfound status as a leading country, wanted the excellent naval bases in the Philippines to project its military might and help open up economic prospects in Asia, the world's largest marketplace.

After much vacillating, McKinley showed that he was not afraid to get up, stick a finger in the wind, and tell a whopper. According to presidential biographer Charles Olcott, McKinley, a devout Methodist, told a crowd, "There was nothing left for us to do but to take them all, and to educate the Filipinos, and uplift and Christianize them . . ."

Quite an achievement, especially since, after three hundred years of Spanish rule, about 90 percent of Filipinos were Christian.

LIKE NEARLY EVERY president in American history, McKinley was not chosen for his foreign policy acumen but for domestic considerations. Indeed, his 1896 electoral triumph over the fabled midwestern Populist William Jennings Bryan was based on questions of monetary policy, specifically whether to allow an inflationary system with the coinage of silver or, as McKinley held, to keep America on a strict gold standard. Foreign policy was barely considered, but by 1898, many leaders with their own well-funded bullhorns (such as Hearst and Pulitzer) were pressing for America to take its place as an imperial power, and a new situation presented a perfect opportunity for the country to gain a place on the world's stage.

Since the election, William Randolph Hearst's and Joseph Pulitzer's newspaper chains had been jointly pushing the story of Spain's harsh crackdown against a three-year-old Cuban insurrection. Cuba's latest uprising began in 1895 after Spain suspended constitutional guarantees, leading to a temporary unity among the bickering rebel groups and starting off a vicious war for independence. Many in America were chomping at the bit to go to war to defend freedom and liberate these poor souls. As an added bonus, America would kick Spain out of the United States' backyard and gain the benefits of liberating the rest of Spain's colonies.

For many of the nation's military and political leaders, a war with Spain had great potential benefit. The acquisition of overseas bases would help project America's nascent naval power far into the Pacific Rim. America had been looking to spread her wings internationally for a number of years, and ever since Alfred T. Mahan wrote his seminal work, *The Influence of Sea Power upon History*, these leaders had been salivating at the prospect of establishing naval bases throughout the world. Spain, with its weakened military might, shaky control over such properties, and recent gross violations of human rights—the Spanish can be credited with coining the term "concentration camps" in this war—was a perfect target.

As popular sentiment for the war increased, McKinley displayed his characteristic indecisiveness and natural wariness to get in front of an almost unsolvable problem. The Spanish were not about to leave Cuba, but their war to keep it was becoming increasingly brutal. Fortunately, other American leaders, such as Assistant Secretary of the Navy Teddy Roosevelt, were there to help by putting the navy on alert and transferring weapons from storage facilities to active military positions without the advice or consent of his boss or the president. All the debates and negotiations became irrelevant on February 16, 1898, when a curious explosion destroyed the USS *Maine*, in Havana Harbor to protect U.S. interests, and America was plunged into war.

The resulting Spanish-American War went swimmingly for the United States. Despite an incompetent secretary of defense, some massive failures in supply and logistics, and a great deal of death caused by yellow fever, in less than three months American forces basically ended Spain's three-centuries-long colonial rule in America. Though mainly seen as a result of Teddy Roosevelt's Rough Riders regiment and their charge up San Juan Hill, the quick, complete American victory was also due to America's naval prowess.

The Philippines, which itself was in the middle of a nearly decade-long revolt against Spanish rule, was also easily conquered, though by no means pacified.

With the dust of the Spanish-American War settling, President William McKinley was finally forced to come to a decision: Should the United States keep the Spanish possessions of Cuba, Puerto Rico, and the Philippines as colonies or should it let them become free? McKinley and many of his Republican colleagues may have wanted to expand the country, but anti-imperialist sentiment ran deep in America. The annexation of Hawaii in 1898 had come with significant opposition, including from the enormously powerful Republican Speaker of the House Thomas Reed, and leading American figures such as Andrew Carnegie, Mark Twain, and Carl Schurz were members of the Anti-Imperialist League. Naturally, the cautious McKinley was worried about the domestic political fight to keep control over any of the new territories.

The two major properties, Cuba and the Philippines, presented different problems. The indigenous Cuban independence movement was obviously too popular both in America and in Cuba for the United States to succeed in taking the country, except by the same force that Spain had tried and failed to use. Besides, Cuba, a mere ninety miles from the United States coast, did not present the same strategic benefits as the Philippines. The Philippines, with its excellent naval base, looked like a perfect place for the United States to establish a presence in Asia. It was a particularly tempting acquisition.

From a strategic point of view, retaining the Philippines was not a hard decision, and to win over the American people, McKinley made a number of claims for keeping the islands. He couldn't let the islands go back to Spanish control. He didn't want another country to take over. He also did not trust the Filipinos to take over their own government. Hence, the American people needed to back his decision. As an inherently indecisive and eager-to-please person, McKinley may have offered one too many reasons to woo the American constituency.

Ignoring the fact that the Philippines had been under Christian dominion for three centuries, he was reputed to have told the General Missionary Committee of the Methodist Episcopal Church that he stayed up all night praying and contemplating what he should do with the strategically valuable Philippines. Divine inspiration eventually came to him and, he said, hours of prayer led him to the revelation that it was his duty to help educate, uplift, and "Christianize the Filipinos."

Unfortunately for America, many Filipinos were not too thrilled with again being "Christianized." Indeed, after having paid Spain twenty million dollars, the United States also became owner of its first brutal colonial insurrection. The rebels, led by Gen. Emilio Aguinaldo, waged a guerilla war that is estimated to have cost more than four thousand American lives, twenty thousand Filipino soldiers and, by some estimates, more than two hundred thousand Filipino civilian lives before the unrest was effectively put down in 1902.

McKinley may have been trying to appease his political base and get America an overseas empire in the bargain, but his religious missionary zeal led the United States into a very costly endeavor. America's expansionist policies didn't hurt McKinley politically—an assassin's bullet ended his worries a few years later—but neither his nor the United States' reputation fully recovered from his lie, which Christianized a country full of Roman Catholics for the second time and gave his nation a Pacific protectorate, the Philippines.

Okay, even history teachers lied to us. . . .

THE MIDNIGHT RIDE OF PAUL REVERE

SILVERSMITH OR POSTER CHILD FOR THE CIVIL WAR DRAFT

James M. Ward

Longfellow, the poet, presents a version of Paul Revere's ride that vastly exaggerates, but that became the accepted myth, of what really happened. To this day, Paul Revere is known as a Revolutionary War hero for an act he was unable to finish.

From "Paul Revere's Ride," by Henry Wadsworth Longfellow:

Listen my children and you shall hear
Of the midnight ride of Paul Revere,
On the eighteenth of April, in Seventy-five;
Hardly a man is now alive
Who remembers that famous day and year.

So through the night rode Paul Revere;
And so through the night went his cry of alarm

To every Middlesex village and farm,
A cry of defiance, and not of fear,
A voice in the darkness, a knock at the door,
And a word that shall echo for evermore!
For, borne on the night-wind of the Past,
Through all our history, to the last,
In the hour of darkness and peril and need,
The people will waken and listen to hear
The hurrying hoof-beats of that steed,
And the midnight message of Paul Revere.

Few people today would know of Paul Revere and his contribution to the Revolutionary War if not for the classic poem written by Henry Wadsworth Longfellow in 1861. The legend that has come down to us is that Revere, in revolutionary zeal, took it upon himself to ride through the nighttime countryside shouting a warning about coming British troops. In actual fact, he was much more the organizer of a mass pony express–style effort than the solo rider portrayed in Longfellow's poem. Ultimately there were at least sixty riders moving about the countryside that night, doing the exact same thing as our hero Revere, and doing it a lot better.

It's highly likely that the British spy who gave away information to Paul Revere was none other than Margaret Kimball Gage, who was known to have deep feelings for her British general husband but apparently even deeper feelings for the developing United States. Mrs. Gage was sent back to Britain and the Gage family mansion shortly after the Concord and Lexington battles.

It's also silly to imagine Revere shouting, "The British are coming, the British are coming!" In those days, everyone thought of themselves as British. It would have been like someone today shouting, "American citizens are coming, American citizens are coming!"

Longfellow's poem so interested the mid-nineteenth-century public that no matter what historians discovered about the ride,

Paul Revere stands today as the man who single-handedly warned the colonies about the British troops coming to Lexington and Concord.

Not only was Revere only one of many to make the ride, he also failed to complete it. A British patrol captured him long before he finished. They probably would have let him go, but he made the mistake, by his own account, of mouthing off to the British and telling them some of their own secrets. From Revere's own words, the roadblock wouldn't have stopped him, but he loudly proclaimed that colonial forces would be out and dealing with the British regiment very soon.

"After they had taken Revere, they brought him within half a rod of me, and I heard him speak up with energy to them . . ." (from the deposition of Elijah Sanderson, December 17, 1824).

Paul Revere's own account of that night states, "In an instant, I saw four of them (British troopers), who rode up to me with their pistols in their hands . . . 'If you go an inch further, you are a dead man, shouted the troops.' . . . 'We are now going towards your friends, and if you attempt to run, or we are insulted, we will blow your brains out.'" Revere wanted to do much more than insult them; he wanted to make war on the entire British Empire.

Paul Revere's life and times are a well-documented tale of a hard worker with some talent. The facts of his life before his ride are very clear in the various records of the day. He was born on January 1, 1735, in Boston, Massachusetts. He took his education in Boston and later fought in the French and Indian War. After the war, he took up his father's silversmith business and married Sarah Orne. Far from being just a silversmith, he was also known for his work in gold and for making artificial teeth, surgical instruments, and printing plates.

Very interested in politics, Revere joined the Sons of Liberty and through them drew many political cartoons, which were printed on the flyers of the day. Such cartoons, and the flyers that bore them, developed into a highly popular means to spread the ideas of rebellion all through the colonies. If Revere where alive in modern times, he would be a very popular political cartoonist, as his images poked brutal fun at the British troops.

In December of 1773, along with other Sons of Liberty, Revere dressed up in a fake Indian costume and rushed a British merchant ship in the Boston Harbor, dumping the ship's tea cargo into the water. This act helped inflame the colonies against the taxes being forced on them by the British government. No one was fooled into thinking Indians had done the deed. There hadn't been an Indian attack on Boston in more than a hundred years.

Months before the now-famous ride, Revere served as a courier for the cause of rebellion against the king of England, riding throughout the northern colonies of Massachusetts, New York, New Hampshire, and Pennsylvania and passing out information to increase the tensions between England and its colonies.

While the Longfellow poem would have us believe that Revere rode alone on that historic night in 1775, two others started with him to make sure the job was completed. William Dawes and Samuel Prescott were assigned to ride too, to ensure that at least one man made it all the way.

Another possible reason for the presence of two other riders with Revere comes to us from information gathered about a small town in Massachusetts, called Medford, that had its own claim on Mr. Revere that night. It seems our Paul mentioned in the account of his ride that he arrived in the town and woke up a captain of the local militia, one Isaac Hall. Mr. Hall was famous for his family's rum distillery. The British also imposed high taxes on the ingredients of rum. French molasses was much cheaper than English molasses, but not after taxes. The distillers making rum were forced to use the highly taxed British molasses and other ingredients to make their goods. This situation naturally caused distillers all over the colonies to be angry, and Captain Hall was among those taking part in the open rebellion. The town of Medford claims there isn't a chance in the world that Paul Revere could have gotten out of town without two or three of the famous Medford distillery rum toddies in his belly. Common knowledge says that such generosity was the way of Isaac Hall for all visitors to his home. Long after the ride was finished, and Paul Revere's version of the trip came out, one other citizen of Medford was supposed to have said, "It's a lucky thing those two escorts were with Paul Revere. I've seen him in town before, and after drinking two or three of our rum toddies it was often necessary to hold him on his horse."

The famous poem that wrongly details Revere's ride was published in 1861, a time when people were talking of civil war between the North and the South. At the time of its publication, Longfellow freely admitted that the poem was an attempt to stress the importance of fighting for liberty and that individuals could make an important difference in history. With people thinking along those lines, maybe more of them would be willing to fight for their country. The poem was an instant success and made Paul Revere and his ride a prime topic of discussion throughout both the North and South.

While the Longfellow poem has Revere making it to Concord, the silversmith was actually captured long before he reached that town. William Dawes, however, made it all the way, and was able to deliver the message that the forces of Gen. Thomas Gage were marching on the town the next morning and that the militias of the area were to form up on the greens of Lexington and Concord to show their opposition against this act.

Colonial spies working among the British troops reported that the purpose of the British expedition to Concord and Lexington was to capture supplies of gunpowder and bullets. However, that was only the secondary mission of the British forces sent into the two settlements. Gage wanted to capture John Hancock and Samuel Adams, both known for leading forces in rebellion. The small roadblock that had stopped Paul Revere was duplicated in several areas around Lexington and Concord that night, hoping to stop Hancock and Adams. It was thought these men would be traveling that night, and General Gage had issued orders for their capture.

In contradiction to Longfellow's poem, which has Revere and others going from house to house in Lexington and Concord, the church bells were rung to assemble the town's militia on the town square. As Revere and his British captors moved toward Lexington, they heard the sounds of gunfire. When asked by Major Mitchell of the Kings Fifth Regiment what the gunfire was about, Paul Revere answered that it was men in open rebellion. He was let go as a harmless fool, and the British troops moved toward Cambridge. Revere later joined Hancock and Adams.

Of that fateful time, Revere was reported to say later, "[A]fter resting myself, I set off with another man to go back to the tavern, to inquire the news; when we got there, we were told the troops were within two miles. We went to the tavern to get a trunk of papers belonging to Colonel Hancock. Before we left the house, I saw the ministerial troops from the chamber window. We made haste, and had to pass through our militia, who were on the green behind the Meeting House, to the number as I supposed, about 50 to 60, I went through them; as I passed I heard the commanding officer speak to his men to this purpose; 'Let the troops pass by, and don't molest them, without they begin first.' I had to go across the road; but had not got half gunshot off, when the ministerial troops appeared in sight, behind the Meeting House. They made a short halt, when one gun was fired. I heard the report, turned my head, and saw the smoke in front of the troops. They immediately gave a great shout, ran a few paces, and then the whole fired. I could first distinguish irregular firing, which I supposed was the advance guard, and then platoons; at this time I could not see our militia, for they were covered from me by a house at the bottom of the street."

His words would seem to indicate that the militia didn't fire first. We will never know.

During the Revolution, Revere commanded a garrison at Castle Williams in Boston Harbor. His life after the Revolution is an open book. He was a proud member of the Masons. He had sixteen children by two wives, fifty-two grandchildren, and there are today many groups throughout the United States claiming kinship to the man. Paul Revere died on May 10, 1818.

We know the facts of Paul Revere's aborted ride from numerous letters, diaries, memoirs, and British troop reports from that time. It would have been totally impossible for Revere, on horseback, to go from home to home rousing the populous of the countryside as the Longfellow poem implies. There just wouldn't have been time.

Some historians would demean Revere's efforts, pointing out that he never made it all the way. They don't point out that at least he tried. They don't point out that he did warn Hancock and Adams in Lexington. The man was there in the thick of things doing what he thought was right. He deserves respect not only for his Revolutionary War effort but also because of his excellent skill as a silver- and goldsmith. Where he *doesn't* deserve much respect is for keeping his own council and not talking to the enemy.

Some think the "shot heard round the world" that started militia shooting at British troops could have been a much less deadly action. That day British troops stood in front of colonial militia, nether side wanted to fire, but someone fired the first shot and there was a short battle.

None of the taverns of that period allowed their patrons to enter with loaded weapons. The only way to unload a flintlock rifle was to fire the weapon into the air. There is a definite possibility that a man thirsty for a quick drink during the day started the war that birthed the United States.

In 1896, in an effort to give William Dawes his rightful due in that ride, one Helen Moore wrote a parody of Longfellow's poem.

The poem begins:

I am a wandering, bitter shade,
Never of me was a hero made;
Poets have never sung my praise,
Nobody crowned my brow with bays;
And if you ask me the fatal cause,
I answer only, "My name was Dawes"
'TIS all very well for the children to hear
Of the midnight ride of Paul Revere;
But why should my name be quite forgot,
Who rode as boldly and well, God wot?
Why should I ask? The reason is clear—
My name was Dawes and his Revere.

At the time of this writing, I wasn't able to find any poems giving Dr. Samuel Prescott equal time.

And he wore dresses . . .

J. EDGAR HOOVER'S NOT-SO-RED MENACE

WASHINGTON, D.C., 1958

Paul A. Thomsen

"A disciplined Party of hard-core fanatical members is now at work, with their fellow travelers, sympathizers, opportunists, and dupes. Communists in our country . . . want to add America to Soviet Russia's list of conquests."

—J. Edgar Hoover, *Masters of Deceit* (1958)

Throughout his life, J. Edgar Hoover exhibited an almost relentless tenacity for hunting down enemies of the United States of America. While the FBI director had apprehended or jailed bank robbers, Nazi spies, civil rights protestors, and antiwar advocates, Hoover held an almost personal, burning hatred for American-based Communists.

Throughout the 1940s and 1950s, the House Un-American Activities Committee (HUAC) and a congressional investigative body led by Senator Joseph McCarthy had spearheaded efforts, in parallel with Hoover's more silent investigations, to purge every facet of American society of a feared Communist insurgency. While McCarthy's red-hunting had ended in the destruction of hundreds of careers and in his own humiliation, Hoover still saw telltale signs of a Communist menace ready to crawl out of the shadows and take over his country.

In his 1958 book *Masters of Deceit: The Story of Communism in America and How to Fight It,* Hoover warned, "A disciplined Party of hard-core fanatical members is now at work, with their fellow travelers, sympathizers, opportunists, and dupes. Communists in our country . . . want to add America to Soviet Russia's list of conquests."

It was a good line, and the book became a bestseller.

Too bad, Hoover's anticommunist claims turned out to be for the most part works of creative truth-telling, strung together by suppositions, innuendo, and bald-faced lies.

When an anarchist bomb (and bomber) exploded on the doorstep of virulent antisocialist and anti-immigrant Wilson administration attorney general A. Mitchell Palmer in June 1919, J. Edgar Hoover became one of the attorney general's lead investigators in the first Red Scare (better known as the Palmer Raids), hunting down potentially dangerous resident aliens, anarchists, and Communists. Though Palmer's own presidential ambitions and public service career went up in flames when it was revealed that he had unlawfully imprisoned several dozen American citizens, Hoover emerged entirely unscathed from the ordeal. Shortly thereafter, he transferred into the new and then-named Bureau of Investigation, and started his rapid rise to the top in a relentless pursuit of Communist insurgents on American soil.

In 1925, J. Edgar Hoover was appointed to the permanent directorship of the tiny, underutilized, poorly staffed, and ill-funded Bureau. In order for his new charge to gain a level of budgetary prominence commensurate with its national duties, Hoover needed to reach beyond Palmer's elusive World War I threats and establish the Bureau's credentials as a productive and autonomous investigative apparatus. With a hefty helping of public relations, Hoover rapidly recast the bureau as the modern personification of the legendary Texas Ranger in pursuit of dastardly villains. Ironically, the Bureau's first targets were, indeed, modern incarnations of the law's Old West adversaries: bank robbers. While John Dillinger, Pretty Boy Floyd, and Bonnie and Clyde may have carted away hefty sums of American greenbacks, their booty did not compare to the metaphoric bounty earned by Hoover's federal agents in tracking down and killing the outlaws. Each new kill or capture of a public enemy earned Hoover and his agents invaluable popular support, political capital, and greater respect as the preeminent law enforcement apparatus in the country. By the 1930s, the Bureau had evolved substantially, with a dramatic increase in its number of agents, cases, and new crime-fighting technologies.

With the advent of radio shows, newsreels, and mass market advertising, it seemed that every kid wanted to be just like Hoover's agents and serve as junior G-men (government men) on the watch for illegal activity.

Still, it seemed that the Bureau had done its job a little too well.

The newly renamed FBI had managed to unceremoniously end the age of bank robbers. Hoover could have turned to the next most sensational target, La Cosa Nostra, but that was a problematic fight, which was being waged largely by the Treasury Department . . . and it was going nowhere fast.

Instead, the FBI next leveled its sights on Hoover's old nemeses: American Communists, which they had been watching infiltrating labor unions, co-opting organized protests, and distributing literature critical of the government. But before a new grand campaign could be established against this hated twentieth-century foe of capitalism, Nazi Germany's chancellor, Adolf Hitler, invaded the Soviet Union and brought the Western powers into bed with the most unlikely of allies: Joseph Stalin and the Communist Party.

Throughout the Second World War, Hoover's FBI challenged that the Soviets were a threat second only to Nazi Germany (according to annual wartime threat assessments, the FBI claimed that the alleged international and domestic elements of the Communist menace were far superior threats to the United States than either the empire of Japan or Fascist Italy), but the Bureau gained little traction with these assertions until the end of the war. With the onset of the Cold War, however, Hoover found renewed support in Congress and with the general public in removing the taint of communism from American soil.

Indeed, public support for the Bureau's new red-hunting preoccupation had grown so popular that FBI agents did not need to make headlines to gain anticommunist notoriety. While agents infiltrated alleged Communist organizations, investigated celebrities, tracked dissidents, and ran counterintelligence operations against the few known Soviet agents in the country, Senator Joseph McCarthy and HUAC were both drumming up support for yet more red-hunting initiatives with their widely public and highly elaborate congressional hearings. As a result, when McCarthy's witch-hunt tactics brought public ire, and HUAC started to fade into the background in the 1950s, Hoover was able to emerge, once again, as the nation's unblemished anticommunist with an audience still willing to drink deep his assertions that Communists may have abounded in the most unsuspecting places (including the National Association for the Advancement of Colored People), that newspapers frequently critical of the government may have been infiltrated by Communist agents, and that the American Communist was plotting to take over the United States.

Amazingly, none of it was accurate.

According to Christopher Andrews and Vasili Mitrokhin's archival research, KGB records reveal that the highly publicized Second Red Scare actions of McCarthy had so spooked the Soviet intelligence agency that they dared not attempt to recruit agents in the United States during this period for fear of vast negative political repercussions. Instead, they decided to use Soviet mission personnel to gather intelligence, train illegals to create backup safe houses, and wait for Americans to come (or be driven) to them. Furthermore, only a handful of publications outside the established Communist literature were subsidized by world Communist Party entities, and those, again according to Andrews and Mitrokhin, were largely minor conspiracy theorist publications.

Finally, far from thriving, when Hoover published *Masters of Deceit*, his handbook on discovering American-based Communist Party agents, the American Communist Party was about to fall apart, for at least the fourth time in the nation's history, with the retirement of Hoover enemy, Communist Party USA general secretary William Z. Foster.

It seemed that the McCarthy era, the revelations about the extent of Stalin's pre- and postwar purges, the loss of most labor union power to the cold-war military industrial complex, Hoover's own red-hunting, and the general growing dissension between American Communist goals and the Kremlin had spelled the doom for the FBI's not-so-Red Menace. Still, with the dramatic rise in civil disobedience and antiestablishment action from the late 1950s through the early 1970s, Hoover would keep the seemingly preeminent American bugaboo around a bit longer to plague the civil rights movement and the antiwar lobby.

To be fair, FBI director James Edgar Hoover likely believed the pervasive threat of the Red Menace to his dying hour, regardless of the facts. Throughout the Cold War, and well until the fall of the Berlin wall, the periodic discovery and incarceration of Americans spying for the Soviets had kept alive tacit credence for Hoover's red fears. But beyond the 1950s, there were very few incidents of Soviet spies committing espionage on American soil for ideological reasons greater than advancing their own personal wealth.

It makes one wonder, who really were the "masters of deceit" the FBI director alluded to?

This lie almost got us all killed: "The Soviet government has never sent and is not now sending offensive weapons of any kind to Cuba" (Soviet ambassador Valerian Zorin, New York, 1962).

THE SOVIETS BLINK

Paul A. Thomsen

In 1959, Cuban Republic leader and former Central Intelligence Agency asset Fidel Castro defected to the Union of Soviet Socialist Republics (USSR). Since then, the United States has kept a wary eye on the Caribbean island of Cuba. On Sunday, October 14, 1962, a United States U-2 surveillance plane flew a routine reconnaissance mission over Cuba and discovered an alarming fact: the USSR was covertly erecting ballistic missiles on the island nation—missiles capable of reaching far into the North American continent. Over the next several days, the United States "quarantined" Cuba and, through U.S. ambassador Adlai Stevenson, demanded that the Soviet Union immediately remove the missiles.

At the October 23, 1962, meeting of the United Nations Security Council, Soviet ambassador Valerian Zorin denied the charges, saying "The Soviet Government has never sent and is not now sending offensive weapons of any kind to Cuba."

Whereas lies have generally been considered bad form and the stuff of poor moral fiber, Zorin's misstatement of the facts might have unintentionally saved the world from nuclear annihilation.

Heated relations between the two superpowers had been rising to a critical point for years. By the mid-1950s, both powers had the capability of delivering nuclear weapons to the other nation's major cities within a matter of hours. In 1961, the United States tried unsuccessfully to seize the Communist nation of Cuba. In May 1961, President Kennedy appeared weak in negotiations with Soviet premier Nikita Khrushchev, and now the Soviet ambassador was lying about the placement of several nuclear weapons systems capable of reaching and vaporizing Washington, D.C., within approximately five minutes of flying time.

With the world approaching the brink of mutually assured destruction, clarity remained both superpowers' most assiduously coveted asset. Yet, through several decades of mutually divisive policies, that item was in very short supply. In order for the Soviets to survive against better-equipped foes, first the White Army (czarist Russia) during their civil war, and later her Western associates (largely Great Britain, France, and the United States), Vladimir Lenin's Communist factions adopted a strategy of clandestine activities, guerilla warfare tactics, and psychological operations. During the Cold War, Denial and Deception (D&D) became a primary tool of Soviet military policy and statecraft, frequently preventing politically inconvenient truths from detonating until readiness had been achieved. After the rise of the iron curtain, the United States, likewise, frequently employed covert means to attack Soviet interests, including periodically manipulating politically delicate democratic elections in Europe and dispatching small insurgency teams to overthrow Communist-leaning Latin American regimes. Ideological rhetoric may have outlined each power's grand designs, but with the exception of human-, signal-, and overflight-provided image intelligence, neither side had more than a general notion of the other's truest intentions or capabilities, nor were their meager assessments even closely approximating accuracy.

According to Central Intelligence Agency historian James H. Hansen, in the spring of 1962 the Soviets crafted a comprehensive D&D plan to shield detection of Khrushchev's ordered transfer of missiles to Cuba. Castro had been after Khrushchev for months about adequately defending Cuba from another potential American invasion. The Soviet leader, looking to trump the United States' positioning of similarly lethal weapons on Russia's European borders, saw a way to do it with a few well-placed weapons systems embedded right outside his adversary's back door—weapons to be revealed in the premier's forthcoming November trip to the region.

Prior to the discovery of the Cuban-based medium- and intermediate-range ballistic missiles, the CIA had believed that the Soviet Union would never arm Cuba with offensive-capable weapons systems (weaponry with the capacity of reaching beyond an immediate zone of military conflict). They had been duly duped by the Russian D&D plan of hidden shipments and nocturnal-moving schedules. But the covert Russian effort did have one large hole in it. Once the weapons systems were brought into Cuba, many realized that they could be seen from the sky. While the Soviets hoped to fool American overflight missions, as they had their adversary's human and signal intelligence assets, with yet another set of well-placed props (in this case, floral arrangements to disguise the missiles as tropical trees), the October 14 U-2 and its successor flights were undeterred by what they saw and, hence, the Soviets had no backup plan in place in the event of a United States naval embargo of Cuba.

Still, what the United States found was also not the whole picture. After several more U-2 overflights of Cuba, the intelligence community estimated that the island held twenty-four offensive weapons systems, but they did not believe any of the missiles carried nuclear payloads. According to Kennedy administration secretary of defense Robert McNamara's and Watson Institute scholar James Blight's later investigations: "The Soviets had already delivered 162 nuclear warheads to Cuba and had them in a secure storage depot at Bejucal, southwest of Havana . . . the warheads were divided equally between those for the strategic missiles capable of threatening the U.S. directly, and those for cruise missiles (which would be used to attack U.S. ships involved in any invasion) . . . and for short-range tactical weapons (which would be used to attack the invading U.S. forces as they arrived at the island)." Moreover both administrations also enlisted untested and, in at least one case, compromised intermediaries to convey administrative positions and intentions throughout the conflict, including teletype machines, secondary-level embassy officials, undercover intelligence operatives, and a journalist. To further complicate the matter, the Soviets had also given discretionary power over nuclear torpedoes to the theater submarine command.

As a result of this incomplete picture, the Kennedy administration arrived at what they thought were three realistic options: full embargo, air strike, and invasion. While the United States initially chose to pursue the more diplomatic option, quarantine, if that had failed, diplomacy was to be followed by military action, and unbeknownst to the Americans (who thought they would have several hours or days to prepare for the next phase of the war), that act would have triggered an immediate, devastating nuclear attack on the continental United States.

The situation was equally precarious on the floor of the United Nations. According to historian Michael Becheloss, ambassadors Adlai Stevenson and Valerian Zorin were similarly diplomatically ill-equipped walking into the crisis. Stevenson, a Democratic Party powerbroker who had at one time stood in the way of John Kennedy's election, was believed by administration officials to be ready to give away every security concern to the Soviets for the sake of peace. Zorin, on the other hand, was a former teacher and little-utilized party diplomat who a few contemporaries later claimed was losing his mind.

Yet, over the course of their lengthy arguments on the floor of the United Nations Security Council, each of the two was also the main spokesman for his side, hoping not only to directly influence the other into backing down but also equally to sway the world leadership, who had been living under threat of imminent nuclear attack for decades, to their side. Like their supernumerary counterparts, Stevenson and Zorin continued to hammer each other with challenges, rhetoric, and denials, but when Zorin adamantly refused to believe Stevenson's assertions, and Stevenson, subsequently, revealed the missile-ridden U-2 overflight images, an opportunity to resolve the conflict peacefully opened with the loss of only one person's and party's honor.

The USSR had blinked.

Immediately, the Cuban missile crisis took on a new dimension. World opinion suddenly shifted in favor of the United States' position, but that was not all. Like the falling of dominoes, this increased pressure polarized Khrushchev's advisers, dividing them into two extreme and opposite camps: those who would rather retain their honor in protecting a fellow Soviet state with wide-scale war and those who saw absurdity in the retention of dignity in the shadow of nuclear suicide. In response, Khrushchev drafted and sent a letter of agreed phased ballistic disarmament of Cuba, if the United States would also remove its Jupiter missiles from Turkey. Finding himself now exposed to the critical eyes of the hard-liners, he drafted and sent a harsher, more confrontational letter. The Kennedy administration, realizing that this was their last chance at avoiding nuclear annihilation, agreed to the contents of the first letter, and ignored the second. In the following months, the Soviets withdrew their missiles and, in a separate agreement, their bombers from Cuba. The conflict had ended.

During those thirteen days in October, everything seemed to be going wrong for both the United States and the Union of Soviet Socialist Republics. Had Valerian Zorin admitted to placing offensive weapons in Cuba, there would have been no further room for diplomacy and nuclear war would have followed, but one man's lie had actually saved the day.

This editor was actually there in Chicago, Illinois, in 1968. I was lucky the only thing a cop broke was my watch. Even my memories of all this seem strange today.

DALEY COUNTRY

CHICAGO, ILLINOIS, 1968

Peter Archer

Richard J. Daley was the last of the big city bosses. For twenty years he ran the city of Chicago like a private fiefdom, dispensing patronage to the enormous Democratic Party machine that ensured his reelection by fair means or foul.

Perhaps his greatest crisis came halfway through his reign. Ironically, it occurred at what should have been one of his greatest triumphs: Chicago's hosting of the Democratic National Convention in August 1968.

The year 1968, probably more than any other, embodies the spirit of the sixties. The war in Vietnam dragged on as Lyndon Johnson announced he would not seek another term as president. In April, Martin Luther King, Jr., was assassinated in Memphis, Tennessee, as he stood on a hotel balcony, and in June, Robert F. Kennedy was shot and killed as he walked through a hotel kitchen in California, on his way out of a triumphant political rally backing him for the presidency.

So there was no question that the meeting of the Democrats to select their presidential candidate was going to be full of controversy. For months Daley had lobbied energetically to hold the convention in Chicago. Chicago is, after all, in the words of Norman Mailer, "the great American city." And the added business the convention would bring would certainly benefit Daley at the polls.

But even as the announcement was made that thousands of delegates would be converging on the Windy City in August, storm clouds loomed on the horizon. The candidacy of Eugene McCarthy, around which opponents of the Vietnam War had rallied, was gathering steam and seemed likely to attract many young, idealistic people to the convention. Along with them would be thousands of other young people intent on demonstrating their contempt for the war, the president, most of the candidates—and Mayor Daley himself.

Among them would be the Yippies—anarchistic, irreverent, fun loving—led by Jerry Rubin and Abbie Hoffman. Rumors flew that the Yippies planned to release LSD into the city's water supply, though neither Hoffman nor Rubin had announced anything of the sort. What Rubin and Hoffman planned, though certainly colorful, was, in fact, considerably less exciting. They would hold a Festival of Life in the city's Lincoln Park, including music, poetry readings, workshops, religious ceremonies, and training in karate and self-defense. As a highlight of the festival, they would mock the convention by nominating a pig, Pigasus, for president. Pigasus's political platform would include free love, community control of the police, the abolition of money, and an end to pay toilets.

Daley and the city administration took this nonsense very seriously. The city denied the Yippies a permit to sleep in Lincoln Park. They mobilized a force of twelve thousand police, five thousand soldiers from nearby Fort Sheridan, and six thousand National Guardsmen to maintain law and order.

A few minor skirmishes occurred between police and demonstrators the week before the convention began. Interestingly, that week also saw the Soviet invasion of Czechoslovakia. Demonstrators began referring to Chicago as Prague West. The administration had a different image they wanted to project. Arriving delegates were greeted with signs declaring, "You Have Arrived in Daley Country."

On Sunday night, the police launched a sweep through Lincoln Park to clear it of the Yippies by 9:00 P.M., two hours before the park's closing. When the protestors taunted the police with shouts of "Pig!" the men in blue responded with a rhythmic chant of "Kill! Kill! Kill!" as they swung their clubs.

Tensions continued to run high through Wednesday morning, both on the convention floor, when the more conservative forces mobilized to nominate their candidate, Hubert Humphrey, and on the streets, where antiwar demonstrators marched and shouted. On Monday and Tuesday there were more police attacks, more arrests, and more angry words between the young demonstrators and the cops.

On Wednesday evening, demonstrators marched along Michigan Avenue, the street that was flanked by Grant Park on one side and a line of impressive hotels on the other. In front of the Conrad Hilton, where many of the delegates were staying, the protestors were halted by a line of police. Another group of policemen cut them off from behind, trapping them in front of the hotel.

Then, in the glare of the television lights, as hotel guests watched from their balconies, the police attacked. Swinging their batons, they charged, re-formed, and charged again, cutting through the crowd like a buzz saw.

The violence grew more and more random. The police charge drove spectators behind a barrier against the plate-glass windows of the hotel's coffee shop. The windows shattered, and screaming men and women fell through, struggling to avoid the jagged shards of glass. The police leaped after them through the window, beating and arresting them.

The police turned on reporters filming and photographing the scene. "Hey, you dirty bastard! Gimme that notebook!" one cop told a reporter.

Even as the attack continued, the protestors shouted in defiance. "The whole world is watching! The whole world is watching!"

On the floor of the convention, delegates heard with horror accounts of the violence outside. Senator Abraham Ribicoff rose to nominate Senator George McGovern for the presidency. His voice quavering with indignation, he looked straight at Mayor Daley and said, "With George McGovern as president of the United States, we wouldn't have those Gestapo tactics in the streets of Chicago."

It was the last straw for the mayor. He leaped to his feet, joined by his son Richard and other supporters, and shouted at Ribicoff. Though his words were drowned by others' shouts, he was captured on film. Most analysts of the footage agree he said, "Fuck you, you Jew son of a bitch. Go home!" (A county Democratic official later tried to explain that Daley and others had been shouting "Faker!" at Ribicoff. "If you move your lips to form 'faker,' it looks just like you're saying that other thing.")

To Daley, it was doubly tragic that this should be happening when the convention was poised to select Humphrey, his chosen candidate. He should be receiving accolades as a kingmaker. Instead, here was some senator from Connecticut, of all places, accusing him of "Gestapo tactics."

The following day, August 29, Daley struck back at his critics. He made himself available for a special interview with Walter Cronkite, dean of American newsmen, whose integrity was unimpeachable. Cronkite had been critical of the police violence in the past few days, especially of their attacks on reporters and photographers.

Daley at once seized control of the interview and read a statement defending his police and his administration. The demonstrators, headed by the Yippies, he said, were "terrorists" who had come equipped with maps, medics, weapons, and a strategic plan to disrupt the convention. Their leaders were known Communists.

Beyond that, even, the mayor had evidence of a plot, the details of which "I never said to anyone." Intelligence reports told him that "certain people" planned to assassinate Senator Eugene McCarthy and—horror of horrors!—Mayor Daley himself. Said Daley, "I didn't want what happened in Dallas or what happened in California to happen in Chicago."

When Cronkite asked about the attacks on members of the press, Daley lashed out. "Many of them are hippies themselves. They're a part of this movement. Some of them are revolutionaries and they want these things to happen. There isn't any secret about that." It was a secret to the editors and publishers who had hired these so-called revolutionaries.

Surprisingly, Cronkite did not argue with Daley's clearly self-serving assertions. Nor did he ask for evidence of the assassination plot. The mayor's assertions, which seem wild and improvised in the searching light of history, were allowed to stand unchallenged.

Despite this, Daley wanted even more justification for his actions. After the convention's end, the mayor's office published *Strategy of Confrontation*, the official account of the disturbances. The report asserted, without evidence, that there had been a plot to murder a young female supporter of McCarthy and blame the death on the police. It showed weapons supposedly brought to Chicago by the demonstrators, including a baseball bat.

Daley commissioned a filmed version of the report, retitled, *What Trees Do They Plant?*, a dig at his critics in Chicago. Though all three of the major networks refused to air it, Daley found 140 stations in the United States, Canada, and England that would.

By and large, the population of Chicago supported the mayor and didn't question him too much about the secret assassination plot, which, like the tear gas that repelled the demonstrators, vanished in the wind after the convention. Chicagoans were mostly happy with the way their city worked, and they had more sympathy for the cop on the beat than the demonstrator in the street.

Possibly as a result of the extensive television coverage of the violence, and probably as a consequence of Richard Nixon's announcement of a "secret plan" to end the war in Vietnam, Hubert Humphrey went down in defeat in November. The Yippies and hippies apparently weren't the only ones with "secret plans" that year. The events of the convention produced a bestselling book by author Norman Mailer, *Miami and the Siege of Chicago*, and a film, *Medium Cool*, that used actual footage from the events of August 1968 as the backdrop for its story.

In December an investigative commission headed by future Illinois governor Dan Walker, issued a report titled *Rights in Conflict*. The report characterized what had occurred as a "police riot" but sought as well to assign blame to the demonstrators who had provoked the police.

When Abbie Hoffman threatened to put LSD in the city's water, no one except Mayor Daley believed him. That stuff was expensive and something like a few tons of the drug would have been needed. Still, looking back in embarrassment, one can see that there was a lot of rhetoric on both sides that a lot of people believed.

Daley himself probably gave the best summary of the Chicago Democratic Convention disorders, albeit an inadvertent one. On September 9, 1968, at a news conference, he snapped, "The policeman isn't there to create disorder. The policeman is there to preserve disorder."

THE FIRST CASUALTY OF WAR IS TRUTH

That sort of says it all. Deception as a tactic is different from just plain lying, and it has been successful from Joshua and Hannibal to Rommel and Schwarzkopf. Lies are the general-purpose tool of those who make war. They are told to start wars, to justify wars, to win battles, and occasionally even to end a war. In fact, people seem able to lie in wars for just about every purpose except to prevent them. But, then, if a successful lie has prevented a war, it seems ironically likely we would not know of it.

A divided Congress, a semi-plausible excuse for war. Sound familiar? It's not 2003, but 1846, when a president bullied Congress into declaring war.

JAMES K. POLK'S FABRICATION TO CONGRESS

WASHINGTON, D.C., 1846

Robert Greenberger

Sam W. Haynes, professor at the University of Texas at Arlington, said of him, "He was a man with a very strong sense of duty and professional obligation that made him seem cold, aloof and distant to many people. He was not a man who made friends easily or who had many interests. As far as we know, as President, his only reading materials were government documents and Bible scriptures . . . [He] was very methodical—a man who paid scrupulous attention to detail. He was a man whose mind was closed to abstractions and new ideas. But one of the truly striking things about [him] was his self-confidence. In the diary he kept as President of the United States, there's absolutely no evidence of self-doubt."

David M. Pletcher, of Indiana University, added, "Some people believe that [the] President . . . intentionally provoked the war with Mexico . . . he was willing to create a threat of war to do this. If he had to fight, he wanted a short war and a quick victory. He never expected a long-drawn-out war. The Army was not ready for war and had never fought so far from home before. The country was divided."

How little things change.

In 1846, President James K. Polk reported to Congress that American troops had been shot at by Mexican troops in American territory and that a swift reaction was called for. Some in Congress disputed the rationale but had to support the troops, so they ratified the call to war.

What was it all about? When Polk took office at age forty-nine, he was one of many who believed in a then-new notion known as "manifest destiny"—described back in the day as the idea that acquiring Western lands was proper and necessary in order to secure the noble purposes of the United States. He was also the first president since James Monroe who vigorously applied the Monroe Doctrine to his policies.

In 1836, Texas had declared its independence from Mexico and subsequently applied for statehood, although the exact boundaries remained in dispute. Mexico was experiencing its own political problems as it went through a series of presidents since Santa Ana lost Texas. What Polk never seemed to grasp was the depth of feeling in Mexico over Santa Ana having been forced to give up Texas years earlier, or that the Mexican government never recognized the American annexation.

Mexico was deeply in debt to the United States and Britain, and Polk had hoped to settle matters by offering to wipe out that debt by settling the disputed border at the Río Grande. Mexico refused. At the same time, many in Washington, D.C., were concerned that Britain might want to extend its own North American holdings by demanding the California territory in lieu of repayment.

As it was later learned, Britain never desired the land, but it stayed out of matters during those years due to its own internal problems. Still, Polk was concerned, since Britain was proving difficult on settling the Oregon border with Canada, which led to the famous rallying cry of "Fifty-four Forty or Fight!" The border was eventually settled at latitude forty-nine.

Polk decided to try a different approach. He knew that Mexico had rejected an offer of outright purchase of California in 1835, but he decided to try again. The president dispatched John Slidell to Mexico, charging him with four tasks: resolve the Río Grande border, settle the American citizens' financial claims against Mexico, and attempt to purchase California and New Mexico. President José Joaquín de Herrera wanted nothing to do with the envoy, so he found a technical flaw in Slidell's credentials and refused to see him. The Mexicans even showed their displeasure by recalling their minister from America's capitol. Undeterred, Slidell settled in a few towns over and waited, and an infuriated Polk named him permanent minister to Mexico.

Nearby, in Texas, Zachary Taylor commanded troops positioned in the disputed Texas territory as Slidell's backup.

The conflict with America led Herrera's government to be overthrown by General Mariano Paredes, who named himself president and proved to be even more anti-American than Herrera. He continued to refuse to recognize Slidell for fear that he'd be forced into concessions, which would result in his own coup.

To counter Taylor's forces, Mexico saw to it that there were troops also at the disputed Río Grande. Their general sent men across the river to ambush an American detachment and killed the soldiers. Taylor reported back to his commander in chief, "I presume this means the beginning of war."

Polk began to prepare his declaration of war, at no time recognizing that the ground where the attack had occurred was disputed land. By not addressing the point, he was able to make the strongest case possible to a skeptical Congress. Among the skeptics was Illinois congressman Abraham Lincoln, who was among those to challenge the facts as presented. He knew that the border was indeterminate and not worth going to war over. However, he was dwarfed by the support Congress wanted to offer the army.

In 1846, America found itself going to war against Mexico.

Polk thought the mere threat would attract Paredes to the negotiation table, but when that failed, he was convinced that the Mexican army would fold quickly. Instead, they fought valiantly, with the struggle dragging on. In fact, as the war passed the one-year mark, people wondered how the conflict would be resolved, if ever, and when their boys would be coming home.

Dissatisfaction with the president's war grew so that in January 1848 the Congress actually tried to censure Polk. They added the censure as an amendment to a resolution being prepared to praise the efforts of Maj. Gen. Taylor. The censure's language referred to the conflict as a "war unnecessarily and unconstitutionally begun by the President of the United States." The entire resolution, though, died in committee.

The war ended that summer, and America suddenly gained land that would one day became the states of New Mexico, Arizona, and California, while also settling the Texas border dispute once and for all.

The Whig Party, who detested Polk and his unnecessary war, made a hero of Taylor, nominating him for president. Loyal to his commander, Taylor refused to issue public criticism, and Polk didn't oppose his officer in the election, honoring his promise to stay in office for only one term. In fact, Polk passed away 103 days after leaving office, the shortest post-presidency on record.

"'Veni, Vidi, Vici' *(I came, I saw, I conquered)*" *(Julius Caesar)*.

HOW THE ROMAN EMPIRE LOST ITS GALLIC WARS BUT JULIUS CAESAR BECAME EMPEROR

Paul A. Thomsen

On March 15, 44 B.C.E., Roman emperor Julius Caesar was stabbed in the back, front, and sides by a group of once-close friends and senators. As he lay dying in a pool of blood, history records the Roman emperor's shock at the personal betrayal in his final famous words, *"Et tu, Brute?"* (Latin for "And you, Brutus?"). Yet, the joke would be on his assassins.

In only a few decades, Caesar had risen from a minor philandering nobleman to a legendary battlefield commander and the ruler of one of the greatest nation-states in the history of Europe all because of a single piece of wartime propaganda, beginning with the words "All Gaul is divided into three parts . . ."

Sent to patrol the outskirts of the then-Roman republic by political victims of his charismatic ways, Caesar had been expected to die in obscurity with his meager army, but the young nobleman had other plans. In 390 B.C.E., the nascent Roman republic had been burned to the ground by the Gauls, and for centuries Romans had lived in fear that the blue-painted and half-naked-seeming savages of the north might one day return. With stylus and gladius in hand, the young Caesar managed to push forward the northern borders of the republic and set his people's fears at bay.

Through frequent dispatches home, which recounted his army's many battlefield victories, Julius Caesar's *Commentaries on the Gallic Wars* carved out a grand reputation from the dark forests beyond the Himalayas, but the general also misled his admirers. His stories frequently characterized his enemies as inferior, his own campaigns as a series of nearly unblemished victories, and his opposers as soon-humbled subjects of the Roman Empire.

None of this was true.

Gaul was replete with cunning warriors armed with advanced war machines and sailing vessels to rival Rome's own arsenal, and were kept from attacking neighboring nation-states solely because they too were too busy fighting each other for the fertile resources of northern Europe. Others had previously tried and succeeded in subduing regions of Gaul, but it was Caesar who pacified the region and declared victory over the north . . . or so he told everyone.

While he had, indeed, eventually beaten every Gallic army to rise against him, had expanded the republic with new allies in the region, and had eventually bested all domestic political rivals to become Roman's first emperor, Julius Caesar had never really managed to either divide or truly conquer Gaul. Over the next several hundred years, as the legendary emperor's body turned to dust, Rome spent millions in denari and hundreds of thousands of soldier's lives trying to suppress a veritable plentitude of rebellions in this supposedly conquered land. After a while it seemed that each time one faction would be pressed down by bloody Roman sandals and gladii, another would soon rise to take their place. In response, the Romans tried everything from poisoning wells to practicing diplomacy to giving rewards, and after about forty years of trial and error, it seemed that they had finally bought off the Gauls with the rewards of Roman citizenship . . . or so they thought.

In the intervening years, many Gauls living in what today is both France and parts of Germany had forsaken their old ways and risen to fairly high levels in both military and political circles. Several leaders of Gallic factions had even become the veritable toast of the Seven Hills of Rome. But while many of the blue-painted clans had, indeed, grown old and fat sucking on the imperial tit, others being trained in the arts of warfare and engineering by the Roman military itself were plotting the empire's downfall.

In assimilating surrendered factions, Roman imperial policy dictated that the children of the conquered leadership were to be taken to Rome to be raised as proper citizens of the empire. On the surface the policy seemed sound. The precarious position of the Gallic children's lives often squelched ideas of rebellion in their parents before they could gather steam, and upon completion of their decade-long education as new Roman citizens, the children seemed to be ideal vassals to rule their ancestors' conquered land for the empire. It was a clockwork system. But eventually the synchronized mechanisms began to break down.

In A.D. 9, the Roman governor of Germania, Publius Quinctilius Varus, learned of the formation of yet another Gallic rebellion. His source, a Romanized German prince named Arminius, implored him to put down the forming insurrection before the factions could launch an attack against their shared interests. Varus, a descendent of the Roman emperor Caesar Augustus (the adopted nephew of Julius Caesar), saw an opportunity for glory in the intelligence. Never questioning Arminius's word, he gathered together three legions of troops, six cohorts, and three squadrons of cavalry, and rode out to subdue this new threat.

Over the next several weeks, Varus, directed by Arminius, led his several-thousand-strong contingent through untamed wilderness, cold winds, torrential rains, and thick mud of the Teutoburg Forest (presently northeastern North Rhine–Westphalia land) in search of the enemy. Periodically small groups of rebels were sighted on the periphery of the military column, throwing rocks and insults, but before orders could be given to subdue them, the rebel Gauls disappeared into the thickening fog. A few days later, now spoiling for a fight, the frustrated column of soldiers stumbled across a small group of rebels massing ahead of the column. With swords at the ready, the men charged at the enemy, but in a matter of moments the retreating enemy party stopped, turned around, and joined a wall of several thousand rebel Gauls emerging from fog and cover to attack the Roman column.

Varus was stunned. Arminius, having orchestrated the ambush with the rebels, was nowhere to be found. In a matter of minutes, the once-lengthy show of Roman regional prowess was pressed into a tiny mass of screaming men fighting for their very lives. Unwilling to be captured, and knowing he would receive a far worse fate should he survive the battle to return to Rome, Varus drew his own gladius and fell on the blade. By day's end, only a handful of soldiers had escaped the Roman-educated Arminius's power play and the vengeance of the Gauls. In response to the staggering loss and the sudden vulnerability of the Italian peninsula, Roman emperor Caesar Augustus reportedly shouted, "O, Quintilius Varus! Give me back my legions!"

Shortly, thereafter, the entire region was plunged into unchecked rebellion. Over a year passed before Rome sent another army into the region. Finding only piles of skulls and splintered bones to mark the site of the massacre, the army retreated, and for the next several hundred years, the Rhine River became the new northern boundary of the empire until it was likewise pushed back by Gallic armies.

In A.D. 410, the progenitors of those whom Julius Caesar had "conquered" spilled over the Alps, sacked Rome, and, once more, burned it to the ground. There was no spin to be put on this occasion. Julius Caesar, it seemed, had finally gotten the last laugh on his assassins and their progeny. The Gallic Wars had never ended, the region was never completely divided, and Gaul was never truly Rome's.

RADIO RAIDERS OF THE POLISH FRONTIER

GERMANY, SEPTEMBER 1, 1939

Douglas Niles

"Poland attacked Germany first!"

—Adolf Hitler

Although the Japanese had been sporadically fighting in China for nearly a decade, the generally accepted outbreak of World War II occurred on September 1, 1939, with the German invasion of neutral Poland. The Nazi attack had been in the works for many months, with the final cornerstone of the strategy falling into place during August. At that time, Adolf Hitler's Nazi government and Joseph Stalin's Communist regime set aside their intrinsic differences to sign one of the most cynical and ruthless treaties in modern history.

The pact went into effect on August 23, and guaranteed that neither dictatorship would interfere with the other as they went about reclaiming "ancestral lands" that had been granted to Poland at the end of World War I. In a further burst of cynicism, the Nazis agreed that Stalin could have a free hand moving his armies into the Baltic states of Latvia, Lithuania, and Estonia—despite the fact that these small countries included a significant population of Germanic and Prussian descent.

Germany was poised to devour western Poland like a wolf ready to gulp down a rabbit. A glance at the prewar map confirms this—the geographical positions resemble nothing so much as widespread jaws. East Prussia, separated from Germany by the Danzig corridor connecting Poland to the Baltic Sea, lay directly north of the Polish heartland and was garrisoned by the German Third Army. West of Poland stretched Germany proper, where the Fourth, Eighth, and Tenth armies awaited action. Finally, as a result of the Nazi seizure of Czechoslovakia in the previous year, the mountainous country south of the Polish border was also in German hands. Here the Fourteenth Army coiled, ready to strike north. Fully trained, and supplied with ammunition and fuel, the troops moved into their attack positions and awaited the command to move out.

But Hitler still had an ear, however muted, turned toward world opinion. With a sense of public relations that would fall ever more soundly by the wayside as the war progressed, he concocted an elaborate propaganda trick. He intended it to gain at least a perfunctorily plausible reason to claim that his well-planned, long-sought, and utterly aggressive invasion of Poland was at heart merely a simple act of self-defense.

Though the Nazi regime had not yet progressed to the era of death camps and routine incarceration of Jews and other "undesirables," the party had already established concentration camps. Prisoners, both of political causes and mere criminal behavior, were gathered in these centers in great numbers as virtual slaves, bereft of rights, representation, or communication with the outside world. Now the pool of manpower represented by these camps would provide the Nazis with useful tools of propaganda.

Early in August, Heinrich Himmler, chief of staff of the Shutzstaffeln—the notorious SS—ordered thirteen unfortunate prisoners moved from a concentration camp in eastern Germany, at Oranienburg, to a schoolhouse near the Polish frontier. At the same time, he ordered a number of Polish military uniforms from the German army quartermasters. The uniforms were provided, and the scheme—code-named "Operation Canned Goods"—was ready for implementation.

The plan would consist of two parts, each executed with ruthless efficiency and utter contempt for the truth. On the last day of August 1939, the prisoners were ordered to don the Polish uniforms. Immediately thereafter, twelve of the thirteen men were killed by lethal injection. The bodies were taken to remote woods in Germany, some ten miles from the Polish frontier. There, the dead men were shot, raked by rifle and automatic-weapons fire to simulate the wounds of actual combat. The bodies were then gruesomely posed, some draped over tree limbs or tangled in fences, to make it look as though they had died in action.

No sooner had the smoke cleared than German police forces began closing in. Immediately the word went out to the press: "Poland has staged an invasion of Germany!" Reporters and photographers—transport-expedited by the Wehrmacht, the German army—quickly arrived on the scene to take pictures and dutifully record their observations for the world. Although the reports were subsequently overwhelmed by the massive and irrefutable news of the Nazi invasion, Hitler had this first piece of wartime propaganda broadcast throughout Germany as justification for the attack.

The second phase of the operation went into effect later that day, one of the final acts in prewar Europe. The remaining prisoner, still in his Polish uniform, was hustled to the nearby town of Gleiwitz by a small squad of SS men led by a major. The prisoner was secured, and the SS men—dressed in civilian clothes—charged into the town's small radio station and evicted the broadcasters. Seizing the microphone, one of the SS men, who was fluent in Polish, sent out a frantic call to arms in that language. Claiming that this was the vanguard of a Polish attack against Germany, he urged all who felt loyalty to Poland to rise up and help overthrow the Nazi dictatorship.

There followed a scuffle that would have done any radio-drama director proud. Shouts and cries were heard against the background of further violence. Finally, a volley of gunfire erupted. All of the carefully choreographed action went out over the open microphone, broadcast live to this little corner of the world—and recorded on tape for posterity. The final piece of the plan was simple: shoot and kill the remaining prisoner-in-Poles'-garb, and leave his body in the studio, where all could see that the seditious agitator had met his just fate.

In an address to the Reichstag the morning of the next day, September 1—while his tanks and infantry were already pouring into Poland from the north, west, and south—Hitler used the faked attack on the Gleiwitz radio station as public justification for his long-planned war of aggression. According to the script laid out in Operation Canned Goods, the Germans were just defending themselves!

History, even beginning that first week in September 1939, already knew better.

Whodunit? Now we know . . .

MURDER MOST FOUL

POLAND AND THE USSR, 1939–1943

Douglas Niles

"It was the Germans who killed all those Polish officers!"

—Joseph Stalin

It was the hot summer of 1939, barely more than a year after British prime minister Neville Chamberlain returned from meeting Adolf Hitler in Munich and signing the pact that, according to Chamberlain, had won "peace for our time." (He was not the first, nor the last, to be taken in by a Nazi lie.)

But the agreement signed between Nazi Germany and Communist USSR in that August of 1939 certainly set a new standard for cynicism and betrayal. Named after the two foreign ministers who hammered it out, the Ribbentrop-Molotov Pact essentially carved up Poland between the voracious dictatorships to her east and west. The Soviets and the Nazis promised not to interfere with each other's operations, even going so far as to arrange, in advance, the line along which they would divide the formerly free country.

The pact was signed on August 23, and Hitler wasted no more time, launching his invasion on September 1. The Poles fought valiantly but were utterly overwhelmed by the revolutionary Blitzkrieg tactics that were revealed to the world for the first time. The Germans won complete air superiority by the second day of the war, leading with slashing armored attacks that swiftly penetrated and isolated the Polish defenders—some of whom rode horses into battle against Nazi tanks! Inevitably, the German armies were closing in on Warsaw within the first week or two of the war.

When the Soviets struck, on September 17, Poland's doom was sealed. Even so, some Poles viewed the Russians as the lesser of two evils, even to the point of believing that Stalin's troops were coming in to help protect at least part of Poland from the Nazi aggressors. Warsaw fell on September 27, and the last organized resistance of the Polish army ceased only a few days later. In one month, Hitler had won his first military victory—and hurled the world into the conflict that would rage for nearly six more years, and end only with the utter devastation and defeat of the Nazi homeland.

But in the immediate aftermath, the nations of Europe settled into an uneasy waiting game—mockingly dubbed the Sitzkrieg. England and France had declared war on Germany within days of the invasion but were helpless to do anything to prevent the swift conquest. Hitler quickly moved his victorious troops from Poland to the Western Front, where in May of 1940 they would be unleashed against France, Belgium, Luxembourg, and the Netherlands. Faced with this clearly lethal war machine, the Western powers did not give a lot of thought to the Russians, who were resting comfortably with their half of Poland.

But those Russians were busy. Spearheaded by the dreaded NKVD (forerunner of the Cold War–era KGB), Soviet agents required all former Polish army officers to register with the new government.

When they did so, they were arrested and shipped to camps in Russia. Exactly how many Poles were shipped to one of three gulags, at Kozelsk, Starobelsk, and Ostashkov, is unknown, but it was certainly more than ten thousand, and probably close to fifteen thousand, people. Polish officers and senior noncommissioned officers made up the bulk of these numbers, but the deportees were not exclusively soldiers. At the Kozelsk camp, the Soviets also held Polish doctors, lawyers, professors, and religious leaders of both Catholic and Jewish faiths.

Initially it seems that the Russians tried to "convert" their captives to the cause of communism, but this effort was soon abandoned. Instead, a colonel from the Soviet Secret State Police visited the camps and the prisoners began being shipped out to an unknown location. Over the months of March and April 1940, all three camps were completely evacuated. The prisoners had, for all intents and purposes, disappeared from the eyes and knowledge of the world.

In June of 1941, the Nazis invaded the Soviet Union, and Stalin's government was thrown into the Allied camp. The Germans met with astounding initial success, advancing hundreds of miles in the first few weeks of the campaign and, by autumn, closing in on Moscow itself. Stalin offered amnesty to any Polish soldiers who would join the Soviet Union in fighting the Nazis, and many Poles answered the call.

Of the more than ten thousand men who had been in the three camps, however, there was no sign. Poles living in England began asking questions about the men's fate, and their whereabouts, but Stalin, predictably, was not forthcoming. No less an emissary than Winston Churchill asked the Soviet dictator for an explanation, and finally Stalin suggested that the captives had escaped and made their way to Manchuria. This was such a preposterous claim that the official story was quickly changed; now the Soviet government explained that the Polish officers had been held in territory that had been overrun by the Germans, and thus the Nazis were the only ones who knew what had happened to them.

The question remained unanswered and, for the most part, forgotten as Germany and the USSR waged a titanic struggle for survival. Moscow was saved by a desperate winter counteroffensive in December 1941 and January of 1942, but the following spring the Nazi juggernaut erupted across the southern steppes of the vast Russian homeland. Even as Leningard (Saint Petersburg) in the north endured its epic siege, the Germans closed in on Stalingrad (Volgograd), the great city whose name had been changed in honor of the current master of the Soviet Union.

From autumn of 1942 until winter of 1943, the great struggle for Stalingrad was waged, as each side made an all-out effort to win the key strategic and symbolic center. Gradually the Soviets gained the upper hand, and with their victory, the tide of the war turned against Germany for good.

But it was in the region of Smolensk, a city that had fallen to the Nazis during the first months of the war, that the façade of secrecy surrounding the Polish captives finally began to crack. A Polish exile living near there told some laborers, also Poles, about a secret compound the Soviets had established in a forest named Katyn Wood. A barbed-wire fence surrounded it and frequent patrols, accompanied by guard dogs, ensured that the locals gave the place a wide berth. As long ago as 1929, the Communist government had executed political enemies in the secure and well-defended installation.

When the laborers, and later the German authorities, went to the site, they found a number of earthen mounds on an area known as the Hill of Goats. The mounds were covered with saplings that, in the spring of 1943, were easily identified as being three years old. When the earthen hills were excavated, the grisly truth was revealed: some 4,500 bodies were found, surprisingly well preserved by the loamy soil. Nearly all of the corpses were wearing the uniforms of Polish military men. Their hands were bound, and most had been shot in the back of the head; although a few had apparently been executed by bayonet.

The Germans trumpeted the news of this find to the rest of the world, but because of the notorious unreliability of the Goebbels propaganda machine, British and American authorities reacted with skepticism.

Stalin made an outright denial, claiming, "The Polish prisoners in question were interned in the vicinity of Smolensk in special camps . . . it was impossible to evacuate them at the time of the approach of German troops and as a result they fell into their hands. If, therefore, they have been found murdered, it means they have been murdered by the Germans who, for reasons of provocation, now claim that the crime was committed by Soviet authorities."

Only the Polish government-in-exile (based in London) placed any credence in the German claims. The Poles broke with the Soviet Union, and could later only watch in horror as their country was "liberated" from the Germans and placed under the yoke of communism for more than four decades following the war.

Of course, the Nazis had committed their own atrocities in numbers too great to easily comprehend. At the Nuremburg trials following the war, the Soviets tried to claim that the murder of the Polish officer corps numbered among them. It wasn't until after the fall of the USSR, in the early 1990s, that the truth was finally revealed from official Soviet sources:

Not only had the NKVD done the killings, but they had done so under the express orders of Joseph Stalin himself.

There is a case to be made that this particular lie won the Pacific War.

LISTENING IN

HAWAII/MIDWAY, MAY 1942

Douglas Niles

"Midway's freshwater distilling station is busted . . ."

—U.S. Navy commander Joseph Rochefort

The first five months of World War II in the Pacific saw a virtual tide of Japanese victories in the air, on land, and at sea. Beginning with the deadly surprise attacks at Hawaii and in the Philippines, American military forces were rocked back on their heels. The war came home to the New World in a series of stunning defeats: Pearl Harbor, Wake Island, Lingayen Gulf, Manila, Bataan, Corregidor. Though in many cases American troops fought valiantly, mere courage was not enough to change the lethal course of history.

The Japanese, conversely, swept through a series of apparently inevitable conquests: Wake Island and Hong Kong during December

1941; Burma and Malaya in January 1942; Singapore and the Dutch East Indies in February; and so on. When the last American forces in the Philippines surrendered on May 6, 1942, the Japanese military considered itself virtually infallible, and possessed a feeling of utter contempt for the enemy. Whatever ships dared to challenge the Imperial Japanese Navy were sent to the bottom. Whatever strongpoints the Japanese ground troops attacked were captured. The Americans had no fighter plane capable of meeting the vaunted Zero in aerial combat, and, increasingly, they had no air bases in range of any important Japanese installation.

Only twice during the period from early December 1941 until the first of June 1942 did the Americans give their Pacific enemy pause. In April, U.S. Army Air Force general Jimmy Doolittle led sixteen twin-engine bombers in a raid on the Japanese homeland, courageously flying the land-based bombers from the deck of the aircraft carrier USS *Hornet*. The raid inflicted little actual damage, but it gave the Japanese a nasty shock. The military commands of both the army and the navy were humiliated by the presence of American bombers over the home islands; and the threat to the emperor's life was viewed as a personal disgrace by the esteemed naval commander Admiral Isoruku Yamamoto.

About a month later came the first check to the Japanese plan for expansion, when the invasion of Port Moresby (New Guinea) had to be put on hold following an inconclusive naval air battle in the Coral Sea. For once, an American fleet had stood in battle against the Japanese, and had not been defeated. The fact that in both the Doolittle Raid and the Battle of the Coral Sea the American aircraft carriers—the ships that had fortuitously escaped damage at Pearl Harbor—had proven decisive did not go unnoticed by the Naval Command staff.

But Japanese ambitions remained unchecked, and in fact the American resistance—in particular the Doolittle Raid—had convinced Admiral Yamamoto that the Imperial Japanese Navy needed to be more aggressive in challenging the enemy, and in particular sinking those vexing carriers. And the admiral, the most highly regarded naval officer in the country, had conceived of a plan that would do just that.

The target was located just about a thousand miles from Oahu. The twin islands of the Midway atoll stood out on a map of the Pacific as a very forlorn, lonely, and advanced American outpost. Through the past century, the island had been a coaling station for whaling ships, a relay station for transoceanic telegraph transmissions, and, most recently, a refueling center for the Pan-Am China Clipper. Now it was occupied by some American Marines (Japanese estimates ranged from seven hundred to fifteen hundred of the leathernecks) and a few single-engine fighters and bombers.

The capture of Midway Island, Yamamoto reasoned, would put a Japanese base within a thousand miles of Hawaii, and this was too great a menace for the Americans to ignore. An attack on the atoll would be certain to draw the American carrier fleet out for battle, and Yamamoto—as well as every other Imperial Japanese Navy officer and aviator—was convinced that Japan must certainly win such a battle. The plan for taking Midway had been in the works for several months, but the Doolittle Raid clinched it: the imperial fleet would strike at the island, the Americans would come out to challenge the invasion, and the Japanese would inevitably win a decisive, even a strategic victory.

In attempting this invasion—and, more important, in bringing about the desired fleet action—Japanese leadership felt, logically enough, that it possessed all the advantages. Flush with the confidence of its long string of victories, the Imperial Japanese Navy outnumbered the American Pacific Fleet in battleships, cruisers, destroyers, and, most important, aircraft carriers. Furthermore, the quality of IJN naval air forces had proven to be a match for American air power whenever they had met.

At the recent Coral Sea battle, both sides had given, and gotten, a few licks on the carrier front. The Japanese had lost a light carrier, *Shoho*, and suffered damage to one of the six fleet carriers, the *Shokaku*. A second fleet carrier, *Zuikaku*, also retired to the home islands after the battle, having suffered serious losses of airplanes and air-crew. That still left Japan with four fleet carriers and four light carriers available for the battle at Midway. The Americans, on the other hand, lost the venerable fleet carrier *Lexington* at Coral Sea, while the *Yorktown* had suffered serious bomb damage; estimates were that she would require ninety days of repair. This left only the two carriers from the Doolittle Raid, *Enterprise* and *Hornet*, available to counter the Japanese move against Midway.

There were several hidden advantages on the American side, however, that helped to level the playing field. The island of Midway itself had a seaplane base and an airfield. A number of planes were based on the island, including Marine Corps fighters and dive bombers (many of them admittedly obsolete) and more than twenty army bombers, including long-range B-17s. The total was more planes than any flattop could carry, so in effect, the island would function as an unsinkable aircraft carrier. Secondly, the ninety-day repair estimate for the *Yorktown* was, through heroic efforts on the part of the Pearl Harbor Navy Yard, trimmed to fewer than three days actual port time, allowing the ship (which the Japanese had recorded as "sunk" at Coral Sea) to take part in the Midway battle. Since the Japanese dispersed their light carriers among far-flung auxiliary fleets, this meant that the main showdown would occur between the four fleet carriers of the Imperial Japanese Navy and the three of the U.S. Navy.

Most important of all—indeed, the component that gave U.S. Navy admiral Nimitz the confidence to fight the battle in the first place—were the activities of the Combat Intelligence Office at Pearl Harbor, commonly known as "Hypo." The analysts there, under the tutelage of the unconventional commander Joseph Rochefort (he often worked in slippers and a red smoking jacket), had broken the Japanese navy's most important code, and were busily decrypting the enemy's communications, right up to the highest level of radio traffic.

Although even a broken code is far from an open book (best estimates were that Rochefort and his staff could read some 15 percent of a typical message), by late spring of 1942, the Hypo cryptanalysts were fairly certain that they could pinpoint the position of most important Japanese ships to within a few hundred miles. Furthermore, Rochefort was certain that the enemy was up to something big—a major offensive operation—and managed to convince Admiral Nimitz of the same thing. The target of this operation appeared in coded messages with the designation "AF." Both officers guessed that the enemy target AF would be Midway Island.

But officials in Washington, as well as Lt. Gen. Delos Emmons, the army commander in charge of the defense of the Hawaiian islands, remained skeptical. Emmons feared—logically enough, given the legacy of the Pearl Harbor attack—that the enemy might attempt a landing on Oahu. The chiefs of staff in Washington were worried about an attack on Alaska or the West Coast.

This is where, with Nimitz's blessing, Rochefort cooked up a little white lie. He had a message passed to Midway over the secure telephone cable connecting the island to Hawaii. The garrison of the island was ordered to make a radio report "in the clear" (that is, uncoded) claiming that their freshwater distillation equipment had broken down. The report, a lie, went out over the airwaves.

Within forty-eight hours the Hypo cryptanalysts picked up a coded Japanese navy message reporting the news that "AF" was short of fresh water. Rochefort's little white lie exposed the truth, the U.S. Navy confirmed the Japanese objective for the upcoming battle, and the American carriers would be waiting—exactly where the enemy did not expect them to be. In a stunning reversal of the fortunes of war, Japan would lose all four of her fleet carriers, claiming only one American flattop, the *Yorktown,* in exchange.

Midway would go down as probably the most significant naval victory in all the wars of the twentieth century, and the whole plan hinged on Joe Rochefort's little white lie.

Racism as national policy all based on a lie of omission. Just what we were fighting for . . .

THE YELLOW PERIL THAT WASN'T

Paul A. Thomsen

"In the war in which we are now engaged racial affinities are not severed by migration. The Japanese race is an enemy race and while many second and third generation Japanese born on United States soil, possessed of United States citizenship have become "Americanized," the racial strains are undiluted . . . The very fact that no sabotage has taken place to date is a disturbing and confirming indication that such actions will be taken."

—FROM THE "FINAL REPORT: JAPANESE EVACUATION FROM THE WEST COAST, 1942," HEADQUARTERS WESTERN DEFENSE COMMAND AND FOURTH ARMY, OFFICE OF THE COMMANDING GENERAL, PRESIDIO OF SAN FRANCISCO, CALIFORNIA

In the aftermath of the December 7, 1941, surprise Japanese attack on Pearl Harbor, long-standing class and racial hatred erupted in a cacophony of Caucasian-spearheaded threats, demonstrations, and riots against the Pacific Rim Issei and Nisei. Amid cries of outrage over the near destruction of the entire Pacific Fleet, many Californians claimed that leaving those residents of Japanese ancestry on the West Coast would only be inviting acts of sabotage or, worse, a second attack, the uprising of a large Fifth Column of resident Japanese troops, and an invasion of the American homeland.

Although the federal government held classified information to the contrary, and the Roosevelt administration stalled the issue for several weeks, in early 1942 General John DeWitt was authorized to remove the entire Issei and Nisei populace from the West Coast, because, he said, "In the war in which we are now engaged racial affinities are not severed by migration. The Japanese race is an enemy race and while many second and third generation Japanese born on United States soil, possessed of United States citizenship have become 'Americanized,' the racial strains are undiluted . . . The very fact that no sabotage has taken place to date is a disturbing and confirming indication that such actions will be taken."

While United States expansionist policies had encouraged industry and government to form closer ties with Asia (or, at least, with its resources and markets), few Americans felt hospitably toward Asian immigration, but as economic downturns in China and Japan forced many to immigrate to the United States, that lukewarm antipathy, especially on the American West Coast, turned to bitter loathing. Whereas other Asian immigrant groups, such as the Chinese and Filipinos, were able to assimilate relatively quickly, Japanese immigrants remained largely isolated in self-contained fishing and farming villages along the Pacific coastline. Much to the consternation of their Caucasian neighbors, efforts to check the Japanese (Issei) and Japanese-American (Nisei) population growth through legal measures (restricting land entitlement and citizenship to natural-born residents), the Issei and Nisei had prospered.

In the late 1930s, the Japanese Empire established a far-reaching network of agents throughout Northern and Central America to watch and report on the movements of Allied shipping, and on cultural shifts, political changes, and war industry activities. While some were American men and women (largely Caucasian) in search of monetary compensation in exchange for their access, most were Japanese citizens. Many of them were naval officers working under diplomatic cover within the continental United States or traveling aboard various transports, observing the density of shipping activities along certain routes. In 1941, after developing technology that would make a long-range attack possible, the Japanese Imperial Navy settled on Pearl Harbor as their target. But they lacked detailed information to ensure the success of their strike. They dispatched a twenty-five-year-old Japanese ensign by the name of Takeo Yoshikawa, under diplomatic cover, to gather the needed intelligence on the Pacific Fleet headquarters in the Hawaiian islands. Due to the lax peacetime security, Yoshikawa was able to take boat rides around the area by day and tour the hills overlooking Pearl Harbor by night. With camera in hand and United States counterintelligence agents in tow (and helpless to stop him), he managed to gather enough data to allow Yamamoto's team to replicate the entire harbor facility in large-scale miniature and to provide his pilots with timetables for crew changes and target positioning.

After the Pearl Harbor attack, many Americans believed that the intelligence coup that made the attack possible had come from a wide number of sources.

It did not.

Others feared that the presumed savages who had been the object of the so-called White Man's Burden for the past several decades had finally grown into the much-feared Yellow Peril and were just waiting in their isolated American communities for the proper signal to rise up against their Caucasian neighbors. Yet, the federal government knew what had happened almost as soon as the smoke cleared. Furthermore, United States intelligence sources had broken the Japanese diplomatic codes (code-named MAGIC) and had been keeping track of all radio communications between the Empire of Japan's various embassies and consulates and the Japanese home island. Unbeknownst to much of the outside world until well after the conclusion of the Second World War, the MAGIC decrypts contained the names, dates, targets, and gathered intelligence of the Japanese spy network in North America.

Of still greater value to American intelligence efforts were the directions of the Japanese high command involved in recruitment and intelligence management. Contrary to everything the general public believed at the time, the MAGIC decrypts reveal that the Empire of Japan *forbade* its intelligence agents from recruiting any Nisei in the pursuit of their war aims or intelligence-gathering agendas for fear that, when the Japanese finally attacked the United States, their ancestral sisters and brethren would suffer greatly under the social backlash if there were any evidence tying them to the Japanese Empire. As MAGIC was one of the most vital war secrets the United States held, only a handful of people had access to the decrypted intelligence and fewer still knew from whence it came.

Gen. John DeWitt, as the military commander of the Western Defense Command (WDC), had been apprised by government sources that there were Japanese intelligence operatives in the California area, but his fears were not limited to the facts. The real operatives were known Japanese nationals who were independently visited and taken into custody by the FBI in the aftermath of the Pearl Harbor attack (when the agency could no longer gain any further intelligence from watching their activities). The FBI paid similar visits to the West Coast's Issei and Nisei civilian populace, even though the federal leadership knew, through their own intelligence sources, that most of these people had had no knowledge of nor taken part in the prewar Japanese intelligence network. Still, the general feared his command might yet become the site of another Pearl Harbor attack, beliefs that led him to embrace the region's growing anti-Asian lobby as more nationals were detained. Both Roosevelt administration attorney general Francis Biddle and FBI director J. Edgar Hoover attempted to privately correct the army general's misjudgment regarding the remaining Issei and Nisei populace through appropriate channels, but the efforts were too little and too late. Swayed by political pressure and feelings of national insecurity, by 1942 General DeWitt had come to ardently believe the long-standing lie that the Issei and Nisei populace constituted a potential threat to WDC operations.

While some within the government knew that both the anti-Asian lobby and General DeWitt were wrong, they could never be certain and, as the Roosevelt administration rapidly found, the facts were far less potent than the populace's belief in the lie of the "Yellow Peril." Instead, rather than reveal the United States' own intelligence sources, tools, and methods, the federal government allowed DeWitt's lie to stand. By mid-1942, the entire populace of WDC residents of Japanese ancestry were removed from their homes and placed behind barbed-wire patrolled by members of the United States Army. And there many would stay for the majority of the war . . . all because of fear, prejudice, and economic self-interest . . . and in the service of protecting a national security lie.

Speaking of deceptions that won wars, here is an example that was crucial to the success of the Normandy landings and the break out—without which it might have been another year before we returned to France and the iron curtain would have run along the English Channel.

THE MAGICAL LIES OF QUICKSILVER

ENGLAND AND FRANCE, JANUARY–JULY 1944

Douglas Niles

"The D-Day Invasion Will Come Ashore on the Pas de Calais"

On June 6, 1944, combined British and American forces under Field Marshal Bernard Montgomery landed in the strength of some six divisions along a series of beaches along the Normandy coast of France. The German defenders, under the command of Field Marshal Erwin Rommel, fought tenaciously, and for many weeks the landing forces, reinforced by a steady stream of fresh divisions from the United States, the United Kingdom, and allies battled mightily in a vain effort to break out of the enclosed beachhead.

Though the attackers faced outnumbered (and outclassed) German troops and possessed the benefit of virtually uncontested air superiority, the rugged boscage-strewn countryside, with high, sturdy hedges that rendered every small field into a strongpoint, proved almost impenetrable to the Americans. The British, meanwhile, struggled for a month before finally evicting the Germans from the coastal city of Caen—a city that had been scheduled for liberation on the first day after the invasion! It was not until late July that the stalemate would finally be shattered—in dramatic fashion—by the breakout of American armor under the command of Gen. George Patton.

During all the weeks of furious fighting in Normandy, the Allies were facing Rommel's Seventh Army, some fifteen divisions entrusted with the defense of a long sector of French coastline north of the River Loire and west of the River Seine. Although the Seventh was gradually reinforced during the campaign, the greatest German army in France did not participate in that crucial battle.

The twenty divisions of the Fifteenth Army were deployed east of the Seine through the Pas de Calais region of France and Belgium, defending a smaller front, with more troops, than was the Seventh Army. Even as the beachhead defenses gradually gave way in Normandy, Hitler remained convinced that the massive campaign of Operation Overlord in Normandy was only a diversion, and that the real invasion would occur in the neighborhood of Calais. By the time the Germans figured out the truth, it was too late to halt the breakout, and the fall of Nazi Germany—though it would take ten more long, bloody months—was assured.

It was not just the Führer, Adolf Hitler, who believed that Calais would be the objective of the invasion. Some of his most experienced generals, including Rommel and Rommel's theater commanders, Field Marshals Gerd von Runsdtedt and, later, Hans Gunther von Kluge, also believed that the main blow would come against Calais. The Nazis were encouraged in this belief by one of the most elaborately staged military deceptions—one of the biggest lies—ever presented as truth.

"A Force" and a Magician

At this point in the war, the Allies, led by the British, had already raised military deception to a high art. Under the leadership of Winston Churchill—who noted that "in war, truth should be accompanied by a bodyguard of lies"—the United Kingdom stood alone against the overwhelming Nazi war machine for a long, lonely year. Fighting in the North African desert, they needed to take advantage of every asset at their disposal. This clearly included deception, and in January of 1941 the commander of British forces in Africa, Gen. Archibald Wavell, authorized the creation of "A Force," a unit dedicated to deception in military operations.

Under the command of an eccentric but brilliant officer named Dudley Clarke, A Force quickly proved its worth in the fighting against the Italians and, very soon, the German Afrika Korps under the famed Desert Fox, Erwin Rommel. Concealing the true strength of British forces, inventing illusory units, the A Force worked hard to fool the ever watchful enemy.

One of the most colorful of Clarke's officers was a former magician and illusionist named Jasper Maskelyne, scion of a family of renowned performers. Initially given the task of concealing British troops and operations from Axis aerial reconnaissance, Maskelyne gathered a group of a dozen able men, to be known as the "Magic Gang," and went to work with a vengeance. The Magic Gang created countless dummy tanks and aircraft, usually made from plywood and canvas, which served to confuse the enemy and cause the Germans to inflate estimates of British strength. Maskelyne also invented a machine that would create authentic-looking tank tracks in the sand and used the device to create impressions of much military activity where, in reality, there was none.

During the crucial battle of El Alamein, when the tide of war had finally turned in England's favor, the Magic Gang deceived Rommel by making it appear that a great concentration of armor—some two thousand tanks!—had assembled at the southern end of the British position. A fake railroad track and operations center were laid out in the sands, while an illusory water pipeline was slowly extended toward the position; sound effects were even broadcast to mimic the noises of a busy construction site.

Meanwhile, where the real strike force was assembling, Maskelyne and his team busily concealed some one thousand tanks, making them look like trucks. As an added note to the deception, the false water pipeline leading to the fictional troop concentration progressed so slowly that the Germans did not expect the British to be able to attack for another four or five weeks. When Montgomery's Eighth Army struck in October of 1942, not only did the attack occur much earlier than the enemy expected, but it came in the north, at the opposite end of the line from the anticipated thrust.

Perhaps the Magic Gang's most colorful exploit was the creation of a model of the great harbor at Alexandria in a bay along the Egyptian coast. Created with an array of fake buildings, a temporary lighthouse, dummy ships, and extensive mock-up antiaircraft positions (complete with lots of flash and smoke from blank charges), the harbor illusion drew the attention of many enemy air attacks, and saved the real harbor—a key installation—from serious damage.

Operation Torch

In November of 1942 the Americans entered the war in a big way with Operation Torch, multiple landings on the western shores of North Africa, in territory controlled by Vichy France. Deception was not neglected in concealing the actual dates and locations of the landing from the alert Nazis. False radio traffic was broadcast from ships and shore stations ranging from the eastern United States, Puerto Rico, and Cuba, all the way to Cape Town, South Africa. The plan, called Operation Quickfire, was to make the

Germans believe that the American troops shipping out just then were intended to go to Egypt and Lebanon, freeing up British garrison troops who would be moved into action.

One elaborate deception operation involved the planting of a corpse dressed as a British officer carrying plans detailing fake objectives and timetables for the invasion. The Germans found the body, examined the false plans, and gleefully organized defensive preparations around their intelligence "windfall." Other deception plans caused the Germans, and even Hitler himself, to obsess over an imaginary threat to Norway.

Operation Torch also saw the introduction of another notable officer into Allied deception planning. A decorated lieutenant colonel, David Strangeways—a survivor of the Dunkirk evacuation early in the war—had worked with Dudley Clarke in Egypt, and had demonstrated imagination and determination there. Dispatched to Eisenhower to help with Operation Torch, Strangeways quickly established himself as a master in the art of military deception. He helped to plant in German minds the notion that the increased traffic around Gibraltar (which German spies could easily observe from neutral Spain) was the result of an effort to relieve Malta, the beleaguered British-held island in the middle of the Mediterranean Sea.

When the three great fleets showed up off the coast of northwest Africa, the Germans and their Vichy French allies were taken completely by surprise—which is a good thing, because there were plenty of bugs to work out in the Americans' first amphibious landing of the war: paratroopers landed in the wrong places; heavy seas dumped landing craft; the most important supplies were loaded in the bottoms of the ships' holds; and the Vichy French troops were, at least initially, less than delighted to be "liberated." Nevertheless, the campaign was a success.

And as plans for the great invasion of Europe began to gather steam, David Strangeways would play a key role.

Operations Overlord and Fortitude

By the time the Germans and Italians had been ejected from North Africa in the spring of 1943, deception was recognized as an integral part of Allied operations. The upcoming invasion of Europe would be the riskiest and most ambitious attack of the war, and both tactical and strategic surprise would be crucial. Thus, it was clear that the invasion would need an elaborate cover.

David Strangeways arrived in England in late 1943 with a mandate to fool the Germans into believing that a notional invasion was going to occur in a place well removed from the actual site on the beaches of Normandy. As planning for Operation Overlord progressed, Strangeways and his team concocted an array of deceptions to conceal the real objective from German intelligence. The initial deception plan was called Operation Fortitude, and was divided into Fortitude North and Fortitude South. Each was designed to fool the enemy into believing that a sector of Europe was in danger of being invaded. It was hoped that the Nazis would correspondingly deploy forces in the wrong place to meet the real invasion.

Operation Fortitude North consisted of a creating the potential for an invasion of Norway from bases in Scotland and Northern England. Real units were already based there, and aerial reconnaissance and diplomatic efforts—for example, pressuring Sweden to stay out of the upcoming campaign—added verisimilitude to the deception. Although Fortitude North met with some limited success in terms of causing the Germans to expect an invasion, the Nazis never increased their garrison in Norway, estimating that the twelve divisions they had there would be adequate to defend that Scandinavian nation against a liberation attack. Since a key goal of deception operations is to make the enemy do something rather than just think something, the operation must be viewed as a failure.

Fortitude South was a whole different matter, however. A series of plans under the overall name of Quicksilver would be implemented throughout the first six months of 1944, and eventually would continue for more than six weeks after the D-day landings. In total, Operation Quicksilver would paralyze the German defenses, and give Eisenhower and Montgomery's troops the breathing space needed to win the campaign in Normandy.

Operation Quicksilver I–VI

Quicksilver I was the centerpiece of the whole operation (which eventually would include six distinct operations, codenamed Quicksilver I through Quicksilver VI).

Quicksilver I was a background story concocted by Strangeways and fleshed out with the help of several of his staff officers. The basic "plotline" centered on the buildup of a fictional First United States Army Group (FUSAG) located in southeastern England. This massive force would supposedly garrison the ports and area around the Dover coast directly across the Channel from Calais. As the plan was put into effect, it was leaked that General Patton himself—the Allies' most capable offensive commander, in reality and also in German perception—would command FUSAG in the ambitious landings on the French coast.

The fact that the English Channel reaches its narrowest point at the crossing from Dover to Calais lent automatic credence to the idea of the Allies' invading there. Furthermore, a great Allied army ashore on Calais would already be adjacent to Belgium and perfectly poised to strike at the German industrial heartland of the Ruhr Valley. The Nazis would have to defend it. Indeed, the Allies had seriously considered Calais as the site of the actual invasion; Normandy was eventually chosen in great part because Calais seemed just too obvious, and the German defenses were arrayed accordingly to make it a very tough nut.

Once the background story had been created—even to the point of casting Patton in his starring role—the rest of the Quicksilver operations were put into place to try to make sure that the Germans were gradually fed the story in a way that would cause them to believe they were analyzing actual intelligence, instead of being fed falsehoods put out by Strangeways and his team. Contrary to popular conception, this was not done with the creation of a lot of dummy units, tanks, and aircraft, such as had been done in Egypt, for the simple reason that, by this stage of the war, German reconnaissance flights over England were virtually impossible given the state of Allied air superiority.

Instead, the false information was disseminated via two methods: radio signals and the reports of double agents. The latter included more than a dozen spies who had been in England since the beginning of the war. Early on, British counterintelligence services successfully identified every one of these agents. A few were arrested, but most were persuaded to continue sending reports back to Berlin—only, instead of actual observations and conclusions, the reports would contain information crafted by British intelligence. This remarkably successful arrangement lasted throughout the war, with the spies usually reporting over radio channels and feeding carefully scripted information back to their Nazi handlers. The double agents made valuable contributions to Quicksilver, reporting on the false concentration of American and British Forces for FUSAG, providing a wealth of detail about the specific units involved, and even suggesting that these troops were being trained for amphibious or airborne operations.

Quicksilver II was primarily concerned with radio deception. Many small stations were set up throughout the FUSAG area. Basically, a few men in a small trailer or radio shack would put out enough radio traffic to make it seem as if they were an entire division. By moving these units around, and gradually bringing them into the launching zones in southeastern England, the Allied planners fooled the Germans into believing that a great number of divisions, some real and some purely notional, were assembling for a mighty invasion.

Quicksilver III was the closest thing to a dummy force involved in this elaborate plan. The false equipment consisted of, for the most part, fake landing craft and transports. All of these were gathered in the ports of southeastern England, where it was hoped that the German aerial and nautical reconnaissance would observe and report their presence. Additional fake signage was posted on the coastal roads to add to the fiction that a great force was gathering here. After the war, it was learned that the level of German recon was so low that this part of the Quicksilver plan had relatively little impact on the great deception.

Quicksilver IV was the air component of the plan. Key to this operation were a great many actual air raids during the weeks and days leading up to the real invasion. The deception was carried out to such an extent that more bombs were actually dropped in support of the fake invasion than the real landing! Some of the air missions focused on destroying the bridges over the Seine, which had a tangible benefit to the real Operation Overlord (since the bridges would have been useful to German troops going in either direction), but much of it consisted of bombing raids against the coastal installations and nearby depots and transport junctions in the Pas de Calais.

The part of the plan known as Quicksilver V went into effect during the month or so prior to the actual landing, and consisted of increased radio activity around the Dover ports. The wireless activity was intended to suggest vigorous tunneling and hastily erected fortifications and installations. Centered on locations, not units, Quicksilver V put out a lot of traffic and created the impression of a massive amount of military activity.

Quicksilver VI was another short-term operation, consisting of lots of lighting to simulate activity in the Dover ports in the days immediately before the invasion. It was hoped, again, that German forces would observe this extra illumination directly and conclude that the invasion was embarking. As with Quicksilver III, the level of German recon was so low that the effort was mostly wasted. However, this might have been a blessing in disguise, as Strangeways and his men concluded that the fake lighting arrays around the Dover ports were so extreme that a keen German observer might have reached the conclusion that he was in fact witnessing a deception rather than the activity of an actual operation.

D-Day and Beyond

The invasion of the Normandy coast went ashore beginning before dawn on June 6, 1944; but that did not bring an end to the deceptions of Operation Quicksilver. Instead, the double agents immediately stepped up their traffic, reporting that the units of FUSAG remained in place, together with all the transport necessary to launch another invasion. Diversionary air attacks continued at a frenzied pace, and even as the invasion troops struggled to maintain their precarious toehold on the mainland, the German high command, all the way up to Hitler, remained convinced that another, even greater landing was due to occur in the region around Calais.

Rommel pleaded for the reserves to be released to his control, but Hitler remained adamant, and the Fifteenth Army remained in place, defending a part of France that was not in any danger of imminent attack. As the days of battle turned to weeks, and June finally gave way to July, the continuing efforts of Strangeways and his team held the Germans mesmerized. Reinforcements to the Seventh Army trickled up to the front in Normandy, while the Americans and British were bringing fresh divisions ashore daily.

In fact, the arrival of these troops presented a real challenge to the deception central to Operation Quicksilver, since many of them were actually units that had been attached to the notional FUSAG but were now being used in the real campaign. The arrival of Patton himself could not be kept a secret, but Strangeways, Montgomery, and Eisenhower had an answer. Another highly esteemed general, Leslie McNair, was sent over to England from the United States as Patton was brought over to France to command his newly created Third Army. The deceivers explained that Patton's "demotion," from army group to mere army command, had resulted from some of the troubles the always volatile Patton had stirred up in the public relations arena. Finally, a whole new fictional unit, Second U.S. Army Group (SUSAG) was established and staffed with nonexistent units.

On July 17, Rommel was badly wounded by a strafing Allied fighter bomber, and his role in the campaign was concluded. Shortly before his death (by forced suicide) later that year, he would confess to his son that leaving the Fifteenth Army in place instead of bringing at least some of these divisions into the battle had been one of the great mistakes of the war.

Operation Quicksilver had done its work very well indeed.

Very few things are worse than being caught in a lie. One of these is being caught in a whole series of lies in front of the whole world. This was not President Eisenhower's finest hour.

AND U-2

Brian Thomsen

LIE: A NASA weather research plane on a mission inside of Turkey may have accidentally drifted into Soviet territory.

In 1960 the so-called Cold War was heating up, and in an effort to defuse the tensions a summit meeting in Paris was scheduled for May 16, bringing together the four heads of state of the United States, Great Britain, France, and the Soviet Union.

Unfortunately on May 1, a U.S. Lockheed U-2 plane disappeared over the sovereign territory of the Soviet Union. The pilot was a civilian in Lockheed's employ by the name of Francis Gary Powers.

Four days after Powers disappeared, NASA (not Lockheed, which was supposedly in charge of the flight) issued a very detailed press release noting that a weather research plane had "gone missing" north of Turkey, distancing the U.S. government from any involvement with the matter. It was suggested in their release that perhaps the pilot might have fallen unconscious while the autopilot was engaged. They also stated that "the pilot reported over the emergency frequency that he was experiencing oxygen difficulties," and as a result may have uncontrollably drifted off-course.

A photo of a U-2 plane painted in NASA colors was also provided to the media by Lockheed.

Quickly thereafter, the Soviet Union went public with an announcement of their own.

Soviet premier Nikita Khrushchev declared that a "spy plane" had been shot down, whereupon the United States issued a statement reaffirming the claim that the plane was a "weather research aircraft," and allowing that it may have strayed into Soviet airspace after the pilot had "difficulties with his oxygen equipment during a mission over Turkey," as was previously stated. Furthermore they attested "there was absolutely no deliberate attempt to violate Soviet airspace and never has been." NASA attempted to strengthen their case by grounding all U-2 aircraft to check them for "oxygen problems" to avoid further potential "accidents."

In all actuality, the United States was lying through its teeth.

The U-2 piloted by Francis Gary Powers (who had left the air force in 1956 with the rank of captain to accept civilian employment with the Central Intelligence Agency), had left Preshwar, Pakistan, intending to overfly the Soviet Union and land at Bodo, Norway, with the intention of photographing Soviet intercontinental ballistic missile (ICBM) development sites in and around Sverdlovsk and Plesetsk, far within the borders of the Soviet Union. At its cruising altitude, the U-2 was able to avoid being intercepted by Soviet fighters on patrol and those dispatched in pursuit, but eventually a 14 SA-2 Guideline surface-to-air missile disabled the plane and brought it down.

As was standard in such spy missions, Powers was under strict orders to destroy the plane and himself rather than risk being captured, even though such an event was considered unlikely since the U-2 had the capability of flying higher than Soviet surveillance was able to monitor—but no one was 100 percent sure exactly how high an altitude Powers had reached when his U-2 disappeared.

Still, the United States was confident that its secret mission was still safe . . . that is, until May 7, when Khrushchev made a startling revelation: "I must tell you a secret. When I made my first report I deliberately did not say that the pilot was alive and well . . . and now just look how many silly things [they] have said."

Powers's aircraft was indeed wrecked, having crashed near Yekaterinburg, but Powers had been captured after making a parachute landing. Moreover, the Soviets managed to recover the surveillance camera and its film and were even successful in developing the incriminating photographs it contained. Also damning was Powers's survival pack, including 7,500 rubles, Soviet currency that left little doubt about his intended flight path, and could not be considered standard issue for a civilian pilot on a mission involving meteorology.

Powers was put on trial for espionage, pled guilty (to avoid being executed), and was convicted on August 19. He was sentenced to three years' imprisonment and seven years' hard labor, of which he served one and three-quarter years before being exchanged for Soviet master spy Rudolf Abel on February 10, 1962, and returned to the United States.

The Paris summit was left in shambles, and the long-anticipated meeting between Eisenhower, Charles de Gaulle, Harold Macmillan, and Khrushchev, in an effort to cool tensions, was preempted by further escalation.

The only saving grace had been that President Eisenhower himself had not made the false statements concerning the U-2's status as a "weather research aircraft," though he had issued frequent denials in the past in the face of Soviet allegations that the United States had encroached on sovereign Soviet airspace and undertaken spy missions within the Soviet Union.

According to Eric Alterman in his book *When Presidents Lie*,

Eisenhower admitted to his secretary that the entire incident made him want to resign from the presidency. Several stories were quickly put out that suggested that Ike may actually have been unaware of the spy program, and that he was pursuing an investigation into what exactly happened, since he should have been informed about what was going on.

A cloak of deniability was quickly fashioned for the president to protect him from the scandal. Secretary of State Christian Herter contended that the news and status of the U-2 program had never crossed the president's desk—but this did little to restore U.S. credibility and made public the severe mistrust that existed between the two superpowers. The incident brought more chill to the growing Cold War.

A large part of the U-2 wreckage, and items from Powers's survival pack, are still on display at the Central Museum of Armed Forces in Moscow.

In 1998, information was declassified revealing that Powers's fateful mission had actually been a joint USAF/CIA operation, with Lockheed and NASA acting in camouflage.

In 2000, Powers was posthumously awarded the Prisoner of War Medal, the Distinguished Flying Cross, and the National Defense Service Medal—and an admission that he had been following direct orders on his surveillance mission.

When asked how high he was flying on May 1, 1960, he often replied, "evidently not high enough."

The Vietnam War was one of the most divisive in our history. It changed the nation and deeply affected a generation. The way we perceived that war was the eventual cause of our losing it. We didn't have to; we chose to. Here is the beginning of why that happened.

HOW NOT TO SELL A WAR

William Terdoslavich

The truth is that every war is a contest between the good guys (us) and the bad guys (them). But in a democracy, the president must frequently remind the people regularly that the war is a struggle between "us" and "them."

Patriotism does not endorse a blank check of political goodwill that a president can draw on to support a war. This is a basic rule in politics, yet one that President Lyndon Johnson overlooked when underselling the Vietnam War. Johnson was one of the sharpest politicians ever to serve as president. But he left office branded a liar because he could not tell the whole truth about the war.

What Should Be Done?

It was a simple question. What should be done to win in Vietnam?

By late 1964 it was pretty clear that the United States would have to do more than just supply and train South Vietnam's army. The

South was losing its war against indigenous Communist Viet Cong guerillas, supported and supplied by North Vietnam. The loss was being compounded by the political game of musical chairs played by South Vietnam's generals, who preferred infighting and coups rather than a unified effort to defeat the enemy. All this added up to a South Vietnam that could not fight for itself.

By early 1965, elite South Vietnamese units were losing battles to the Viet Cong. To salvage the situation, Defense Secretary Robert McNamara and National Security Advisor McGeorge Bundy outlined two choices for Johnson: negotiate with North Vietnam or go to war. McNamara referred to this as "the fork in the road memo" in his memoir, *In Retrospect*. Johnson chose war. When it came time for Johnson to explain truthfully to the American people why this was needed, he never really did so.

McNamara saw two reasons why he didn't. First, Johnson was fixated on getting his Great Society programs passed in Congress. The pricey package of social programs was Johnson's effort to raise the poor out of poverty and outdo Franklin Roosevelt's Depression-era New Deal. But, second, Johnson feared political pressure from the right wing of his own Democratic Party, as well as from the Republicans, to fight a more unrestrained war, knowing that a greater war effort in Vietnam might draw in Communist China and the Soviet Union, thus risking World War III.

General William Westmoreland, who commanded the ground forces in South Vietnam for much of Johnson's term, critiqued this lack of candor. "When the President and his Administration failed to level with the American people about the extent and nature of the sacrifice that had to be made, they contributed to a credibility gap that grew into an unbridgeable chasm. . . . If a war is deemed worthy of the dedication and sacrifice of the military services, it is also worthy of the commitment of the entire population," Westmoreland wrote in his memoir, *A Soldier Reports*. Unfortunately, Westmoreland himself also played a major role in presenting a less-than-truthful picture of the Vietnam War, thus undermining the nation's resolve.

Westmoreland's assessment became more haunting because the United States relied on draftees to man a significant percentage of the army it was sending to fight in South Vietnam. An honest reason was needed to send conscripts to war, as they were the ones who would pay the "blood tax."

How Many?

After the questionable Gulf of Tonkin incident involving a supposed North Vietnam attack on U.S. naval ships, Johnson resolved to strike back at North Vietnam using airpower. The bombing campaign was conducted by U.S. warplanes based in the South. The war saw its first escalation in February 1965 when Viet Cong guerillas struck the airbase at Pleiku, killing eight U.S. servicemen. The air campaign was intensified and was named Rolling Thunder.

But the airbases that enabled this campaign needed protection. This required ground troops. Westmoreland requested several Marine battalions to provide base security at Danang, located roughly a hundred miles south of the Demilitarized Zone. He was then granted a mission change from base security to active combat, as the best defense was an offense.

The press would be the conduit that carried Johnson's word, or lack of it, to the American public. While browbeating his press secretary George Reedy over the lack of good stories, Johnson never put Reedy in the loop on any Vietnam policy. He reasoned that if his trusted press secretary did not know anything, he could not leak anything. Reedy directed any questions about Vietnam to the Pentagon, where "no comment" was the standard reply. This created a dangerous vacuum where the slightest unexpected revelation could burst into a maelstrom of outrage.

Not long after the Marines were sent to Danang in early 1965, the dam broke. A State Department spokesman figured out that the Marines' mission had changed from base protection to combat, and told the reporters so. All hell broke lose in the White House as Johnson raged against the leak. But the story was out—there had been a major change in policy, and it had *not* been announced from the top.

While urged by advisers to prepare the American people to support a long struggle, Johnson ignored this advice. He clung to polling data that showed Americans supporting him and the war, as Americans do "rally round the flag" in any war—at first. So there was no need to explain anything. Instead, Johnson pursued a "policy of minimum candor," which historian Stanley Karnow described as "the deliberate tactic to disclose only the barest essentials without blatantly lying." This policy only produced unwanted surprises, blindsiding the press and the administration.

By April 1965, the CIA reported that the North Vietnamese Army (NVA) was sending regular units to augment the combat capability of the Viet Cong (VC) guerillas. Westmoreland and the service chiefs now asked for two divisions and two brigades plus necessary support units. This would boost U.S. force levels from thirty-three thousand to eighty-two thousand. Johnson would not break the news about the troop increase, instead preferring to announce the call-up of units at appropriate times, McNamara recounts in his memoir.

In June 1965, Westmoreland asked for more troops, as South Vietnamese units proved no match against the Communist enemy. The general wanted 41,000 immediately and another 52,000 later in 1965, bringing the U.S. deployment up to 175,000 by that year's end. How did Johnson pitch this? He made the announcement at a midday press conference conveniently timed for the moment when the least number of people would be watching TV.

Manpower estimates for 1966 would be affected by the November 1965 Battle of the Ia Drang Valley. There a battalion of U.S. heliborne troops mauled a pair of NVA regiments (an event well documented in the book and movie *We Were Soldiers Once, and Young*). North Vietnam was having little problem matching U.S. deployments. Westmoreland therefore doubled his 1966 requests from 100,000 to 200,000, which would bring U.S. force totals to about 410,000 by the end of the year. By March 1967, Westmoreland had 470,000 under his command, and was asking for another 200,000!

McNamara recounts how he pressed Westmoreland for an estimate on when victory would occur if he got none, some, or all of what he wanted. It would take five years to win at current troop strength, two years with two hundred thousand more troops, Westmoreland replied.

How Lack of Truth Became a Lie

Westmoreland's approach to counterinsurgency would lay the foundation for failure in Vietnam, unwittingly abetted by McNamara and Johnson.

Traditional counterinsurgency strategy called for the protection of villages by local troops or a constabulary. This effort must be augmented by civil improvements, provided by the government. Once the villagers trust the government, they will provide information on the guerillas, who could then be hunted down by smaller units of highly trained troops.

Instead, Westmoreland preferred "search and destroy," as large U.S. units moved through the jungle, relying on their firepower advantage to wipe out any enemy units they brushed up against. But search and destroy did not kill enough of the enemy to exceed Westmoreland's replacement rate.

The bombing of North Vietnam would complement the strategy by wiping out the few industrial targets that could help the war effort, and interdicting the Ho Chi Minh Trail that supplied Communist troops in the South. But the bombing campaign never dented

North Vietnam's logistics effort. Most weapons the North needed were made abroad and shipped in. Communist units needed so little supply that whatever was lost was easily replaced or supplemented.

These factors created a vacuum that sucked in ever-increasing numbers of American troops, all of whom were needed to produce victory, by Westmoreland's calculus. McNamara endorsed the plan, despite any latent misgivings he might have had.

When Truth Hurts

The Vietnam War was becoming financially and politically exorbitant. By December 1967, U.S. troop strength had reached 485,000, and would peak at 543,000 by April 1969. The intervening event that broke the camel's back was the January 1968 Tet Offensive. NVA and VC units attacked every provincial capital in South Vietnam, banking on a popular uprising that never occurred. Areas the United States declared "pacified" became battlefields overnight. The Communists took Hue, a major city. Even the U.S. embassy in Saigon was attacked. Despite all this, the VC and NVA were soundly defeated everywhere. U.S. casualties were high, but American public opinion suffered more heavily, as political support for the war was destroyed.

Westmoreland's post-Tet request for another 206,000 men did not go down well. It would have required mobilization of the reserves, a politically unpopular move that Johnson could not afford. Polls showed the president's approval rating plummeting from 48 to 36 percent in the weeks following Tet, while those who favored how he was handling the war also fell from 40 percent to 26 percent. Added to that was Senator Eugene McCarthy's surprise showing in the New Hampshire primary, where he garnered over 40 percent of the vote against the sitting president. By March 1968, Defense Secretary Clark Clifford, backed by a bevy of foreign policy alumni from previous administrations collectively known as "The Wise Men," recommended that no more troops be sent to Vietnam, now perceived as an unwinnable war. Johnson halted the bombing of North Vietnam, called for negotiations, and then shocked the nation by declining to seek reelection.

Alan Enthoven, a senior adviser to McNamara, astutely identified U.S. public opinion as the most precious but limited resource of the war. Could the United States build up a viable South Vietnamese Army and government that could hold its own before the American public wrote off the war as a waste of time, money, and lives? Sending in more troops was not the answer, as it increased U.S. casualties while producing empty victories on the battlefield. Johnson had to tell his fellow Americans that the sacrifice was worth it, while at the same time concentrating resources on building a South Vietnamese government that could successfully conduct a pacification campaign. Sadly, Enthoven's memo was overlooked.

Johnson and many of his advisers never understood that Americans make war by the clock. A president can get two or three years of unconditional public support for a war, but he had to show results to justify the sacrifice. An unending war without results only produces political breakdown.

Johnson never lied about the war, but he never told the whole truth, either. He became his own worst enemy, too willing to undersell the war so that he could get his Great Society program enacted and civil rights legislation passed. In the end, it no longer mattered what Johnson said. Opinion leaders and voters alike saw the Vietnam War's lack of results every night on the evening news, and concluded that the conflict was not worth the effort.

Lyndon Johnson failed, and the truth was not there to say otherwise.

The worst lies are the ones we tell to ourselves, even when we believe that we know better. The murky beginning of the Vietnam War is a good case study of self-deception. No good reason could be found to justify a war that cost more than 58,000 dead and 150,000 wounded.

INCIDENT IN TONKIN GULF

The Dishonest Truth

William Terdoslavich

The first shot fired in a war is not always loud and clear. The Japanese attack on Pearl Harbor and the Confederacy's firing on Fort Sumter left no doubts as to "who started it." But the Gulf of Tonkin incident was fathered by confusion, born in doubt, and led to a war in Vietnam that was fought with ambiguity on our side. Did the United States start this war? Or did North Vietnam? Our leaders at the time said "they started it," but the information they had to go on was incomplete. In politics, any statement that turns out to be less than true is seen as a damned lie. The falsehood of omission would haunt the war for evermore.

SEALs, Swifts, Spooks, and Snoops

Let us turn back to the "good old days" better known as the Cold War, a political struggle between the United States and its free-market democracy on one side, and the Soviet Union and totalitarian communism on the other. Any gain made by communism was a loss for the U.S.-led West, and vice versa. It meant that even the most irrelevant little nation could be a theater of strategic decision, such as Vietnam.

By the end of 1964, the United States already had more than twenty thousand military personnel in South Vietnam, trying to train the South's army to resist and defeat the Communist Viet Cong, which were native to the South and being supported by the North. Unfortunately, the Communists were winning.

To fight back, U.S.-trained South Vietnamese commandoes tried their hand at raiding North Vietnamese coastal installations in a scheme called Operation Plan 34A (aka "Oplan34A"). These missions would be run concurrently with an unrelated U.S. espionage effort, code-named DESOTO. As described by James Bamford in his book *Body of Secrets,* DESOTO called for a National Security Agency signals-intelligence van to be bolted on to any available navy destroyer. Such a van would steam off the coast of North Vietnam, trolling for any signals intelligence. The Oplan34A raids would bestir North Vietnamese forces to turn on coastal radars and communicate via radio, which a DESOTO patrol would then net and record for later analysis. These two missions were not deliberately coordinated, but destroyers on DESOTO patrol would take advantage of the situation to gather intelligence. On other patrols, the presence of the destroyer alone would not have generated any signal reaction from the North Vietnamese.

The stage was now set for some gross misunderstandings.

One hot summer night . . .

History tends to happen out of the blue, as the ordinary turns into the extraordinary with sudden swiftness. Such a fate visited the USS *Maddox,* on DESOTO patrol on August 1, 1964. The navy assumed that North Vietnam did not claim a twelve-mile limit on territorial waters, so the *Maddox* could come within eight miles of the mainland shore or within four miles of any North Vietnamese island. The *Maddox* sighted Hon Me island, the target of a South Vietnamese commando raid two nights previously, and steamed by without incident. But hours afterward, the NSA signal van on the destroyer's deck intercepted a message ordering an attack on enemy vessels, followed by another report of an enemy vessel giving the *Maddox*'s location. The ship went to general quarters at 2:45 A.M., changing course to sail eastward and away from North Vietnamese waters, though the intercepted radio signals gave no explicit order to attack the *Maddox*.

At 11:30 A.M. on August 2, the *Maddox* sighted five North Vietnamese PT boats headed toward Hon Me island. Forty-five minutes later, the *Maddox* reached the end of its patrol line and turned south. The signal van again picked up signals ordering an attack on an enemy vessel. The *Maddox* again increased speed and set course southeast, away from a trio of North Vietnamese PT boats coming out at thirty plus knots. Each one launched a torpedo at the *Maddox*. None hit. The destroyer returned fire, sinking two of the PT boats. Capt. John Herrick of the *Maddox* wanted to discontinue the DESOTO mission but was overruled by superiors who did not want the destroyer's fighting retreat to look like the United States was being chased out of international waters. The destroyer *C. Turner Joy* would provide an escort to the *Maddox*. Both would sail back into harm's way.

On the night of August 3, South Vietnamese commandoes raided a coastal radar station and security post seventy-five miles north of the DMZ. The two U.S. destroyers were not far away. By August 4, Herrick cabled his concerns to his superiors: that North Vietnam would treat the DESOTO patrols as a supporting element in the South Vietnamese commando raids. From more distant listening posts, NSA intercepted several North Vietnamese radio messages, one specifying the location of the two destroyers, another ordering PT and patrol boats to be readied for attack. Word was passed to the Pentagon, then on to Herrick aboard *Maddox* at 7:15 P.M. local time.

One hour later, Herrick radioed for help. Radar on the *Maddox* had picked up three blips on the surface, closing fast. The nearby carrier USS *Ticonderoga* scrambled its fighters. The night was moonless. The cloud ceiling was low. Despite this, fighters arrived at the scene and sighted . . . nothing.

For the next two hours, the *Maddox* and *C. Turner Joy* reported being shot at and torpedoed, but for this information the ships were going on sonar and radar data, perhaps receiving false signal returns owing to the stormy weather. No enemy PT boats were ever seen. Herrick cabled his doubts to his superiors in Honolulu and Washington, urging caution until events could be fully evaluated.

Perhaps there was no attack after all?

Playing Telephone

What followed can only be described as a good case study in confusion. President Lyndon Johnson, thousands of miles away in Washington, had to make a judgment call. He did not want to retaliate unless North Vietnam had actually "started it." He leaned on Defense Secretary Robert McNamara to get all the information. McNamara then pressed Joint Staff chief lieutenant general David Burchinal (Air Force) to get the straight dope from the commander in chief, Pacific (CINCPAC) Admiral U. S. Grant Sharpe. Sharpe in turn communicated with Herrick on the *Maddox*, trying to get an answer to the question "What happened?"

McNamara recounts in his memoir, *In Retrospect*, that he had definite word that the first attack of August 2 did happen, but that there was the possibility that the second attack of August 4 might not have happened. Reviewing the facts as they were known at the time, McNamara concluded that the second attack had happened, based on fragmentary information pieced together. Reports indicated that the *C. Turner Joy* was fired on; that PT boat cockpit lights were sighted by one of the destroyers; that two of the navy fighters were fired on by AA guns on one of the nearby islands; that North Vietnamese message traffic indicated two PT boats lost; and that Sharpe declared that the second attack had taken place.

Roughly twelve hours after receiving news of the second attack, President Johnson decided to do two things: order retaliatory air strikes against North Vietnam and seek a resolution from Congress authorizing him to take action.

The carriers *Ticonderoga* and *Constellation* launched planes to hit nearby North Vietnamese PT boat bases and a fuel complex.

The war was on, but Congress did not make it official until August 7, when it passed a resolution authorizing Johnson to take any action, including military, to help any U.S. ally in Southeast Asia. And of course, close consultation with Congress was promised. The vote was unanimous in the House, and there were only two "nay" votes in the Senate. Little did the legislators know that they just handed a blank check of power to Johnson. And he would draw freely against that account, with dire results.

Oops

Years later, the errors of the moment would become known. In 1972, deputy NSA director Louis Tordella testified before Congress that North Vietnamese radio intercepts surrounding the August 2 attack were misinterpreted as ordering the August 4 "attack."

But worse was yet to come to light.

Writing in his memoir, McNamara recalls a meeting with his counterpart from the war, North Vietnam defense minister Vo Nguyen Giap, on November 9, 1995. McNamara asked him about the second attack on the destroyers. Had it occurred? Finally the answer came from the other side: no.

The decision to fight was based on faulty information, and McNamara had had a hand in it. The rush of events, the political pressure to act, the lack of complete information, and the need by

Johnson to be seen as forceful and decisive in a crisis (especially during an election year) only compounded the wrong decision.

The small fight between the *Maddox* and the North Vietnamese PT boats did not justify an all-out war. (Similar incidents in later years were resolved by smaller doses of force and greater use of diplomacy.) The North Vietnamese probably felt they were being baited by the Americans and their South Vietnamese proxies, writes James Bamford. The truth won't be fully known until Soviet and North Vietnamese archives are opened to outside scholarship, adds McNamara.

Perhaps the decision making that arose from the Gulf of Tonkin incident can be called an honest mistake. But Johnson and McNamara jumped to conclusions rather than taking the time to get to the truth or letting the matter drop. If the truth that later emerges is at variance with the facts, then average Americans will call the episode a lie. The court of public opinion renders simple judgments, for anything that is not 100 percent true is a falsehood. Thus Lyndon Johnson stands guilty of lying about the Gulf of Tonkin incident, even if he and his associates lacked all the facts needed to deliberately deceive their fellow Americans.

This is a rather extended look at a period in history when it seems just about everyone was lying. The consequences of those lies still reverberate today all through America.

SINK OR SWIM WITH NGO DINH DIEM

Teresa Patterson

During a state visit to Vietnam in 1961, Vice President Lyndon B. Johnson praised South Vietnamese president Ngo Dinh Diem, proclaiming, "President Diem is the Churchill of the decade . . . in the vanguard of those leaders who stand for freedom."

Earlier, Senator John F. Kennedy had stated that Diem's regime was "the cornerstone of the free world in Southeast Asia, the keystone to the arch, the finger in the dyke." President Eisenhower had hailed Diem as the "miracle man" of Asia.

In fact, they all knew that Ngo Dinh Diem was none of those things. At best he was a petty mandarin. At worst, a self-absorbed dictator who, with his brother Nhu, was responsible for turning the people of South Vietnam against their own government or driving them over to the Communists. As early as 1954, Eisenhower's advisers in Vietnam considered Diem "hopeless," and warned that underwriting his administration was a "gamble." The French prime minister Edgar Faure called him "not only incapable, but mad."

Three years after Johnson's enthusiastic endorsement, the United States gave up all pretense of support, secretly authorizing a coup that ended with the bloody assassination of President Diem and his brother Nhu in the back of an armored personnel carrier.

So why did the United States support and even lie about Ngo Dinh Diem? On board the plane shortly after Johnson gave his speech, journalist and historian Stanley Karnow asked him about the comparison to Churchill. "Did you really mean it?"

Johnson's answer, spoken with his customary drawl: "Shit, Diem's the only boy we got out there."

The truth was that the United States needed someone to hold the line against the growing encroachment of communism in the world. The Geneva Accords had drawn that line at the sixteenth parallel. The French, still smarting from their defeat at Dienbienphu, no longer had a taste for fighting, and the Vietnamese no longer had a taste for French colonialism. South Vietnam was a fledgling country looking for guidance. The accords specified that elections be held in 1956 to unify the country, which gave South Vietnam little time to gain the strength and stability necessary to win those elections.

Diem's rise began with those 1954 Geneva Accords. The Communists controlled the North, leaving Emperor Bao Dai, installed by the French in 1949, in titular control of the South. But Bao Dai, who spent his days in a luxurious château near Cannes and his nights in Monte Carlo, needed someone to run his country—preferably someone who could bring in the Americans to supplant the French. He also needed someone who had access to political clout in Vietnam. He found that man in Diem. Diem was a puritan to Bao Dai's playboy, but they both believed they could use each other. Bao Dai wanted U.S. involvement, and Diem wanted power for himself and his family. The United States wanted a government in the South strong enough to hold off the Communists.

For many Americans, Diem seemed the perfect choice for a Western-style regime in Vietnam. A devout Catholic who had spent years in exile in New Jersey, he proved to be passionately patriotic, fiercely anticommunist, brave, and personally incorruptible. He wanted a Vietnam that was free of both the French and the Communists, and a legacy to pass along to his family.

Unfortunately he also had no idea how to run a democracy. His Catholicism, so valued by the Americans, was actually a major disadvantage in a country that was 95 percent Buddhist. He was rigid, autocratic, a poor administrator, and a clumsy politician. Rather than create a government inclusive of the many factions within Vietnamese political society, he closed ranks, choosing to govern primarily though his family and a select group of Catholics loyal to him. His primary advisers were his brothers, Can, Thuc, and Nhu, whose rival factions included covert political, security, and labor groups, all organized in the tradition of Asian secret societies. Nhu became Diem's chief political adviser and head of the secret police. Together, Diem's brothers spread a web of corruption throughout the country.

Since Diem was a bachelor, his sister-in-law Madame Nhu became the de facto First Lady, playing her role to the hilt while promoting herself as the reincarnation of the Trung sisters, legendary heroines who had led Vietnam's struggle against China in the first century. Madame Nhu used her power to establish a series of edicts that offended the normally permissive Vietnamese population. In the name of protecting Vietnamese traditional values, she abolished divorce and made adultery a crime. She banned abortions, contraceptives, beauty contests, and boxing matches. She also closed Saigon's nightclubs and ballrooms—except for those frequented by the inner circle of the regime—but allowed cafés to remain open. The bar girls there, most of them prostitutes, were required to wear white tunics resembling those worn by dental assistants in the States. Madame Nhu's sanctimonious decrees might not have been as offensive to the Vietnamese if her own family had not been so involved in corruption themselves.

Even though Diem courted the West and spoke of Western democracy, he was at heart a mandarin who believed in divine rule. He came from a family of mandarins, or ranking Vietnamese officials, who had served at the imperial court in Hue. His father had been counselor to Emperor Than Thai before the French deposed him. Diem believed: "A sacred respect is due the person of the sovereign . . . He is the mediator between the people and heaven as he celebrates the national cult." Ogden Williams of the CIA saw Diem as "A man who if he hadn't been a politician would have been a priest or a monk. Very prissy. Very authoritarian. Rather pompous."

Once Bao Dai had elevated Diem as prime minister, the United States promoted him as the great democratic hope in Southeast Asia. They ignored warnings about his flaws, believing and hoping he could be managed. When, in 1955, he came into conflict with Bao Dai, his CIA advisers suggested that it was time to depose the emperor and declare South Vietnam a republic. Diem immediately staged a plebiscite, or major countrywide vote, to decide the issue. But the true concept of a democratic vote eluded him. He claimed victory with a margin of 98.2 percent, tallying more votes in Saigon and other cities than the total number of voters registered within those cities. His claim of a landslide victory was the first of many lies that would taint his regime, while pulling the United States deeper into a quagmire of deceit.

After the elections some American advisers wanted Diem replaced, considering him incompetent, but Diem won their respect that spring by crushing the Binh Xuyen gangsters in Saigon and coming to terms with armed religious sects in the countryside. He then embarked on a massive campaign to eliminate any remaining Vietminh elements in the South. Believing the Communist threat was simply a matter of security, he began the Khu Tru Mat program, to build *agrovilles*, later known as strategic hamlets, to protect the peasants from the Vietminh (members of the national liberation movement that had been founded in 1941 to secure liberation of Vietnam from France). The success of his campaigns, and the resulting growth of peace and security, convinced the United States that, like it or not, they would have to "sink or swim with Ngo Dinh Diem."

In 1959, Diem staged another sweeping—and fraudulent—victory in U.S.-backed elections to set up a national assembly. This time the government registered voters, invited their critics to run for office, and vowed to respect the sanctity of the secret ballot. But on election day that promise proved to be yet another lie. In rural areas, peasants were either coerced to vote Diem's ticket or ballot boxes were simply stuffed. In places where ballot stuffing was impractical, popular opposing politicians were disqualified. To ensure victory, Diem even brought large contingents of his own troops into Saigon to vote. Those American advisers not involved in the scheme were dismayed, but at that point, the United States had a terrible dilemma: If not Diem, then who? There were no other Western-leaning candidates, and the United States was spending a million dollars a day propping up Diem's regime.

Diem claimed that the election proved he had won the support of the people, but in actuality he was driving them away—in many cases right into the arms of the Communists. His *agroville* program, and the "strategic hamlet" program that grew out of it, proved disastrous. Peasants were forced from their native villages, leaving their ancestral graves behind, to move into fortified villages that were often miles from their fields or markets. The construction of these villages required many more workers than could actually live there, so at least half of the peasants were forced to abandon their crops to work for free building other people's homes. Diem saw this as the civic duty required of any citizen. The peasants saw it as forced labor. The strategic hamlets were not even useful for protecting the peasants from the Viet Cong. The rapid and sloppy pace of the project often left as many Viet Cong on the inside as on the outside. The chief administrator of the project even turned out to be Viet Cong himself.

When pressured to help the farmers, Diem brought in prominent American experts on agrarian reform, then promptly discarded their advice. He also required peasants to pay for their own land—the land they had been given for free by the Vietminh during the war against the French. This made the Viet Cong look particularly good in comparison. The fact that Diem was so focused on security that he spent little on the things the people really needed—such as schools, medical care, and social services—further alienated the peasants. Corruption flourished everywhere. Many people joined the Viet Cong just to "get Diem."

American advisers realized that Diem was losing touch with his people, and insisted that he make an effort to connect with the population by visiting rural areas. But all the peasants wanted was for the government to leave them alone. Government attention usually meant that government troops would steal their rice and chickens, capture and imprison innocents accused of insurgency, or initiate indiscriminate artillery bombardments of innocent villages. On Diem's rare visits to the countryside he was so heavily protected that the people could not even see him through his guards.

The peasants were not the only ones disenchanted with Diem. He alienated the liberals and the left wing very early. He then lost most of the intellectuals and professional politicians because of his refusal to consider inclusive policies. Doctors, lawyers, teachers, and other professionals were disturbed by his rigidity. Madame Nhu's "reforms" managed to alienate much of the remaining urban population. Diem's American advisers, including Colonel Edward G. Landsdale, realized the problem but had little success persuading Diem to implement reforms. Ogden Williams, CIA assistant to Landsdale, recalls, "He wouldn't reach out . . . to try to win over elements who were patriotic but not Catholic, not from his background. He would treat them with suspicion, and they would resent it."

American support of Diem's regime had been based largely on his apparent success against Vietminh insurgents, now nicknamed "Viet Cong." In reality, the Communists had been holding back, deliberately avoiding escalation—primarily in the hope that the unification elections, promised by the Geneva Accords, would actually take place—but also because Diem was doing such a good job of alienating his people without their help.

By 1959, Ho Chi Minh realized that Diem had no intention of holding the elections. Ho took the gloves off, releasing the Viet Cong to begin a brutal program of assassinations and sabotage against Diem's government. Stanley Karnow reports that between 1959 and 1961, the number of assassinated South Vietnamese government officials soared from twelve hundred to four thousand a year. Unprepared for the escalation, Diem reacted by appointing army officers loyal to him to manage the rural bureaucracy. Often paired with American advisers, these officers were unfamiliar with their areas and exacerbated the situation by neglecting the economic and social needs of the population. Most of them lived in fortified bunkers and went out only by day. By night the villages belonged to the Viet Cong.

In 1960, Hanoi moved one step further, announcing the formation of the National Liberation Front in the South. Designed to bring together disparate groups opposed to Diem, the group particularly appealed to surviving members of the Binh Xuyen gangsters, and to other groups and sects Diem had oppressed. The war had begun.

But Diem's focus remained on his domestic adversaries. In April 1960, eighteen distinguished nationalists, including several former members of his cabinet, presented him with a modest petition urging him to reform. Their primary request was that he broaden his entourage. They even offered to serve him.

Diem's response became characteristic of the rest of his regime. Turning to brother Nhu for advice, he rejected the request, then, in retaliation, closed opposition newspapers and arrested a number of journalists, students, and assorted intellectuals for "Communist affiliations."

By this time, the United States had funneled more than a billion dollars into South Vietnam. But even as the bill increased, American leverage over Diem decreased. He knew the United States needed his regime as an anticommunist bastion, so he had no qualms about resisting U.S. pressures for reform. But he was perfectly happy to keep taking American money, channeling most of it into his personal military and police—building and supplying conventional units to protect him from his rivals in Saigon—rather than toward an army to fight Viet Cong. Only a small fraction of U.S. aid was left for economic development. He had become, as one U.S. official put it, "a puppet who pulled his own strings."

In November 1960, the cry for reform grew stronger. But this time, instead of a polite petition, three crack paratrooper battalions and a marine unit surrounded the palace. But the rebels, intent on encouraging reform rather than staging a coup, had left the phone lines into the palace intact and failed to take the radio station or block the roads into the city. They gave Diem thirty-six hours to comply with their demands. He used that time to tape a speech promising the requested reforms, then called his loyal contingents for rescue. Just as his concessions were being broadcast over the air, his loyal troops rolled in and crushed the rebels, indiscriminately killing inquisitive civilian bystanders along with the rebels. Of course, once the crisis ended, Diem immediately reneged on his promises. Nhu later claimed that the regime's enemies were "not only Communists, but foreigners who claim to be our friends," clearly suggesting that the United States had backed the rebels.

Angered by the insinuation, Elbridge Durbrow, the U.S. ambassador to South Vietnam, warned Diem that Nhu and his wife were a liability to his government and should be sent abroad. Diem refused, denouncing criticism of Nhu as "Communist propaganda." In a message to Washington on December 4, six months before

Johnson gave his flattering speech, Dubrow wrote: "We may well be forced, in the not too distant future, to undertake the difficult task of identifying and supporting alternative leadership."

Diem, unaware of Dubrow's misgivings, began to view himself as indispensable, especially after Johnson's speech that May. But when Johnson broached the idea of deploying American combat troops in South Vietnam, Diem was less than enthusiastic about the idea. More American troops would give the United States more leverage over his government. Six months later, however, Diem had a sudden change of heart after the Viet Cong viciously attacked army posts in two provinces. Stung by heavy losses, Diem declared that a "real war" was developing and announced that he would welcome American combat soldiers as a "symbolic" presence. He also proposed a bilateral defense pact between his country and the United States.

Faced with the growing Viet Cong insurgency, President Kennedy accepted a plan that included drastically increasing the number of American advisers in Vietnam—but that plan required going against the terms of the Geneva agreement, which specified that foreign military personnel could be assigned to Vietnam only as replacements. To avoid repercussions from this deceit, Kennedy was counseled to avoid consulting Britain, co-chair of the Geneva Conference, or the International Control Commission, which was supposed to monitor adherence to the Geneva Accords. The additional advisers would be placed in varied locations throughout the country to attract less attention.

By December 1961, in direct violation of the Geneva agreement, the United States had increased its commitment of advisers to well over three thousand, including several squadrons of helicopters. American pilots soon began to fly combat sorties out of an airbase north of Saigon, camouflaging their flights as training exercises for the Vietnamese.

Stanely Karnow recalls one morning in December of 1961: "I was sipping coffee with a U.S. army press officer on the terrace of Saigon's Majestic Hotel as an American aircraft carrier, the *Core*, turned a bend in the river and steamed toward us, the first shipment of forty-seven helicopters strapped to its deck. Astonished, I grabbed the officer's arm, shouting 'look at that carrier!' He directed a mock squint in the direction of the gigantic vessel and replied: 'I don't see nothing.'"

In a news conference on January 15, 1962, President Kennedy was asked if U.S. troops were engaged in fighting in Vietnam. His one word answer: no.

Kennedy's lie was simply part of the growing tradition of deceit that soon escalated into a method of doing business in Vietnam. Positive results and attitudes were rewarded, negative reports or realistic assessments often meant missed promotions. On a fact-finding mission in 1961, Maxwell Taylor reported that South Vietnam "is not an excessively difficult or unpleasant place to operate." He also stated that "North Vietnam is extremely vulnerable to bombing . . . There is no case for fearing a mass onslaught of Communist manpower into South Vietnam."

Unfortunately Kennedy's influx of advisors and material did not have the desired effect. Convinced that the war was strictly conventional, Diem refused to consider necessary political, economic, and social reforms. But he also refused to take the war seriously. That was up to the Americans. He instructed his soldiers to avoid casualties, believing their primary role was to protect him against possible coups, not to fight the Viet Cong. Some advisers believed he wanted the war to stumble along inconclusively so that he could continue to receive U.S. aid.

Frustrated by his incompetence, two formerly loyal South Vietnamese pilots attempted an aerial assassination of Diem by bombing the palace in February of 1962. Diem and his family survived mostly unscathed, but the incident convinced him he was right. He began sequestering himself with his family, leaving most of the country's daily affairs to his brother Nhu.

On the battlefield, Diem's army battalions continued to follow his orders, becoming increasingly reluctant to confront the Viet Cong directly. They relied on U.S. air strikes and artillery to do their job for them, a policy that, in January of 1963, led to disaster outside the village of Ap Bac. On a mission to destroy a VC radio transmitter, the ARVN (Army of the Republic of Vietnam) Seventh Division was soundly defeated by a Viet Cong force they outnumbered ten to one. The operation, which should have been an easy offensive, turned into a rout for the government forces, primarily because key ARVN officers either refused to fight, or were too indecisive to deploy their troops effectively. In the end, sixty-one ARVN soldiers and three Americans lay dead with a hundred others wounded. Many of the dead and wounded were hit by friendly fire in the chaos of mismanaged deployments. The Viet Cong disappeared, leaving only three bodies behind.

Two days later, Admiral Harry Felt, the American commander for the Pacific, called the battle a South Vietnamese triumph. He insisted that the South Vietnamese army had won because the Viet Cong had abandoned its positions. The U.S. military adviser in charge of the Ap Bac operation resigned in disgust.

By the time of the Ap Bac debacle, the U.S. presence in South Vietnam had increased to more than sixteen thousand service personnel. As the number of advisers continued to grow, it seemed inconceivable to most that "we could lose Vietnam." Yet the sense began to grow that "Diem was losing it for us." But the United States insisted on continued support for Diem. Then, as if it wasn't enough to alienate the peasants and intellectuals, Diem turned on the Buddhists.

Though they had been treated as second-class citizens in Diem's pro-Catholic government, the Buddhist majority had primarily kept to themselves, focusing on improving their own organization. But on May 8, 1963, during a celebration of the Buddha's birthday, one of Diem's Catholic deputy province chiefs decided to prohibit the flying of the Buddhist flag, even though he had encouraged the Catholics to fly their banners at an event a week earlier. That event had been different; it commemorated the anniversary of Diem's brother's ordination. In response, the Buddhist scheduled an address by one of their leaders at a local radio station. Buddhists and interested civilians gathered at the station, but the station management cancelled the address—because it had not been censored—and called out the guard. Five armored cars sped onto the scene. The commander ordered the crowd to disperse, then, before they could comply, he ordered his men to fire. The crowd stampeded in terror. A woman and eight children were killed.

Diem's regime blamed the incident on the Viet Cong—despite the fact that a prominent physician confirmed the Buddhist's account after examining the bodies. The government proceeded to suppress the doctor's report. Infuriated, the Buddhists demanded that the officials responsible for the killings be punished. Diem ignored them.

The Buddhists responded by mobilizing their members. They organized massive protests, rallies, and hunger strikes in a feat of efficiency worthy of the Communists. Their nonviolent protests were often brutally suppressed. The Buddhist leader Tri Quang, turned to the United States, telling officials, "The United States must either make Diem reform or get rid of him. If not, the situation will degenerate, and you worthy gentlemen will suffer most. You are responsible for the present trouble because you back Diem and his government of ignoramuses."

Even with U.S. prodding, Diem refused to retreat from his assertion that the Viet Cong were involved. On June 7, Madame Nhu exacerbated the situation by publicly alleging that the Buddhists were being manipulated by the Americans. The United States warned Diem that he might lose all American support if repression of the Buddhists continued. Diem did nothing.

On June 11, an elderly Buddhist monk sat down in a busy

intersection in Saigon, issued a "respectful" plea to Diem to show "charity and compassion" to all religions, and then allowed his brothers to douse him with gasoline and set him on fire. He prayed as the fire consumed his flesh.

The monk's great sacrifice failed to move Diem. Not only did he refuse to budge, even after repeated American entreaties and several more immolations, he also allowed Madame Nhu to publicly declare the self-immolations a "barbecue." She told a reporter: "Let them burn, and we shall clap our hands."

It was time to take stronger action. The United States, through CIA operative Lucien Conein, began working with some of Diem's disaffected senior generals in preparation for a possible coup. But Kennedy still hoped Diem would compromise with the Buddhists.

Then, in August 1963, Diem and Nhu hatched a scheme that would prove to be their greatest—and most disastrous—lie yet. Diem declared martial law, then set in motion a plan to attack the Buddhists using his own loyal forces disguised as regular soldiers. Their plan was calculated to turn the Buddhists and their sympathizers against the army to Diem's advantage.

On August 21, shortly after midnight, Nhu's men began to attack Buddhist temples in cities throughout the country. In Saigon, they ransacked the pagoda and arrested at least four-hundred monks and nuns. In Hue, monks and nuns managed to barricade themselves inside the Dieude Temple, fighting off Nhu's assailants for eight hours while thousands of people rioted in the streets in protest. Other cities also reacted in horror to the attacks. By the end of the operation, Nhu's men had rounded up more than one thousand monks, nuns, student activists, and bystanders. Many were injured, and many others disappeared, presumably killed during the attacks.

But Diem's plan to blame the army backfired. Vietnamese youths, many of whom were sons and daughters of the army leadership, poured into the streets to demonstrate against the regime. Even Madame Nhu's father, then South Vietnam's ambassador to the United

States, quit his post to denounce the government. The foreign minister resigned and shaved his head like a monk in protest.

Nhu almost succeeded in getting the Americans to believe that the army had been behind the attacks by cutting the U.S. embassy and residential phone lines. As a result, the Voice of America radio station initially broadcast his version of the events, blaming the army. But Diem and Nhu did not know their generals were working with the CIA through Lucien Conein. Outraged that they were being blamed for the attacks, the generals made certain that Conein knew the truth, and pushed for public absolution for the army. They also pushed for U.S. support to go ahead with the coup.

On Saturday, August 24, the newly appointed U.S. ambassador to Vietnam, Henry Cabot Lodge, received a message from Washington that Diem should be "given the chance" to remove his brother from power. If Diem "remains obdurate and refuses . . . we must face the possibility the Diem himself cannot be preserved." Several days later, on orders from the White House, the Voice of America absolved the army of any responsibility for attacking the temples and suggested that the United States "may sharply reduce its aid" to Diem unless he dismissed the organizers responsible for the raid.

But when Ambassador Lodge met with Diem later to present his credentials, Diem refused even to discuss the matter. Realizing they were on thin ice with the Americans, Nhu began negotiations with the Communists. His machinations, partially designed to blackmail the Americans, angered them instead. Pressure increased for Kennedy to approve a coup.

Despite the lack of viable alternatives, it took two more months before the United States was actually willing to consider such a drastic step. Conein continued to keep in touch with the generals, who continued to plan but refused to move forward with the coup until they were certain they had U.S. approval. Rumors began to spread of other groups preparing their own plans for takeover. The Kennedy administration realized they had no choice but to allow the generals to remove Diem before someone else did. In October Ambassador Lodge gave the green light to Conein, using carefully crafted wording to specify that the United States "will not attempt to thwart" the coup, and would continue to supply material and aid to the country.

On November 1, 1963, Ambassador Lodge paid a last courtesy call on President Diem. Lodge recalled that Diem mentioned hearing a rumor of a coup but did not seem at all disturbed by it. In fact, Nhu had gotten wind of the conspirators' plan and prepared a complicated counter-coup of his own. But Nhu did not know that the commander of his own forces, the man he counted on to command the counter-coup and save him, was actually part of the conspiracy.

When the attack came, Nhu tried to put his plan into effect only to discover that his loyal general was neither his nor loyal. Despite this failure, the brothers managed to escape from the palace and remained at large for many hours. But they had no place to go. Diem finally agreed to resign. The brothers were picked up at a church in Cholon and promised safe passage, via armored personnel carrier. But that, too, was a lie. The original plan called for delivering the brothers to a safe house until they could be transported out of the country, but the original plan did not count on the hatred of the men Diem and Nhu had mistreated. The two never made it back to Saigon alive.

In an article for the *New York Times* on June 30, 1964, Henry Cabot Lodge stated: "The overthrow . . . of the Diem regime was purely a Vietnamese affair. We never participated in the planning. We never gave any advice. We had nothing to do with it."

Diem had come to power through U.S. support of his fraudulent elections, and stayed in power only as a result of U.S. support, even when the United States had to lie to its own people to keep him there. When Diem's military proved inadequate against the North Vietnamese, the United States escalated its own military involvement to support him in direct violation of the Geneva Convention, then President Kennedy denied the escalation. As Diem's incompetence grew, so did the lies it took to support him, until it was routine for upper U.S. military personnel and U.S. officials to declare victory where there was none. In the end, the lies turned against Diem as the United States assisted Diem's disaffected generals in staging a coup, then denied American involvement.

It took twelve more years and many more lies before the United States managed to get out of Vietnam. Many scholars argue that the South Vietnamese government fell because it never recovered from the damage done by Diem's regime.

Sometimes a lie is a very necessary evil. "Of course your new hairstyle looks great, dear" springs to this married man's mind. If ever there was a justification for a national leader to lie, this was it. Unfortunately, there is almost always a price to be paid later.

KING HUSSEIN'S TRUST ISSUES

AMMAN, JORDAN, 1967

Joshua Spivak

Trust is a dangerous thing.

At the start of the 1967 Six-Day War, King Hussein bin Talal of Jordan had already shown that he was one of the twentieth century's wiliest political figures. Yet, inexplicably, he swallowed whole a lie of his old adversary, Egyptian president Gamal Nasser, who had claimed, "Our planes have been striking at Israel's airfields since morning." Unfortunately for King Hussein, at that time, the validity of this statement was extremely unlikely, as the Egyptians no longer possessed an air force.

On May 30, 1967, King Hussein of Jordan had flown to Cairo to sign a joint defense agreement with his longtime enemy and soon-to-be-regretted ally, President Nasser. Nasser had long denounced King Hussein as an "imperialist lackey," but that was now water under the bridge. Faced with this unusual alliance and an impossible political situation, once Egypt shut off its Straits of Tiran and blockaded the port of Eilat, the beleaguered state of Israel decided on a preemptive strike against its most dangerous enemy, Egypt.

In the early morning of June 5, the well-prepared Israeli air force caught the Egyptians with their pants down, inflicting one of the greatest surprise attacks in history, with losses at a bare minimum. The Israelis completely annihilated the Egyptian air force. According to historian Michael Oren, in the first 100 minutes of battle, the Israelis destroyed 286 Egyptian combat aircraft and killed almost a third of their pilots. This alone would have represented a great victory for the Israelis, but fortunately for them, the Egyptian's didn't just stop there and concede defeat.

With their air force annihilated and their army now sitting ducks for a sweeping attack that would kick them out of the Sinai Peninsula, the Egyptians promptly struck a pose and announced themselves the winners of the first battle of a new war to destroy Israel. Egypt's early news reports proudly announced that eighty-six enemy planes, including an American bomber, had been shot down, with a loss of only two Egyptian planes. Parades were held in the streets of Egypt, and as hard as it may be for a retrospective observer to believe, nobody in the military was willing to tell President Nasser just how big an actual catastrophe had occurred.

The Egyptian government decided that living the lie of victory was better than facing the reality of defeat . . . but that was not all. The military officials also decided that others should live the lie as well. Egyptian field marshall Abdel Amer (who conveniently committed suicide several months after the end of the war) assured the Jordanian general Abdal Riyad that 75 percent of the Israeli air force had been destroyed.

The Jordanians were a bit suspicious, as they had radar reports of hundreds of planes flying into Sinai. So King Hussein's men checked with their Egyptian counterparts.

Rather than acknowledge the truth—that what his allies were seeing were Israeli planes coming back to refuel and reload for yet another successful bombing run, and that, in fact, there was no longer an Egyptian air force to speak of—the Egyptian military leadership lied. According to them, the planes the Jordanians were seeing on their radar were Egyptian planes bombing their hated enemy, Israel. Better come and join the party, before the war's all over.

And so, King Hussein, the grandson of an assassinated monarch and the Mideast's great survivor, invaded Israel.

The Jordanian leadership gave the Egyptians too much credit. The Egyptian leaders knew that taking the Sinai would be precarious enough. They had warned off King Hussein, but, perhaps trusting his allies instead of his better senses, the king jumped into a military rout that cost him control over the West Bank and the holy city of Jerusalem.

What possessed King Hussein, a realist's realist, to blind himself to this lie?

Yes, President Nasser was a charismatic leader, but King Hussein, possessor of the only really decently trained and run Arab army, must have noticed the incompetence of the Egyptian regime.

Unfortunately for him, his tiny kingdom had other problems. If he failed to fight, he knew he would be blamed for not backing up his Arab brethren. And as the possessor of a kingdom filled with restless Palestinian refugees, Hussein could not risk being blamed for a defeat of this magnitude and the shattering of the Arab alliance. Instead of a realistic assessment of the Egyptian army, he gambled on President Nasser—and lost half his kingdom.

On the second day, after it became apparent that the Israelis had struck a crippling blow to both Egypt and Jordan, President Nasser persuaded King Hussein to join him in what United States president Lyndon Johnson would call "the Big Lie." In attempting to cast themselves as victims, both King Hussein and President Nasser agreed to claim on the second day of the war that it was American and British forces, alongside the Israelis, that had attacked them. In their conversation, gleefully disseminated by the Israelis, as it was made on a tapped phone line, President Nasser couldn't help but tell his Jordanian counterpart a second lie: "We are with you with all of our hearts and we are flying our planes over Israel today. Our planes have been striking at Israel's airfields since morning."

The 1967 Six-Day War has since become a legend among military planners and historians for the breathtaking speed with which Israel completely decimated its enemies. The lies about defeating the Israeli air force had helped mollify the Egyptian citizens, but it didn't help the Jordanians in maintaining their military position.

By the end of the third day, the Israelis owned Jerusalem and the West Bank, and King Hussein of Jordan had learned a lesson no one would have thought he needed to understand: trust no one, especially those who claim to be your allies.

HISTORY BOOKS LIE TOO

Even if you take into account nationalistic bias, it is amazing what has crept into the history books we've all studied. George Washington never threw a dollar across any river, since the currency then was the pound sterling. There is actually no record of a young Abraham Lincoln walking miles to return a penny he had shorted someone. In fact both these tales were created in the late nineteenth century to sell patriotic flyers.

Even works of art are suspect. Since the Delaware was full of pack ice when General Washington led his army across it to take Trenton and revive the Revolution, it would have been suicidal to stand up in the small boats, except maybe to get a quick glance to see through the sleet and snow that marked the crossing. Nonetheless there is a very inspiring picture of such a scene, painted years later by someone who was not there.

Okay, so we've just given some examples of how you can't trust what your generals or political leaders say. Since history is written mostly by the generals and politicians, why should what follows be a surprise?

Here's an easy one: Is there any reason to question the stories about this woman? She was a politician competing for the throne of the richest land on the Mediterranean, and she married two of Rome's leaders in a time of civil war, and bore the son of the first Roman emperor. So in whose interest was it to have Cleopatra be depicted as larger than life and as the great beauty of her age? The Julian dynasty had to make their founder, Julius Caesar, look not just good but godlike. An affair with a plain-looking woman who had political power he wanted would not exactly have been an impressive story. But if one of the greatest temptresses in history had gone after their ancestor, then that made him look . . . well, imperial.

CLEOPATRA

Looks Were Not Deceiving

James M. Ward

"For her own person, It beggar'd all description . . . Age cannot wither her, nor custom stale Her Infinite variety."

—William Shakespeare, about Cleopatra, in *Antony and Cleopatra*

Throughout the ages, since the fall of Egypt to the end of the Roman Empire, historians, storytellers, and poets have written much about the last queen of ancient Egypt. Almost all of them have wondered at the charms of a woman who could beguile two of Rome's most powerful leaders. Surely, such a woman must have been the great beauty of her time—or was she? What is the truth about Cleopatra's beauty?

The presentation of Egypt's Cleopatra as one of the most gorgeous women of ancient times comes to us most recently from movies. In those movies, some of the most beautiful women of the film industry have played the Egyptian queen. All of the films on this topic depict a young and beautiful Cleopatra who uses her physical charms to woo Roman leaders into saving her and favoring her country. Down through history, legends also speak of her beauty and ability to physically charm leaders of Rome to her way of thinking.

The fact is she wasn't a great Egyptian beauty, neither by the standards of her day or by our own. She wasn't even Egyptian. She was a Macedonian Greek—and instead of beauty, she used her wealth and power to compensate for her physical features.

In 69 B.C., Cleopatra VII was born to the ruling family of Auletes Ptolemy XII. The first Ptolemy was a Macedonian, one of Alexander the Great's generals, who came to rule Egypt when Alexander died. The Ptolemys had ruled over Egypt for a little over three hundred years, controlling the country with an iron hand from 301 to 30 B.C.

Rather than interbreeding with the Egyptians, the Ptolemy family maintained the traditions of marrying Macedonian lords and ladies down through their three centuries of power. They did, however, adopt the Egyptian tradition of marrying brothers and sisters in the royal family line. Egyptians of the time didn't think any others were worthy of marrying their rulers, whom they considered gods on earth. The male heirs were all called Ptolemy or Alexander, in honor of the first general and his king. The female heirs in the line were usually named Arsinoe, Berenice, or Cleopatra, as the names meant "Glory to the Father."

Indeed, there were many Cleopatras, with the most famous one being Cleopatra VII. She came from a family of seven. Cleopatra V had died early in her father's rule. Cleopatra-Tryphaina and Berenice were Cleopatra VII's older sisters, Cleopatra VII was a middle child, with Ptolemy XIII, Arsinoe, and Ptolemy XIV as younger brothers and sisters. She was to be the last of the Ptolemy line who would rule in Egypt and the first of Ptolemy rulers who could actually speak Egyptian.

We know Cleopatra wasn't a great beauty from the images of her that have survived the ages. There are several whole statues of her; several carved marble busts, minted coins, and even some Egyptian-style hieroglyphics on temple and royal walls. All of these agree on several features. She had a very long, Greek-style hooked nose. Her face was thin while her form was plump. The coins depicting her image show thick eyebrows and a severe-looking face. One image shows her teeth as large and uneven.

If the coins are to be believed, both Caesar and Mark Antony were more befitting the title of "eye-candy-in-chief" than Cleo was.

When talking about the ancient ruler, most people have assumed beauty to have been a major factor in her many accomplishments. People constantly say the same thing: "She had the children of Caesar and Antony; she must have been the beauty of her time. These were the most powerful men of their age. They could have had any woman they wanted. In picking Cleopatra, they must have selected her because of her face and figure."

These type of people might also have said that Anna Nicole Smith married her octogenarian husband for love. Arguments of that type are fun to enter into and have been so for thousands of years.

Although it was a lie that Cleopatra was the beauty of her age, she did have qualities that made her quite attractive. As a child of the powerful Ptolemy family, she gained skills that allowed her to beguile and control the most powerful men of her age. Her father believed in a sound education. From an early age, all the children of the ruler were tutored in the six different languages of the area, in math and science, and in the laws of Egypt. While her brothers and sisters had the same training, Cleopatra worked hardest to understand Egypt, the country she was destined to rule.

When the famous Cleopatra was sixteen, her father, Auletes, went to Rome to ensure his rule over Egypt with the approval of the then-most-powerful empire in the world, which was marching all over the Mediterranean taking over countries. The Ptolemys had worked with Rome for several hundred years as the empire grew to be the most powerful force in the world. During the negotiations, Auletes Ptolemy received news that his oldest daughter, Cleopatra-Tryphaina had led a revolt in Egypt to replace him. Before he could finish the journey back to Egypt, her younger sister Berenice killed Cleopatra-Tryphaina and took over the reins of government. The chaos that followed allowed those loyal to Auletes to take back control from both of his daughters. For two more years, Auletes ruled, and when he died, his will placed the Cleopatra we know on the throne, with her twelve-year-old brother as co-ruler.

Since Egypt's laws forbade a female from having sole rule of the country, Cleopatra would have to have a relative or her own son assist her in her rule. She didn't like her brother and quickly did everything she could to keep the twelve-year-old away from the reins of government. This factor didn't set well with the boy's three adult advisers, who had advised the children's father.

For the first two years of her rule, hard times struck Egypt. For more than two thousand years, the flood of the Nile had brought fresh earth to the farms along the river. It was rare when the flood didn't come, and its absence was always looked on as a punishment from the gods. As Cleopatra's luck would have it, there was no flood that year, and drought caused the people great hardship.

Cleopatra's enemies soon spread the word that the gods of the Nile clearly didn't want her to rule. Theodotus, Pothinus, and the Greek Achillas were able to take control of the Egyptian army and move the people to riot against her rule. Knowing her brother's advisers were constantly plotting against her, she secretly fled to Syria, as Egyptian public sentiment turned against her. There, she used her political influence to raise a small army to take back her throne when the time was right.

While Egypt struggled in chaos, the Roman Empire suffered as well. Julius Caesar had just crushed a civil war and chased his former co-leader, Pompey, out of Rome. Pompey ran to Egypt, with Caesar's Legions at his heels, thinking young Ptolemy XIII would support his move to win back Rome. When Pompey arrived, the Egyptian officials, aware that Caesar was following him with four Roman Legions, had Pompey killed as he stepped off the boat. His head was cut off and put on display to be shown to Caesar when he landed.

Caesar's military force was more than enough to take over Alexandria, but Ptolemy's advisers ordered all the armies of Egypt to come to the city. The four thousand Roman troops would be facing twenty thousand Egyptian troops, if the advisers didn't get what they wanted from Rome and Caesar.

Caesar temporarily took over the reins of the Egyptian government to gain the riches of the country. He demanded to see Cleopatra and Ptolemy XIII, declaring that he would restore the rule of Cleopatra. Ptolemy's advisers kept the Egyptian armies on guard around Alexandria, with orders to kill Cleopatra if she should appear. Knowing this, she wrapped herself in an expensive carpet and had the carpet presented to Caesar as just another gift from a grateful people. She rolled out of the carpet and into history as she offered Caesar her army, her country, and herself for him to use. Few men could have refused such an offer, no matter what she looked like, and the Roman hierarchy had already proven themselves to be less than discriminating in terms of physical beauty and attraction when it came to matters of immediate acquisition and/or satisfaction.

Cleopatra had the laws of Egypt on her side, making her what would appear to be the perfect pawn for Rome. She had also enchanted Caesar with her wit, knowledge of Egypt, and open flattery of him and his power as given by Rome. And so Caesar allied himself with Cleopatra, she gave him a son, a half-Roman, half-Macedonian heir to the throne of Egypt. All the while, she gained more lands for Egypt to control as Caesar placed Egyptian officials in positions of control in bordering countries Rome had recently taken over. Caesar wanted a stable power on the Egyptian throne in order for the country to give taxes and, more important, grain to Rome. In those troubled times, mobs ruled Rome and the leaders who fed the people controlled the empire.

When Caesar went back to Rome, he was given many honors, including a ten-year dictatorship of the empire. This made him the effective ruler of all the lands controlled by Rome. Later he brought Cleopatra and his son to Rome with glorious pomp and established her in his home, though notably not as his wife.

Indeed, Cleopatra was in Rome when Caesar was assassinated. After his death, instead of becoming a pawn for Rome, she rushed back to Egypt to wait for Rome's next leader to emerge from the chaos.

Once home, she immediately began to work on the problems of Egypt, taking charge and quelling all who contested her right to power. She reformed the laws and ordered the Nile canals cleared of sediment. Watching the chaos in Rome after the death of Caesar—Brutus and Cassius were killed; Antony, Octavian, and Lepidus rose as leaders of the empire—she contacted Antony, having seen his affection for Caesar, and asked him to come to Egypt.

Eventually Antony gained control of a large portion of the empire in the East and came to Egypt, where Cleopatra plied him with gifts and with control of Egypt's armies and gold. While Caesar had praised her for her conversation and insightful suggestions, Antony learned to accept Cleopatra for the unusual fun she brought into his dull life.

Until he met Cleopatra, he had been a man of Spartan ways.

He liked a good party but didn't have much time for them as he led his armies to crush rebellions. Personal long-term relationships were deemed impractical for his chosen lifestyle. Shrewd Cleopatra quickly came to understand Antony and became his good-time girl. She bore him twins, a boy and a girl, and talked him into recognizing Caesar's child as one of the rulers of Egypt and the nearby lands.

Moreover, Cleopatra took up the role as Isis, goddess of the heavens. This greatly endeared her to the Egyptians, who for more than two thousand years had worshipped their rulers as gods on earth. She cut taxes to farmers to encourage them to make the grain Rome demanded. And when Antony asked for her help in defeating Parthia, she supplied him with a huge fleet of Egyptian warships. In exchange for those ships, he agreed to make her queen of the Eastern territories he controlled—territories owned by Rome. At that instant, she ruled over the largest Egyptian empire throughout all of its history.

In 31 B.C., Anthony divorced his wife, Octavia, at Cleopatra's urging, no longer just a good-time girl to him. Her hooks firmly in the slightly dull Roman military man, she had no desire to share him with someone who had interests counter to her own.

Octavia's brother, Octavian, made public Antony's will, which detailed Anthony's intentions to transfer the capital of the empire to Alexandria. The will also proclaimed his wish to be buried in Alexandria, wherever he died in the empire. This document helped force the Roman senate's hand. Octavian declared war against Cleopatra, and in that declaration never mentioned Antony's name. Rome feared the union of Antony and Cleopatra enough to send powerful Roman armies and navies into battle, with Octavian in command.

Anthony tried to defeat the forces of Octavian near Greece. In a navel battle at Actium, Antony and Cleopatra's forces were destroyed. Antony rushed back to Alexandria. The surrounding empires that once supported Egypt turned against Cleopatra.

When the war came to Egypt, Antony did well in the struggle on the first day. But that night, all of his generals and a good portion of his Roman Legions deserted to Octavian's side. Eventually, Antony committed suicide, dying in Cleopatra's arms. Octavian captured her and planned on parading her in Rome as his slave. She was able to thwart his plans by killing herself with the bite of an asp. Some historians now think Octavian killed her and invented the asp story to keep the people of Egypt from rebelling.

Through the chaos of the times and with a government filled with envious officials wanting to seize her power, Cleopatra ruled and ruled well. She used her family position and her ability to bear sons to hold her control of Egypt. As history spoke of her, the queen of the Nile became a beauty able to charm any man with her form and seductive ways. While Octavian referred to her as the Egyptian whore, there is no historical evidence that she was unfaithful to either of her Roman lovers. She was merely a queen looking to see her country prosper. And indeed, there is repeated evidence that as she dealt with the awesome power of Rome, she had the interests of her people constantly in mind.

If royalty encourages a mythos to separate them from the masses, then the places of Kings also have those who have an interest in weaving tales around those places. Here is one such building that has been painted dark and dangerous. Well . . . it does attract the tourists.

It seems nothing about this woman is as we were told. . . .

DEATH ON THE NILE

Teresa Patterson

In *Antony and Cleopatra,* William Shakespeare wrote:

> *(Cleopatra speaking to an asp, which she applies to her breast.)*
> *Come thou mortal wretch,*
> *With thy sharp teeth, this knot intrinsicate*
> *Of life at once untie: poor venomous fool,*
> *Be angry, and dispatch.*

Shakespeare took his inspiration for *Antony and Cleopatra* from the writings of the ancient Roman historian Plutarch. By the time the Bard wrote his famous play, the romantic story of Cleopatra's suicide by serpent had already survived the ages as one of the great tragedies of the ancient world. But many historians now believe that story to be a lie. According to criminal profiler Pat Brown in *The Mysterious Death of Cleopatra,* that lie was probably concocted by her murderer, Octavian.

There are no firsthand records of Cleopatra's death. The only surviving accounts were written more than one hundred years after the event by Roman historians Plutarch and Cassius Dio. In both writings there are two theories. The most popular describes Cleopatra's servants smuggling an asp into the chamber in a basket of figs. In Shakespeare's version there are at least two asps. The second theory suggests that poison may have been smuggled into the room in a hollow comb. But even Plutarch admits in his own writings that no one actually knows how Cleopatra died, only where and when.

Disturbed by the legend, Brown used modern investigative procedures to reexamine the ancient queen's death. First she disproved the likelihood that a serpent could have killed Cleopatra in the time allotted. After the fall of Alexandria, all records agree that Octavian imprisoned Cleopatra and her handmaidens in her own mausoleum. He then took up residence only a few hundred yards away, in her palace. The story states that Cleopatra wrote a suicide note to Octavian and sent it to him with one of his guards before killing herself. He responded immediately upon receipt of that note, desperate to keep his prize prisoner alive. When his guards arrived on the scene, however, Cleopatra and all but one of her ladies were already dead, and that one lived only moments longer.

A re-creation of the layout of Cleopatra's palace at Alexandria proves that Octavian was only a few moments away from her chambers in the mausoleum. There is no serpent native to Egypt or Rome that could have killed that fast. Most snake venom available at that time would have taken hours to kill its victim—if they received a fatal dose on the first strike. There was also no serpent found when the guards returned to the room to find Cleopatra dead. What was done with the serpent? Poisonous snakes do not simply disappear from sealed chambers, and no one inside the chamber lived long enough to get rid of it. Once the guards suspected a snakebite, they surely would have made the discovery of that deadly serpent a first priority. Yet there is no evidence that they even looked for any snakes.

Most historians agree that the poisoned comb theory is even more preposterous. At the time, hemlock was the poison of choice. It would take a comb larger than a football to have held enough hemlock to kill Cleopatra and her handmaidens. Imagine sneaking a very heavy, sloshing football past the guards. "Its just a comb for the queen." Even then, death would not have been instantaneous.

The greatest problem with the suicide theory is the profile of the victim. Pat Brown points out that suicides happen to people who are capable of becoming suicidal. Over its turbulent three-hundred-year reign, there was no history of suicide in Cleopatra's family. Cleopatra herself was a proven survivor, outliving much worse than imprisonment many times throughout her life, and always finding a way to turn defeat to triumph. Why would she have killed herself when all she had suffered was royal imprisonment, the loss of her empire, and Antony? Compared with the travails of her youth, that was a relatively minor setback. All her children were still alive at the time. Cleopatra had sent her firstborn son, Caesarian, to Ethiopia before Alexandria fell. Surely she would have wanted to live for him if nothing else.

Octavian's stated plan was to take Cleopatra back to Rome in chains. But that may not have been such a terrible fate for the queen. In Rome she was known as the mother of Caesar's only son. And she had friends there. Because she was Greek, she did not look like a foreigner. She certainly would have had reason to believe she could turn defeat around once she reached Rome—which is precisely why Octavian had a motive to make certain that this did not happen.

Octavian had taken Caesar's throne, but Cleopatra's son was Caesar's only blood heir. Both mother and son were a grave threat to the new emperor. The fact that he later had Caesarian hunted down and killed is undisputed. But he could not just kill Cleopatra outright. The people of Egypt—the very people Octavian intended to rule—revered her as the embodiment of their goddess

Isis. Cleopatra's open murder might have incited riotous unrest among Egyptians. But if she took her own life, especially if she did so using the serpent symbolic to Egypt, there could be no rancor directed at Octavian.

As Pat Brown points out, the method was easy. Octavian controlled the crime scene and all information about the event. His soldiers could have simply entered the mausoleum and killed everyone. He could then have honestly stated that Cleopatra was dead before he arrived. If he said it happened a certain way, who would dispute him? Every witness loyal to Cleopatra was dead, and Octavian was the emperor.

The truth of Cleopatra's death will probably never be known; her body has never been found, her palace lies in pieces under the waters of the Nile, and the ashes of her great library are lost under the shifting sands. But there is little doubt that the last of the Ptolemy Pharaohs, embodiment of Isis and royal Egypt and mother of the heir to Rome would never have considered suicide. It is ironic that her most enduring legacy may be the legend built around that lie.

When it comes to deceit, nothing is sacred. In this case sacred bows to the practical. Yes, Virginia, there is a Christmas, but. . .

CHRISTMAS—IN MAY?

James M. Ward

"O Holy night . . . the night when Christ was born."

—"O Holy Night"

To most Westerners, the word "Christmas" conjures images of baby Jesus in a manger, decorated fir trees, and of course snow. Everyone knows that Christmas, and the birthday of Jesus, is in December. However, according to most biblical scholars, everyone is wrong.

The New College Edition of the *American Heritage Dictionary of the English Language* defines Christmas in the following manner: 1. December 25, a holiday celebrated by Christians as the anniversary of the birth of Jesus. 2. The Christian church festival extending from December 24 (Christmas Eve) through January 6 (Epiphany). In this sense, also called "Christmastide."

The larger edition of that same dictionary defines a certain pagan holiday this way: "Sa-tur-na-li-a: Roman 7-day festival to Saturn beginning on December 17, known for its unrestrained revelry."

The way these two holidays became one is one of the greatest lies of the Christian faith.

The Christmas holiday is celebrated around the world, often with mistletoe, brightly lit trees, family gatherings, and presents. During the course of the holiday season, Christians are encouraged to think about the birth of Jesus and the religious implications of God giving his only son to us, and all that this gift implies. Even though Christmas is celebrated on December 25, the Bible does not give a specific date for Jesus's birth. In fact, it is much more likely, given the evidence, that his birth actually occurred in the spring. The Bible mentions shepherds herding sheep; they don't do that in the winter. The whole reason Mary and Joseph were traveling was because the Romans were collecting taxes and putting people on the tax rolls, a thing they historically did only in the spring.

In fact, Christmas was not celebrated in winter until the fourth century A.D., when the converted Roman emperor Constantine made the official celebration of Jesus's birthday December 25. Why did he pick that date of all dates? Saturnalia provides the happy holiday answer to that question.

Saturnalia was the largest and most popular of all the pagan holidays within the extensive Roman Empire. Named for the god Saturn, it combined his Roman elements of agriculture and feasting with the holiday elements of the Greek god Chronis, the father of the gods and controller of time and history. The holiday centered on the druidic winter solstice, December 22, a time to celebrate and pray for good weather and healthy crops throughout the year. The Romans folded in the holiday of Juvenilia, which was a feast to honor children and keep them safe, a good excuse to trade presents back and fourth, with the best gift given providing a year of good luck to the giver.

The origins of Saturnalia harken back to a time when the seasons were important and there weren't twelve months in the year. Saturn ruled over this holiday as the oldest and kindliest deity. Worshipers thought of him as a god from the golden age, when man and beast lived together in harmony. This concept of a golden age and the desire for the return of peace and plenty was an important theme among druids throughout the ages. While the idea of peace toward men and goodwill to all seems a Christmas concept, it harkens back to earlier times of man.

Many thousands of years before the birth of Jesus, a good part of the world celebrated the winter solstice using the same traditions of feasting and gift-giving. There was clearly a calculation on the part of the Christian leaders that if the birth of Jesus were folded into the solstice date, it would be far easier to get pagans to come into the ranks of the Christian faithful.

In the forced mixing of the holidays, some of the druidic elements were left out. For example, divination/fortune-telling, a magical part of the pagan holiday, could still be found in the territories that became the USSR. In the rite, a virgin girl was sent into a dark room lit by candles armed with a list of questions. By angling mirrors into the candlelight, she was supposed to be able to find the answers to her questions. The Gauls burned fir boughs in their hearth fires, and the smoke from those fires was said to guide the wise in dreams after the holiday feast; smoking certain weeds today does the same thing. In Scandinavia, families would place all of their shoes close to the fire as a way to bring about harmony and good luck for the entire year. The Yule log was a large pagan rite, because it was supposed to shed light from sunset to sunrise so that good weather and luck would be ensured all year round and the evil spirits would be kept out of the house for another year.

Especially during classical Roman times, sex was a large part of Saturnalia. Many illustrations in the documents of the day reflect Roman women's desire to conceive babies during this holiday, and thus ensure that the newborns, with the luck of the holiday on their side, had the greatest chance of surviving.

A special cake was made for Saturnalia in which a dried bean and a dried pea were baked. The person getting the bean was pronounced the king of the holiday, and destined to be lucky all the next year, and received kisses from all the unwed women at the table. The one finding the pea was able to name a queen, or if she was a female, she became the queen and gave kisses to the unmarried men. The queen was said to get married or bear a healthy baby or be lucky in harvesting all year long, depending on her nature. The recipe, in case you are curious, is:

3 cups flour
1 teaspoon ground cinnamon
1 teaspoon ground nutmeg
1 teaspoon mace
1 cup almonds, finely chopped
1 large dried pea
1 large dried bean
1 lemon, peeled and finely chopped
1 cup dark rum
2 cups butter
1 cup raw sugar
4 large eggs
1 cup normal raisins
1 cup golden raisins
1 cup currants

In a large bowl combine the flour, cinnamon, nutmeg, mace, almonds, the pea, and the bean. Add the lemon to the dry ingredients. Beat in the rum, and let stand for three hours at room temperature with a damp cloth over the bowl. In a separate bowl, beat the butter, sugar, and eggs, and add the dry ingredients in portions. Mix. Add the two raisins and the currants. Let stand for an hour with a damp cloth over the bowl. Pour it into a deep cake pan and cook until the top is golden brown and a toothpick thrust into the cake comes out clean.

It's almost certain two different people will have luck all year long from baking the cake. After all, several thousand years of festival-cake-baking tradition can't be wrong, can it?

It was believed that some spirits roamed only during the seven days of the Saturnalia holiday. Keeping lights on constantly through the darkness of night was said to keep them away. However, the only real way to stop the spirits from entering the house was to burn old shoes in the holiday fires, because the smell from the shoe smoke would keep away the spirits for sure.

Another light-themed tradition of the winter solstice comes from the ancient Greeks. The solstice brought darkness, and with it a fear of the worst of spirits, the Kallikantzaroi, monsters of chaos with a fearsome aspect. The Greek gods were able to keep them at bay most of the year, but at the solstice, and for seven days after, these monsters were free to roam, causing terrible calamities for the Greeks. These spirits especially liked to set fire to houses. To scare them away it was necessary to burn large logs treated with special aromatic herbs. The scent filled the house, and the monsters, hating the delightful odors, stayed away.

Some of the more obscure traditions of Christmas clearly come from the earlier Saturnalia holiday. For thousands of years battles were stopped for this holiday and overtures of peace, in the form of food and gifts, traded over battle lines. We see a reflection of this in modern times, when on Christmas, Union troops traded food across Confederate lines during the Civil War, and British troops traded coffee for sausages with the Germans in the trenches of World War I. During the Korean War, Christmastime always presented an opportunity to advance the cause of peace.

The Saturnalia and Christmas holidays have for thousands of years been a time for businesses to close. Historically, there were few other times one would close a business during the year, especially during ancient times.

Worshiping a spirit and bringing honor in the form of holy

contributions to the temple appears the same with both holidays. Saturn and God, and Mother Mary and the goddess of nature are especially honored at this time of year. The use of lights and the lighting of candles for religious significance were practices both then and now. Holiday greens in the form of wreaths and garlands were diplayed in exactly the same way then as is done now.

For many hundreds of years the Romans made this holiday important all over the known world. Saturnalia encouraged happiness and merrymaking at least once a year, not to mention feasts—especially feasts that brought together families. The halls of Romans and their allies were covered in scented boughs of all types, especially pine tree branches. Candles were lit so that hovering spirits, afraid of the light, would be gone during this time. Bonfires were built as high as possible to help the sun rise in the sky during the darkest of nights. Presents wrapped and given to family and loved ones served as honors to the gods. Candles of all shapes and sizes were especially valued gifts. The religious thought of the day claimed the light from these could help the sun overcome the darkness.

For Romans, one of the pleasures of the holiday was to bring family and friends to the Roman baths. The group would then play trivia games, and when questions stumped the entire assembly of naked bathers, laurel crowns were bought and dedicated in Saturn's temple. The gods only know where they kept their coins during the bath for the purchasing of the crowns.

Libanius, an ancient Sophist, wrote, "The impulse to spend seizes everyone . . . People are not only generous towards themselves, but also towards their fellow men. A stream of presents pours itself out of all sides." Another great quality of the festival is the teaching of men not to hold fast to their money, but to part with it and let it pass into other hands.

Saturnalia was a time of relaxed laws and restrictions. Gambling was allowed in public. Slaves had more freedom and were permitted to don the clothes of their masters. People took the entire seven-day festival as a nonworking holiday. In Roman towns, people drank themselves silly and then went singing naked in the streets. Faces of important people were painted on apples, which were tossed into huge buckets of icy water. Bobbing for those apples was said to bring the luck of personage depicted on the apple to the person who successfully retrieved it.

So, when you find yourself getting Christmas presents, remember that you have the Romans to thank for that. When you are enjoying the lights on your Christmas tree, think of the huddled ancients watching their fires burn from dusk till dawn and thank them for that. When you find yourself feasting and your brothers and sisters have come from far away to be with the family, thank the druids and their like for that. Finally, if you get a little sex during the Christmas holiday, think briefly of Saturnalia, but thank yourself for that.

This may be the best example there is of a lie getting out of hand. The source were superstitious teenage girls with a grudge. The results made the entire fiasco a word still known to everyone more than three hundred years later.

WITCHES, DEVILS, AND PURITANS IN MASSACHUSETTS

Peter Archer

A clapboard meeting house jammed with solemn-faced people clad in simple black and white. At one end of the room a group of men, visages stern, sit facing the crowd. Apart and in front of them stands an old woman, bent with age, sad-faced, but with a calm expression. And rolling on the floor, kicking, screaming, clawing, biting, is a group of girls, joined by one or two grown women.

The scene is Salem, Massachusetts, in the summer of 1692. Since the town is the site of one of the most notorious miscarriages of justice in American history, it's ironic that its name derives from *shalom*, the Hebrew word for "peace."

The first settlers in Salem arrived in 1629, and it was the first town settled in the Massachusetts Bay Colony. It was ruled by a theocracy of Puritans, religious believers with little or no time for humor, fun, or much of anything else apart from church and labor.

They lived in a dark world bound by mysterious forces they sought to exorcise through rituals and superstitions. It was also the world of a small village, sometimes divided by petty jealousies and feuds that turned neighbor against neighbor. That summer, those feuds took on a sinister aspect.

Sometime around March, nine-year-old Betty Parris, daughter of the minister of Salem Village (present-day Danvers), and her eleven-year-old cousin Abigail Williams, were playing with Tituba, an Indian slave Betty's father had brought back from Barbados. Some accounts suggest the girls were playing at fortune-telling, trying to read something of their future husbands with a raw egg dropped into water, interpreting their spouses' appearance from the patterns created by the swirling egg. Whatever the case, when their father discovered them, he suspected the presence of witchcraft. He questioned Tituba, who denied using any mysterious magic.

Meanwhile the girls began to behave strangely. An observer said they were "pinched and bitten by invisible agents; their arms, necks, and backs turned this way and that, and returned back again. . . . Sometimes they were taken dumb." Perhaps they discovered that if they behaved this way, adults would lavish attention on them—and they could break the confining bonds of Puritan society, saying and doing exactly as they pleased.

As news of the afflictions spread in the community, other young girls began to show similar symptoms. The more they were around one another, the more the strange manifestations increased. Sometimes the girls would lie on the ground howling and foaming at the mouth. They interrupted the minister in his preaching at church and shouted and stamped their feet.

And after a few days or weeks of this behavior, the girls put a name to the cause of their suffering: witchcraft, being practiced by Sarah Good and Sarah Osborne, two women of the town. They also accused Tituba of being a witch.

At this point, Thomas Putnam, one of the leading men of Salem, asked the authorities to arrest the three women. His daughter Ann was part of the group of girls supposedly plagued by witchcraft.

Three local men served as judges, all of them prominent in Salem's affairs. They saw their job as searching out evil, and when Sarah Good, Sarah Osborne, and Tituba were brought before them, the judges assumed they were guilty.

The girls, who were present at the hearing, along with much of the population of the town, seemed to confirm the accused ones' guilt. Whenever one of the three women so much as looked at them, the girls howled and shrieked and said they could see "a dark man" whispering in Sarah Good's ear or standing next to Sarah Osborne.

Under pressure from the court and terrified because of her slave status, Tituba confessed. Indeed, she expressed every desire to cooperate with her accusers and to help them root out the evil that had come to Salem. She told of riding with the devil, of calling familiars, magical assistants, in the form of birds and animals. To the judges, this fit in with everything they'd previously believed about witches. And as long as Tituba was confirming their story, the afflicted girls were free of torment.

Quickly the circle of accused widened, and now, instead of relatively marginal women such as Good and Osborne, it began to touch more prominent families. The girls accused Martha Corey, a good, church-going woman and a pillar of respectability. According to Ann Putnam, this was merely a clever disguise, for Martha often appeared to her in a spirit body and tormented her. When Ann made this accusation, the men who noted it asked her what clothes Martha was wearing when she appeared. If the terrestrial Martha wore different clothes from those the girl described, Ann must be lying.

Seeing the trap, Ann seems to have devised a spur-of-the-moment answer. She said that Martha's spirit had blinded her so she couldn't describe its clothes. The answer apparently satisfied the men, who didn't pursue the issue.

The girls' antics became even more extreme. They claimed they were being pierced with pins, bitten, bruised, and could hear the beating of invisible drums. The judges listened solemnly to all these stories. Even when some of the stories were proven to be false, the hysteria went on. One girl claimed to have been stabbed with a knife by a witch and offered the court the broken knife. Another townsman, though, said he'd broken the knife the day before and had thrown it away. The judges cautioned the girl, but her credibility was unimpaired.

One of the most important accusations made by the girls—whose circle had now grown to include a few adult women, among them Ann Putnam's mother—was against Rebecca Nurse. Rebecca was old, with an unimpeachable reputation in the town. Her husband owned much land in the area. None of this did her any good when Ann Putnam, Sr., led the charge against her. In the court, she demanded, "Did you not bring the Black Man with you?" Rebecca was thrown into prison with the others.

The accusations spread wider and wider, reaching John and Elizabeth Proctor, a respectable couple. When Elizabeth defied her accusers in court, they shrieked that they could see her husband sitting on a beam directing her. By May, twenty-seven accused witches were in Salem's jail.

The trials of the accused witches now began, organized by Sir William Phips, governor of the Massachusetts Bay Colony. The court tried and condemned Bridget Bishop. On June 10, she was taken to Gallows Hill, northwest of the town, and hanged.

The hysteria was now in full swing. The girls accused George Burroughs, former minister of Salem, who had left the town some years before to take up a post in Maine. He was arrested and returned to Salem to stand trial. He was condemned to death, and on the gallows, turning to the crowd, he did what was thought impossible for a witch: Without a mistake or hesitation, he recited the Lord's Prayer.

Some in the crowd began to mutter that something was wrong

and that they had condemned an innocent man. Suddenly a young man dressed in black and riding a horse stood in the stirrups and addressed the crowd. He told them that the devil could take many forms, even an angel. Burroughs was duly hanged, and the young man, Cotton Mather, went on to become one of the most prominent religious figures in early New England.

More and more of the accused witches were sent to trial. If they confessed, they were saved from hanging (though still subject to imprisonment and general excoriation by the community), and several did so. Others refused to make false confessions and were executed. Rebecca Nurse defended herself with impressive skill, and the jury acquitted her, but the accusing girls flew into hysterics, and the judges demanded the jury reconsider its verdict. Rebecca was condemned, and on July 19 she was hanged.

The last of the accused to be killed was Mary Easty. She was at first acquitted, but Mercy Lewis, one of her accusers, had a fit of lockjaw lasting for days, and on this evidence, and the renewed accusations of the girls, Easty was retried. In a letter to her judges before her execution, she begged, "If it be possible no more innocent blood may be shed." Perhaps the plea fell on more receptive ears this time.

Another turning point was when the girls, swollen with pride in their success, went to nearby Andover to root out witchcraft in that village. When they began to accuse townspeople, twenty-four residents of Andover signed a petition denouncing the girls as "distempered." The girls went to Gloucester, and although four women were accused of witchcraft there, the girls' tricks and screaming was beginning to wear thin. By the end of 1692, the witchcraft craze had passed. Those who were still in jail were pardoned and set free. The girls themselves sank back into family life. One of them later told someone, "[I] did it for sport, [we] must have some sport."

On August 25, 1706, Ann Putnam, Jr., made a public address in which she admitted that she and the other girls had lied. She was careful to place the responsibility for these lies elsewhere, saying, "It was a great delusion of Satan that deceived me in that sad time." Nonetheless, it was a confession of sorts.

There have been many theories among historians as to the cause of the witch hunt. One suggested that contaminated rye flour had caused the girls to have hallucinations. Other, more practical-minded, historians have seen in the event a conflict of village interests, with some families in Salem trying to profit by eliminating their rivals. Others have suggested that some of the women who were accused might have been midwives and have provided abortions secretly when requested. Whatever the reason for the girls' lies, the term "witch hunt" has entered the English lexicon.

Today Salem is a popular tourist destination. Visitors flock to see Nathaniel Hawthorne's House of the Seven Gables and visit the Witch Museum, with its hokey presentation of the witchcraft scare.

A quarter mile away from the Witch Museum, abutting the Charter Street Burial Ground, is a more quietly moving monument to the hysteria's victims. A small, tree-lined plot of grass is surrounded by a low stone wall, with a path running along it. At the entrance to the park, on stone slabs set in the ground, are engraved the last words of some of the accused: "I am no witch. I am innocent. I know nothing of it" (Bridget Bishop); "Oh, Lord, help me! It is false. I am clear. For my life now lies in your hands" (Rebecca Nurse). And along the wall are inset twenty benches, each bearing the name of one of those hanged in that strange and terrible summer of 1692.

After I read this I felt betrayed . . . by Walt Disney. I wonder if Fess Parker knew the truth.

SO HUMBLE IN GREEN COUNTY, TENNESSEE, 1834

Brian Thomsen

"I would rather be politically dead than hypocritically immortalized."

"Hypocritically immortalized": to be credited for deeds, accomplishments, and honors that one did not actually do or merit or earn. The author of this quote is none other than the larger-than-life hero of the early-nineteenth-century American frontier, Davy Crockett, a man eager to toot his own horn for fun, profit, and political expedience. The bestseller *A Narrative of the Life of David Crockett by Himself* (1834), his autobiography, is most likely to be the actual work of Thomas Chilton, who is credited as the book's editor. Indeed, much of the other writing attributed to Crockett was actually penned by numerous ghost writers (presumably due to Crockett's lack of formal education) and possibly approved by Crockett before publication.

They were all, of course, proofed against a factual record . . . Crockett's own factual record, which generally credited him with far more accomplishments than were humanly possible.

His official congressional bio is as follows:

> CROCKETT, David (father of John Wesley Crockett), a Representative from Tennessee; born at the confluence of Limestone Creek and Nolichuckey River in the State of Franklin, present day Greene County, Tenn., August 17, 1786; attended the common schools; served in Creek campaign, 1813–1814; member of the Tennessee state house of representatives, 1821–1823; unsuccessful candidate for election to the Nineteenth Congress in 1825; elected as a Jacksonian to the Twentieth Congress; elected as an Anti-Jacksonian to the Twenty-first Congress (March 4, 1827–March 3, 1831); unsuccessful candidate for reelection to the Twenty-second Congress in 1830; elected as an Anti-Jacksonian to the Twenty-third Congress (March 4, 1833–March 3, 1835); unsuccessful candidate for reelection to the Twenty-fourth Congress in 1834; fought at the Battle of the Alamo, San Antonio, Tex., 1836; died about March 6, 1836.

Nothing about staring down bears during his infancy, nor his skills as a woodsman, nor anything that would suggest that he was the new-generation Daniel Boone (the title of whose own pseudo memoirs Crockett successfully co-opted).

More to the point, Crockett was married twice (with numerous periods of spousal abandonment), had a taste for hard liquor and an aversion to hard work, fathered seven legitimate children of record, and served a largely undistinguished congressional term before heading off to be killed at the Alamo.

Indeed, his death defending Texas is also a case of his being "hypocritically immortalized." Far from going down swinging, as Walt Disney might like you to believe, he probably died during the first day of the siege, or, as some believe, may have been executed while trying to talk his way out of Mexican custody.

One source even ascribes the following statement to him:

> I am David Crockett, a citizen of the state of Tennessee and representative of a district of that State in the United States Congress. I have come to Texas on a visit of exploration; purposing, if permitted, to become a loyal citizen of the Republic of Mexico. I extended my visit to San Antonio and called in the Alamo to become acquainted with the officers, and learn of them what I could of the condition of affairs. Soon after my arrival, the fort was invested by government troops, whereby I have been prevented from leaving it. And here I am yet, a noncombatant and foreigner, having taken no part in the fighting.

Not exactly what one would call a heroic defense of one's position as a defender of Texas. One might say that "hypocritical" is exactly the word that should be ascribed to this "legendary folk hero."

It should be also noted that Crockett's reaction to being "politically dead" (following his defeat for reelection in 1835) was to curse the voters of Tennessee by telling them all to go "to hell."

Some lies reappear time after time to justify some of history's darkest acts. This is also an object lesson about when deeply held prejudices overwhelm a system of law.

J'ACCUSE!

Peter Archer

On January 5, 1895, at 8:45 in the morning, an assembly of soldiers formed up in the courtyard of the École Militaire in Paris. As they looked on, guards brought out a prisoner, his face lined with care, his hair graying. However, he walked proudly and ignored the shouts that came from the crowd beyond the soldiers. "Death to the Jew!"

A mounted officer confronted him. "Alfred Dreyfus," he cried, "you are no longer worthy of bearing arms. In the name of the people of France, we dishonor you!"

Dreyfus's reply was almost drowned out by the shouts of acclamation from the crowd. A sergeant tore the decorations from Dreyfus's cap, sleeves, and trousers. All the while the crowd shouted, "Coward! Traitor! Dirty Jew!" The ceremony was complete, and Dreyfus returned to the prison from which he had come.

The Dreyfus case—often referred to simply as "The Affair"—was among the most controversial of trials during the nineteenth century. It divided families, destroyed a government, and in the end weakened the dominant position the army had held in French society since the days of Napoleon.

The curious thing about the case was that the lies the prosecution told were in many instances both obvious and easily refuted. Yet the prosecution succeeded by making the case less about Dreyfus's innocence or guilt on the charge of espionage than about the honor of the French army.

In the 1890s, tensions between France and Germany ran high. Germany had defeated France in the Franco-Prussian War, which brought a humiliating peace for France, the destruction of the Third Empire, and the episode of the Paris Commune of 1871. Virtually everyone in France expected war between the two countries to break out again in the near future.

Spies for both sides infiltrated the ranks of the armies, seeking military advantage. In the summer of 1894, the French received reliable information that a spy was operating in the upper ranks of the army. The indication was a discarded draft of a letter from a German spy to his superiors reporting that a French officer was prepared to have dealings with the German government. In addition to this letter, the French acquired a document that gave a description of a new type of field howitzer under development.

Suspicion fell upon Capt. Alfred Dreyfus, a member of the French General Staff, who, it was argued, had access to the kind of information contained in the document. He was also the highest-ranking Jewish officer in the army. In a period when anti-Semitism was rife in France, this automatically made him suspect. When officers compared Dreyfus's handwriting to that in the document, they concluded that he had written it. He was arrested on charges of high treason and sent to await trial.

There was indeed a spy in the French high command, but it wasn't Dreyfus. The spy was an officer named Ferdinand Walsin-Esterhazy, who had a long, dishonorable career plagued by gambling and debts. However, the army rushed ahead with their trial of Dreyfus, supported in this by a coalition of right-wing politicians, anti-Semitic journalists, and the Catholic Church.

The court-martial of Captain Dreyfus was held in late 1894, and not surprisingly, he was convicted. He was sentenced to life in prison, stripped of his rank and medals, and sent to Devil's Island, off the coast of French Guiana. There, with little contact with his wife and children, and neglected and insulted by the prison warders, he languished.

However, other forces were at work, some of which were unknown to Dreyfus. His brother, Mathieu, in particular, was tireless in defense of the imprisoned man, demanding a new trial. He appealed to a wide range of public figures, calling for the army to take up the case again.

What the Dreyfusards (as the defenders of Dreyfus became known) did not know was that the original trial and conviction were based on forged evidence. An army officer known as Henry had concocted some of the papers on which the prosecution had based their case. Henry did this, it would seem, to ensure a conviction, since he had no doubt of Dreyfus's guilt. The forged papers were accepted as genuine by officers all the way up the chain of command to War Minister Auguste Mercier.

In 1896, Lt. Col. Georges Picquart was appointed chief of the army's intelligence unit. An anti-Semite, Picquart was utterly convinced that in convicting Dreyfus, the court-martial had made the right decision. Nonetheless, in examining the papers of the case, he slowly began to come to a different conclusion. There were too many holes in the evidence, too many signs that pointed away from Dreyfus and toward someone else. Picquart concluded that Esterhazy was, in fact, the guilty party.

But when he brought this to the attention of the authorities, he was politely told to mind his own business. A Jew had been convicted of the crime. Who cared if the conviction was wrong? It was only a Jew, after all. And what would be gained by reopening the case, calling into question the authority of the army and its officers?

Picquart made contact with Dreyfus's brother, Mathieu, and the two joined forces to free an innocent man. They gained support from Georges Clemenceau, among the most respected of French politicians and a future premier.

As a concession to the pressure of the Dreyfusards, Esterhazy was charged and put on trial. Army officers, though fully aware that they might be supporting a traitor and a spy, testified on his behalf. Incredibly, he was acquitted, and as he walked down the steps of the courthouse he was greeted with cheers and flowers flung by an adoring mob.

Among the most important figures to take up the defense of Dreyfus and the demand for a new trial was the writer Émile Zola. In 1898, Zola published his famous open letter to the French premier. Titled *"J'Accuse!"* ("I Accuse!"), the letter accused the army and the government of engaging in a cover up.

"I have but one passion," Zola cried, "one for seeing the light, in the name of humanity which has so suffered and which is entitled to happiness. My fiery protest is but the cry of my soul."

The government responded by charging Zola with libel. Tried and convicted, he fled to England and refused to return to France until he was granted amnesty.

Meanwhile, another officer had discovered Henry's forgeries in the original trial documents. Faced with possible disgrace, Henry committed suicide. Right-wing newspapers declared he had been driven to his death by a Jewish conspiracy.

In 1899, under overwhelming pressure from at home and abroad, the army agreed to hold a new trial of Dreyfus. He was brought back from Devil's Island, having no idea of the efforts on his behalf and the controversy his case had engendered. The court deliberated amid threats of a possible army coup supported by right-wing politicians if Dreyfus were found innocent. The defense attorney, Fernand Labori, was shot and wounded, preventing him from attending the hearing for a week.

Astonishingly, the army introduced no new evidence at the second trial. Rather, they relied upon the same discredited batch of forged papers that had been used to convict Dreyfus the first time. At the start of the trial, War Minister Mercier declared, "This trial will show that either I or Dreyfus am a liar." Thus he placed his own reputation and that of the army in the balance.

At last the verdict was announced. By a vote of five to two, the court upheld the original verdict. Once again, Dreyfus had been convicted. General Mercier, ignoring the evidence of Henry's forgeries, announced that the second conviction had vindicated the army.

The government, anxious to hush up the controversy, which had led to the fall of the previous cabinet, pardoned Dreyfus. At last, after five years in prison, he was set free and could return to his family. But the verdicts against him were still a black mark on his record, and the chorus of anti-Semitism continued to resound.

Among those who had witnessed Dreyfus's original humiliation in the courtyard of the École Militaire was a Jewish journalist, Theodor Herzl. He concluded that the Dreyfus affair showed that Jews could not successfully assimilate into European society but must find a homeland of their own. His movement, Zionism, would one day result in the founding of the state of Israel.

In 1906, the French government formally rescinded the verdicts against Dreyfus in both courts-martial. Dreyfus later wrote, "I had never doubted this triumph of justice and truth over error, deception, and crime."

Oh well, it made for a great movie.

SEVENTY-NINE BRIDGES

ARABIA, 1916–1918

Brian Thomsen

"I personally blew up 79 bridges during the campaign against the Turks."

—T. E. Lawrence, aka "Lawrence of Arabia"

Lt. Col. Thomas Edward Lawrence was posted to Cairo in 1916. He was assigned to British military intelligence, as the knowledge of the Arab people he had gained through numerous prior trips to the Middle East (as part of archeological expeditions) made him the ideal liaison between British and Arab forces.

Working with Arab irregular troops under the command of Emir Faisal, a son of the Sharif Hussein of Mecca, Lawrence's objective was to distract German allies through extended guerilla operations against the armed forces of the Ottoman Empire while taking advantage of the never-ending power struggle between tribal interests and religious factions in the area. In essence, Lawrence's major contribution to World War I was persuading Arab leaders to coordinate their seemingly never-ending revolt against the government to aid British interests.

Seven Pillars of Wisdom: A Triumph, the autobiographical account of his experience with the rebel forces during this so-called Arab Revolt from 1916 to 1918, is the primary source for most of the so-called legend of "Lawrence of Arabia," the British officer who led the Arab insurgents against the Turks in their guerilla war during World War I.

Though no doubt a true war hero, Lawrence was also a bit of an "odd duck," prone to embellishing the truth (such as his having personally blown up seventy-nine bridges) in the service of his own ego. He also adopted the tribal lifestyle as his own, and soon became known for wearing white Arabian garb (given to him by Prince Feisal, they were wedding robes originally given to Feisal—a clear case of Arab re-gifting) and riding camels and horses in the desert. Far from blending in with the insurgents, Lawrence's very ostentatious manner garnered their attention.

As he gained the respect and awe of the rebels, he soon taxed the tolerance of his superiors. He was quite insubordinate and even refused to accept the honor of being made a Knight Commander, leaving King George V with the box containing the medal in hand, with no one to give it to at a very public ceremony.

After the war, Lawrence reenlisted in the ranks of the RAF in 1922, under the alias of John Hume Ross. His ruse was discovered within weeks and he was quickly discharged. He then joined Royal Tank Corps in 1923 as T. E. Shaw, and reinsinuated himself back into the RAF again in 1925.

Perhaps one of the most memorable scenes in *Seven Pillars* deals with his temporary captivity in the city of Deraa:

> They took me upstairs to the Bey's room; or to his bedroom, rather. He was another bulky man, a Circassian himself, perhaps, and sat on the bed in a night-gown, trembling and sweating as

though with fever. When I was pushed in he kept his head down, and waved the guard out. In a breathless voice he told me to sit on the floor in front of him, and after that was dumb.

. . . When I saw what he wanted I twisted round and up again, glad to find myself equal to him, at any rate in wrestling. He began to fawn on me, saying how white and fresh I was, how fine my hands and feet, and how he would let me off drills and duties, make me his orderly, even pay me wages, if I would love him. I was obdurate, so he changed his tone, and sharply ordered me to take off my drawers. When I hesitated, he snatched at me; and I pushed him back . . . The Bey cursed me with horrible threats: and made the man holding me tear my clothes away, bit by bit. His eyes rounded at the half-healed places where the bullets had flicked through my skin a little while ago. Finally he lumbered to his feet, with a glitter in his look, and began to paw me over . . .

"You must understand that I know: and it will be easier if you do as I wish." I was dumbfounded, and we stared silently at one another, while the men who felt an inner meaning beyond their experience, shifted uncomfortably . . .

. . . They kicked me to the head of the stairs, and stretched me over a guard-bench, pommelling me. Two knelt on my ankles, bearing down on the back of my knees, while two more twisted my wrists till they cracked, and then crushed them and my neck against the wood. The corporal had run downstairs; and now came back with a whip of the Circassian sort, a thong of supple black hide, rounded, and tapering from the thickness of a thumb at the grip (which was wrapped in silver) down to a hard point finer than a pencil. He saw me shivering, partly I think, with cold, and made it whistle over my ear, taunting me that before his tenth cut I would howl for mercy, and at the twentieth beg for the caresses of the Bey; and then he began to lash me madly across and across with all his might, while I

> locked my teeth to endure this thing which lapped itself like flaming wire about my body. To keep my mind in control I numbered the blows, but after twenty lost count, and could feel only the shapeless weight of pain, not tearing claws, for which I had prepared, but a gradual cracking apart of my whole being by some too-great force whose waves rolled up my spine till they were pent within my brain, to clash terribly together (Book VI, chapter 80).

The entire scene is particularly riveting in its portrayal of the savage and uncouth enemy, as well as praised as being psychologically revealing of Lawrence's guilt over being caught and of his metaphoric ambivalence about some of the decisions that are being made by the British government. This passage is also often cited as evidence of his rumored homosexual and masochistic tendencies. It is a credit to Lawrence's expertise as a prose stylist that he is able to pull off a scene based on such an obviously painful memory.

The only problem is that in all actuality it probably never happened. The dates and location do not match up with the records of Lawrence's whereabouts at the time. The lascivious Turk depicted was actually a known womanizer, and there was a large reward available for the arrest of Lawrence at the time. Given his distinctive appearance for the locale, it is extremely unlikely that his Turkish captors would not have recognized him or would have preferred his "favors" to the cash reward. Moreover, the medical records show no evidence of any damage on his body caused by the flogging or assault, nor is there a record of a period of convalescence, since he obviously would have needed time off to recover from such a vicious attack.

It is fairly evident that the great war hero made the entire thing up . . . which does indeed call into question the rest of his account of his war in the desert.

What was to be believed as fact, and what was merely the fantastic fabulation of his fevered and creative mind?

Lawrence also crowed about his more traditional "heroic" exploits, particularly about how he mastered numerous strategic demolitions ("I personally blew up 79 bridges during the campaign against the Turks"), not just bridges but railways and outposts, too. He also took credit for the accomplishments of his ragtag irregulars' guerilla warfare, stressing how invaluable they were to the war effort, neither of which can be fairly substantiated in terms of their overall effectiveness during the revolt. Indeed his part in the campaign largely just "pestered" the Turks, rather than causing them any real damage or making a strategic contribution to the major front against the allies of Germany.

Indeed, Lawrence joined the ranks of numerous decorated warriors of the British Empire whose lack of pragmatic effectiveness is more than overshadowed by the patina of heroism and daring.

In the words of the esteemed historian Angus Calder, "The gravest charge against Lawrence is that in the interests of promoting his cause, he exaggerated the potency of *his* Bedouin as auxiliaries and minimized the contributions of other whites, not only Frenchmen who served alongside him, but also the Australians who were in fact first into Damascus" (despite the staged ballyhoo of the arrival of "his" Arabs and their dominance of the city, though in name only).

Lawrence did, however, manage to parley his self-proclaimed expertise into commissions for two articles, "Demolitions Under Fire" (*Royal Engineers Journal* XXIX, no. 1 [January 1919]), and "On Guerrilla Warfare," published in 1929 for the *Encyclopaedia Britannica.*

Though Lawrence did indeed lie about many things, there is one matter in which he was entirely truthful. The first edition of *Seven Pillars of Wisdom* was published as a high-priced private subscription edition. Afraid that the public would think he would make a substantial income from the book, and stating that the book had been written as a result of his war service, he declared that he would not reap any financial gain from its private publication.

He didn't.

As it turned out, the sale price covered only one third of the production costs, leaving Lawrence that much poorer for each copy sold.

FOR THE RECORD, Angus Calder, in his introduction to the Wordsworth edition of *Seven Pillars of Wisdom,* corrects Lawrence's bridge-blowing tally to being closer to twenty-three rather than seventy-nine (and most of those failed to disrupt communications or supply lines for significant lengths of time) . . . but who knew anyone was actually counting?

This lie was the keynote deception for one of the darkest past of European history. I am not sure what so many Germans' believing it says about them or the world just over half a century ago. What do we believe that is just as wrong today?

VILLAGE OF THE DAMNED

FORTY MILES NORTH OF PRAGUE, 1944

Brian Thomsen

Der Führer schenkt den Juden eine Stadt
("The Leader Gives the Jews a Town")

During World War II, the Nazis relocated thousands of Jews from their homes into squalid ghettos. Living conditions in these villages were usually crowded and harsh. When the Red Cross asked to visit one of these Jewish resettlement towns, the Reich agreed.

In the spring of 1944, the Nazis began extensive improvements to the ghetto known as Theresienstadt. In their mission to impress the International Red Cross delegates with the high standard of living the Reich maintained for the ghetto's Jews (and thus dispel the rumors of mass executions, enforced slave labor, and death camps), the Nazis outdid themselves. After the beautification project was completed, they were so proud of their handiwork that they made a movie of their accomplishment, entitled, *Der Führer schenkt den Juden eine Stadt*, or *The Leader Gives the Jews a Town*. The film showed the happy internees leading a pleasant, down-home existence while taking pride in their town as good and loyal servants of the Reich.

Known after the fact as "the Paradise Ghetto," Theresienstadt was quite impressive. The resident Jews were allowed access to several parks, a library, a music pavilion, several cultural clubs, and even a synagogue. Local cafés and shops also seemed to be thriving. There were even charitable institutions such as orphanages, retirement homes, and mental hospitals, as well as work centers for the blind, deaf, and disabled.

On June 23, 1944, two Swiss delegates of the International Red Cross and two representatives of the government of Denmark (whose king, Christian X, had vigorously protested the resettlement of his Jewish citizens while demanding assurances of their safety from representatives of the Third Reich) arrived to inspect the so-called ghetto.

Over the course of the war, the Red Cross tried to maintain a degree of neutrality so as to allow the continued distribution of aid parcels and medical assistance among prisoners and internees. They were obviously concerned about the rumors of horrendous conditions in ghettos and the whispers of such nightmarish facilities as death camps, but they nonetheless agreed to work with the Germans to facilitate their visit. The Germans were more than happy to allow the visit, so long as the delegates understood that such things had to be scheduled several months in advance.

The inspection lasted a mere six hours. Cultural events were scheduled for the entire week, as were extra rations, just in case anyone from the team had second thoughts and wanted to return to give the ghetto another look.

The resultant report painted a fairly objective picture of satisfied internees making do given the wartime conditions they were in. Sure, strict discipline was enforced through overly restrictive rules, and of course living conditions were austere. Certainly. It was war, after all. But the so-called ghetto was indeed governed and regulated by the Jews themselves, who had been allowed to form their own government.

The transplanted citizenry of Theresienstadt included World War I veterans, prominent people of culture who had previously garnered some degree of international recognition, such as artists, writers, and musicians, and other very important persons such as Rabbi Dr. Leo Baeck of Berlin, the man the Nazis called "the Pope of the Jews." These were all, for the most part, people whose presence might be missed, thus attracting some unwanted attention to their overall situation and that of those in their circle. As a result, they were effectively cloistered in plain but secluded sight in their town, while some of the more prominent Jews were even given their own private apartments.

The fact that it was all a sham put on for the benefit of deceiving the Red Cross was not as heinous as the subsequent revelation: that the Nazis' "Final Solution" was at that time well under way.

"The Final Solution of the Jewish Question" (in German, *Endlosung der Judenfrage*) is the full title of the Nazis' diabolic plan to engage in the systematic genocide of Jews as well as that of several other "mongrel tribes."

In his diary entry for December 13, 1941, the day after Hitler's secret speech in Berlin regarding the annihilation of all Jews, Joseph Goebbels wrote: "In respect of the Jewish question, the Führer has decided to make a clean sweep. The world war is here, the annihilation of the Jews must be the necessary result."

Mass killings of more than one million Jews occurred before the plans of the Final Solution were fully implemented, but it was only with the decision to exterminate the entire Jewish population that camps were built to facilitate their segregation and execution and the industrialized mass slaughter of Jews began in earnest. This decision to legally and efficiently kill the Jews of Europe was made prior to the Wannsee conference (which took place in Berlin in the Wannsee Villa on January 20, 1942), where SS general Reinhardt Heydrich conveyed Hitler's instructions to a panel of politicians and "thinkers," including an expert on eugenics, whose jobs it was to justify retroactively the decisions that had already been reached. During the conference there was a pro forma discussion to decide on the "Final Solution of the Jewish Question." The questions at hand were couched never in terms of "if" or "should" but rather of "how" and "when," with an accent on speed and efficiency (matters that would be handled from that point on by Heydrich's right hand, Adolf Eichmann).

Theresienstadt, located about forty miles from Prague, had been made into a ghetto for Jewish deportees from the protectorate of Bohemia and Moravia, Slovakia, Germany, Austria, the Netherlands, and Denmark. These deportees would later be transported to one of the extermination camps farther east, in Poland. The first name that the Nazis gave to the town, which had been renamed Terezin by the Czechs, was Theresienbad, which means "Theresien Spa," implying that it was a place where people could take mineral baths. Then the name was changed to Reichsaltersheim, or "State Old People's Home," as those Jews who were incapable of forced labor were temporarily housed there.

It was very important to the Nazi high command that the truth about the so-called "Final Solution to the Jewish Question" be kept under wraps so as not to further incite agitation or resistance among the incarcerated Jews as they were transported to their dooms. Theresienstadt was thus passed off as a typical resettlement center in order to assuage the fears of the transportees.

There was indeed a Jewish "self-government" that ran minor day-to-day operations there . . . but they were also charged with selecting the candidates for the transports, to locations that turned out to be either slave labor centers or extermination camps.

Indeed this "self-government" was also given an important task during the beautification process: It was determined that the number of internees in the ghetto far exceeded the number that would be allowable under sanitary regulations. Ergo, the next step was to relieve the overcrowding so that the International Red Cross would not realize the actual inhuman living conditions there. To accomplish this, the "self-government" was charged with picking candidates for deportation. As a result, in September 1943, December 1943, and May 1944, just before the scheduled Red Cross visit, there were a total of seven transports to the east, in which 17,517 Jews were sent to the death camp at Auschwitz.

. . . and once the visits were over and done with, things returned to normal.

According to the records: "In Sept. 1944, there were approximately 30,000 prisoners living in Theresienstadt. Eleven transports, totaling 18,402 inmates of the ghetto, were sent to Auschwitz between September 28, 1944 and October 28, 1944, the date of the last transport to be sent to the gas chambers of Auschwitz." These numbers, obviously, do not include the many deaths that occurred within the town on a daily basis from malnutrition and other factors.

The total number of Jews transported from the west to the Theresienstadt ghetto from the day it opened on November 24, 1941, until April 20, 1945, was 139,654. (There were also 13,454 persons who arrived at the ghetto after April 20, after being evacuated by the Nazis from other concentration camps that had to be closed in the face of the advancing Russian army.)

Out of the 139,654 Jews originally deported to Theresienstadt, 86,934 were subsequently transported to the various concentration camps and extermination centers in the east, and 33,430 died in the ghetto. (As many as 207 babies were recorded as being born there, despite the fact that most of the men and women were housed in separate barracks.)

In the end, the so-called Paradise Ghetto was merely a temporary way station and diversion from the death camps, and that which was called "self-government" was merely a coordinating body to carry out the orders of the Nazi high command.

. . . and the film *Der Führer schenkt den Juden eine Stadt* was a masterwork of propaganda moviemaking no different from the fantasy films *Siegfried, The Golem,* and *Metropolis,* all of which were filmed at the Babelsberg Studios just outside of Berlin.

In the annals of "liardom" a few men stand out for the number, import, and depth of deception of their lies. Here is a man so dark and duplicitous that he has to be rated as one of the greatest and most evil liars of history. And that is bucking some pretty impressive competition.

WORLD WAR II'S MASTER OF LIES

GERMANY, 1933–1945

Douglas Niles

"All of Germany's problems are the fault of the Jews!"

—Joseph Goebbels

In November of 1942, as the Battle of Stalingrad was starting in the USSR, Joseph Goebbels gave a speech to the German people summing up much of the propaganda he had been dispensing since the Nazis came to power in 1933. Titled "The Jews Are Guilty," the speech claimed (in part):

> The historical guilt of world Jewry on the outbreak and expansion of this war is so amply proved that is not necessary to lose another word over it. The Jews wanted this war and they have it now. But they must also keep in mind the prophecy of the Führer of January 30, 1939—the outcome will not be the victory of

Jewry, but the extermination of the Jewish race in Europe. We now see the fulfillment of this prophecy.

Pity, to say nothing of sympathy, is entirely inappropriate. We must win this war against the Jews. Should we lose it, then the harmless-appearing Jewish good fellows would exact on our people, women and children, a revenge for which history gives no precedence.

By that autumn of 1942, the campaign against European Jewry was well under way. Already the Jews who lived in lands controlled by the Nazis had been crowded into urban ghettos tightly controlled by the Gestapo. The first death camps would be established soon, and within the next year the ghastly plan of the "Final Solution" would be implemented: genocide on an industrial scale, so vast and merciless that it would come to be known as the Holocaust.

The man who gave voice to that scourge, who justified it to his own people and tried to justify it to the world, was a crippled little fellow who nevertheless could speak and write with an oily fluidity that captivated a large segment of the German population. Physically unprepossessing, he used his words as weapons. Joseph Goebbels was nothing less than one of the masterminds of the Nazis' attempted extermination of the Jewish people.

It seems unlikely that Goebbels himself believed in the racist screed that had become a cornerstone of the Nazi empire. Born in 1897, he was ridiculed and mocked as a child because of a club foot—apparently the result of a childhood illness. As a boy, he withdrew from social contacts, had no close friends, and took solace in reading and in the bitter avenues of his own thoughts. He was intelligent, and contemptuous of the other children whom, while physically more capable than he, he always viewed as stupid and unimaginative.

This view of his juvenile world would expand to encompass the whole citizenry of Germany—the people viewed as the gullible "masses." Manipulating the beliefs, prejudices, and ideals of those masses would come to be Goebbels's life's work. Unfortunately for a great many people, he became very, very good at this chosen vocation.

Turned down for military service during World War I because of his disability, Goebbels instead went to the university at Heidelberg. Claiming that his foot had been injured in combat at the Battle of Verdun, he was at last able to win some acceptance from his peers. Here his natural wit, intelligence, and force of personality began to come into their own. It is perhaps fitting that this first social success in his life was based upon a lie; it was to be but the first of many falsehoods spread far and wide by this master liar as he raised the art of untruth to previously unimagined heights.

Receiving his degree in 1922, Goebbels kicked around at odd jobs in writing, publishing, and broadcasting for several years. There is evidence from this period that he was not personally anti-Semitic: he made no secret of the fact that his favorite teachers were Jewish, he admired Jewish writers, and he was briefly engaged to a woman who was part Jewish.

But, like many other Germans, he was fiercely nationalistic. In 1924 he became friends with some of the young National Socialists (Nazis) who were at that time members of a small, radical party focused on righting the perceived wrongs that had been inflicted upon their country. Goebbels was already a gifted public speaker, and he used his gifts to enhance the reputation of the party as it gained influence, attracted followers in greater and greater numbers, and slowly gathered political power. Because so many Germans bitterly resented the harshly punitive Treaty of Versailles that had ended World War I, he found it easy to tap into this growing nationalism. As the Nazis gained power, Hitler would ever be known as the face of the party, but Goebbels became increasingly famous as its voice.

In the mid-1920s, the Nazis faced a schism in their own party, between left and right wing branches that viewed capitalism as favorable or unfavorable, respectively. Goebbels threw his influence behind the right-wing leader, Adolf Hitler. For the next seven years he functioned as Hitler's spokesman and, effectively, campaign manager, establishing the cult of personality that elevated the soon-to-be Führer to almost godlike status for many Germans. At the time, the nation was a democracy, and during the late 1920s and early 1930s the Nazi Party continued to win more and more votes in every successive election.

Key to Goebbels's success in these years was his ability to verbally skewer the powerful, conservative men who ruled Germany. As the worldwide Depression settled in during the early 1930s, the situation in Germany was even bleaker than in many other parts of the world. It was easy to blame this on the Treaty of Versailles, and on mismanagement and corruption by the old noblemen—such as President Hindenburg—who were more and more obviously out of touch with modern sensibilities.

In great part owing to Goebbels's skill at propaganda, the Nazis finally swept to power in the elections of 1933, with Hitler becoming chancellor of Germany. The Führer moved quickly to consolidate his power, and to reward those who had helped him achieve his high station. Goebbels was given a newly created position: director of the National Ministry of Public Enlightenment and Propaganda.

Yet he found himself facing an unexpected problem. So much of his energy as a speechmaker and writer had been directed at the reigning powers. He found it easy to mock and humiliate such large, tempting targets. With his own party now holding the reins of power, however, he had to change his tactics—it would never do to make fun of Hitler or the Nazis! In casting around for another target, a victim he could blame and accuse and vilify before the country, he found a waiting pawn in the people who had so long been subjected to prejudice, pogroms, racism, and discrimination throughout European history.

The Jews were to blame! The claim was not new to the Nazis,

who had long been loudly anti-Semitic. But the accusation became Goebbels's new rallying cry, and over the subsequent years he repeated it so often, so harshly, so relentlessly, that it became ingrained in the psyche of (many of) the German people. By repeating bald-faced lies so continuously, Goebbels came to prove one of his own maxims: the masses need to be fed a repetitious diet of slogans, and they will come to believe these slogans over even the leanings of their own reason and consciences.

Goebbels was a master at casting the German people as beleaguered underdogs, with the whole world arrayed against them. That world, in Goebbels's propaganda, was a tool of the wealthy Jew, and he unfailingly reminded his listeners that the Jew was dedicated to Germany's destruction. It was only self-defense, he reasoned, that would force the Nazis to strike at the Jews first.

During the prewar years this prejudice became more and more pronounced within Germany, leading to events such as the infamous Kristallnacht in November of 1938, where brown-shirted Nazi thugs went on an orgy of destruction directed at Jewish businesses, synagogues, and homes. Some thirty-five Jews were killed while many thousands more were arrested; the Nazis even confiscated the insurance payments on the damage they'd inflicted.

Many German Jews fled the country during this increasingly violent decade, some going safely to England or the Western Hemisphere. (Albert Einstein found work teaching at Princeton.) Others imagined themselves safe in Warsaw, Prague, Paris, or Amsterdam. By the summer of 1940, all of these historic capitals—and their terrified populations—would be firmly in Nazi hands.

By the time World War II erupted, the Nazi attitude toward European Jewry was well known. As more and more countries fell to Germany, more and more centers of Jewish population, religion, and history were scoured from the face of the continent. The people were gathered, regimented, catalogued, and forced into segregated communities—but the worst was yet to come.

Through it all, Goebbels kept up his furious propaganda barrage. In one speech he enumerated the "case" against the Jews with typical disregard for the truth by enumerating his lies in almost a checklist fashion:

> One: The Jews are our destruction. They provoked and brought about this war. What they mean is to destroy the German state and the nation. This plan must be frustrated.
>
> Two: There is no difference between Jew and Jew. Every Jew is a sworn enemy of the German people. This plan has to be frustrated.
>
> Three: Every German soldier's death in this war is the Jew's responsibility. They have it on their conscience, hence they must pay for it.
>
> Four: The Jews are to blame for this war. The treatment we give them does them no wrong. They have more than deserved it.

By 1943, the ghettoes were being emptied, the Jews transported to the death camps whose names have been seared into history's list of dishonor—Auschwitz, Treblinka, Bergen-Belsen, Dachau, and the list goes on. The great evil was under way across all of Europe, and Goebbels continued to justify it, relentlessly pounding home his repetitious message.

Ironically enough, considering that his whole party's rationale was based on a monstrous lie, when it came to actually reporting the events of the war, Goebbels allowed an unusual amount of the truth to show through his propaganda. While there was little need for exaggeration and deceit when the war was going well, by the time of the Stalingrad disaster in 1943, when Allied air raids were bringing the war home to Germany with increasing ferocity, Goebbels became a rallying figure for his nation.

He would not deny the military debacles, but instead reported on them with comparisons to other great historic times—the campaigns of the Prussian Frederick the Great were a favorite—and with bold exhortations that the people must endure to see their way through to ultimate triumph. With her cities burning down on all sides, Germany was facing troubles clearly dire, and Goebbels urged perseverance, courage, and determination. And he never let his countrymen forget that the Jews were to blame.

Even as the Nazi empire crumbled around him and his nation, Goebbels was the master of morale and motivation. By the spring of 1945, many of the death camps had been discovered by the Allies and the true scope of Nazi villainy was being brought to light. Soviet, American, and British forces had crossed the borders of Germany from all directions, and were closing in on the ruined, battered capital.

On May 1, after Hitler had taken his own life in the bunker underneath Berlin, Joseph Goebbels was named as the Führer's successor. For one day the director of the Ministry of Public Enlightenment and Propaganda ruled the nation of his birth—at least, the few square miles of it remaining under German control.

Finally, as the Russians closed in around Berlin, Goebbels and his wife took their own lives—after killing all six of their children.

It was a fitting end, indeed, for the Master of Lies.

Here is a lie from modern history that will surprise many of you. Sort of also makes you wonder why they got so angry at Clinton, who, when it all comes down to it, simply lied about something that didn't affect the nation. A southern gentleman never told . . .

ARMS FOR HOSTAGES?

Peter Archer

On Thursday, November 6, 1986, Ronald Reagan was fuming. In response to press questions, he said flatly that reports that the United States was selling arms to the Islamic Republic of Iran had "no foundation." In a speech to the nation a week later, he was even more explicit. "We did not—repeat—did not trade weapons or anything else for hostages nor will we."

It sounded great. The United States government was standing firm on its principle of not dealing with terrorists and kidnappers.

The problem was it wasn't true.

The tangled roots of the scandal that became known as Iran-Contra were bound up in various problems confronting the Reagan administration, problems that came together in 1986.

First and foremost was the revolution that had taken place in Nicaragua in 1980, toward the beginning of Reagan's first term. The rebels, calling themselves Sandinistas after the legendary Nicaraguan revolutionary Augusto Sandino, had seized power and overthrown the corrupt and dictatorial regime of Anastasio Somoza. Many of Somoza's followers fled the country, ending up in Florida, where they found common cause with the right-wing anti-Castro Cubans who filled Miami. Though the Sandinista revolution began as a nationalist uprising, its leaders, especially Daniel Ortega, came increasingly to rely on Castro's Cuba for support, and their rhetoric took on Marxist overtones.

The Reagan administration watched these developments with alarm. It worried that a Marxist Nicaragua, linked to a Marxist Cuba, would give aid to the forces in El Salvador, and elsewhere in Latin America, that sought to destroy American power and influence on the continent. Though many of the existing regimes in the region were thoroughly unsavory, often linked to drug dealing and organized murder, the administration believed that their anticommunism made them natural allies of the United States.

The Nicaraguan exiles, circulating through Miami and elsewhere, soon filtered back into parts of Nicaragua, where they launched a series of terrorist attacks aimed at overthrowing the Sandinista government and restoring right-wing rule. They called themselves the Contras and were backed by big landowners in El Salvador and elsewhere. They also received backing from the CIA, organized by the Reagan administration.

Congress viewed the situation with concern. Memories of the Vietnam debacle were fresh in the minds of many. The last thing they wanted was a long, drawn-out struggle amid the complexities of Latin American politics. In 1983, Congress passed a bill sponsored by Representative Edward Boland of Massachusetts. It stated in part that the United States was barred from organizing covert actions "for the purpose of overthrowing the government of Nicaragua." The Boland Amendment, as it came to be known, seemed to definitively end U.S. support for the Contras.

Those in the administration who had been most active in organizing the flow of arms and money to the Contras—particularly William Casey, head of the CIA—weren't about to let a little thing like a law stop them. They continued their activities, but now took care to hide them from any possibility of congressional scrutiny.

In April 1984, Congress was shocked to hear that CIA agents, working with the Contras, had mined the harbors of Nicaragua. Barry Goldwater, the 1964 GOP candidate for president and a crusty, outspoken leader of the Senate, sent a furious letter to Casey. "Bill," he declared, "this is no way to run a railroad and I find myself in a hell of a quandary . . . This is an act violating international law. It is an act of war. For the life of me, I don't see how we are going to explain it."

Reagan and Casey apologized and promised that in the future they would keep Congress fully apprised of any covert activity the president approved. Once again, the president seemed to have no options in his wish to aid the anticommunist forces in Nicaragua.

For a solution, Reagan turned to a group of men in his administration who had been passionate supporters of the Contras. These included National Security Advisor Robert McFarlane, his deputy, Adm. John Poindexter, and McFarlane's aide, Col. Oliver North. It was North who had been most active in working with the Contra leadership, negotiating the tricky waters between the different factions, and soliciting support from the unsavory collection of oddballs, crackpots, would-be mercenaries, and others who floated through the right-wing communities of southern Florida.

Since Congress had prohibited the United States from supplying the Contras, McFarlane's first suggestion was that the administration turn to some of its international allies to fulfill that role. Israel agreed to help. McFarlane also lined up support from the government of Saudi Arabia. In secret, North established a Swiss bank account into which the Saudis could deposit money for the Contras.

This was all carefully kept secret from Congress, violating Casey and Reagan's pledge and skating on thin ice as far as the Boland Amendment went.

North gathered others around him to run the expanding operation. Casey began relying more and more on the young colonel to carry out his wishes. And North began establishing what amounted to a shadow government with its own foreign policy in the basement of the White House.

When word of North's activities began to leak out in 1985, Reagan said "We're not violating any laws." He denounced Nicaragua, linking it to the government of Iran, calling them "the new international version of Murder, Incorporated."

This was an odd linkage to make—the Marxist, left-leaning government of Nicaragua with the Islamic fundamentalist regime in Tehran—all the odder because, unbeknownst to the public and Congress, the administration, through McFarlane, Poindexter, and North, had begun to orchestrate a series of arms sales to Iran as part of the whole operation.

The Iranian revolution of 1979 had removed one of the United States' most loyal allies, Shah Reza Palhavi, and replaced him with a government that was openly hostile. Though the hostages seized at the U.S. embassy in Tehran in 1979 had finally been freed at the very beginning of the Reagan administration in 1980, the Iranian government continued to launch volleys of revolutionary religious rhetoric at Washington. Other Americans had been kidnapped and were being held hostage by various fundamentalist groups in the country—with the implicit support and knowledge of the Iranian government.

Reagan knew the damage a prolonged hostage crisis could do to an American government. He had, after all, seen the original hostage crisis destroy the Carter administration. So he was particularly receptive to an idea of North's. The energetic colonel, looking for more ways to raise money for the Contras, suggested that the United States secretly sell arms to Iran. They would use the prospect of these sales as a way to put pressure on the Iranian government to free the American hostages—in fact, offering arms in exchange for the Americans' freedom. At the same time, the U.S. government would secretly use the funds from these sales to give further aid to the Contras.

Reagan gave his approval. In August 1985, a shipment of U.S. missiles made its way to Iran via Israel, which had volunteered to act as middleman in the transaction. On September 15, the Rev. Benjamin Weir was released by his captors. Two more deliveries of arms were made by the end of the year. In December, Reagan retroactively authorized these shipments and explicitly ordered the CIA not to inform Congress of the transaction.

Under North's control, cash from the shipments flowed through a number of hands, including his own. Some was turned to personal profit by the people involved. Some made its way south to the Contras.

With so many people involved and such a complex, convoluted plot, it was inevitable that sooner or later the plot would become public. The story broke when an American, Eugene Hasenfus, one of the soldiers of fortune employed by the CIA to run money to the Contras, was captured by the Sandinistas in October 1985.

The administration first tried to deny that Hasenfus had any connection to the CIA or the U.S. government. North frantically tried to stop the spread of inquiries about Hasenfus. In a panic, he began shredding documents, including the ledger that contained the names and addresses of those involved in the plot.

When, on November 3, 1986, the government announced that another American hostage, David Jacobsen, had been freed in Beirut, they paid little attention to an article in a Lebanese magazine that reported in detail the U.S. arms sales to Iran. But interest in the story grew, and by the next week, Reagan made his televised speech denying that the United States had traded arms for hostages. Later he asserted, "We, as I say, had nothing to do with other countries or their shipment of arms or doing what they're doing."

Now others began to follow North's lead, destroying and shredding any documents that might implicate them in the widening scandal. North told McFarlane at one point that he was going to have a "shredding party."

Finally, in late November, the administration admitted to the final piece in the puzzle. Proceeds from the Iranian arms sales had been diverted to the Nicaraguan Contras.

Both admirers and detractors of Ronald Reagan generally agreed on his management style. The president had little or no interest in the nuts and bolts of government. He preferred to delegate, focusing on problems of communication rather than substance. In the case of Iran-Contra, Reagan took refuge in this loose-and-easy management style. He hadn't known, he insisted, what was going on in his own administration. Running the CIA was Bill Casey's problem. Foreign policy—that was George Schultz's patch. Oliver North. Fine young man. Who would have thought he'd be involved in something like this?

An initial investigation into the scandal was conducted by Senator John Tower. The report, released in February 1987, condemned Reagan for not knowing what his aides were up to but essentially absolved him of blame for the events. On March 4, in yet another televised address to the nation, Reagan defended his policies, while admitting that their "implementation" had been flawed. He also admitted that, yes, the United States had in fact traded arms for hostages. Of his previous statement denying it, he said, "My heart and my best intentions still tell me that it is true, but the facts and the evidence tell me it is not."

Though a majority of Americans did not believe Reagan when he said he had known nothing of the diversion of funds to the Contras, no solid evidence was produced linking him to the transaction. Poindexter, who might have implicated him in his testimony before Congress, refused to do so. Casey died of a stroke without giving any of the details of the complicated plot.

Oliver North took a more aggressive approach than Poindexter. When he was called before Congress to testify, he lectured the members. Dressed in his Marine Corps uniform, he told the Congressmen that he thought using the money from the arms sales to fund the Contras was a "neat" idea, and he took full credit for it. Congressmen fell over themselves to praise his patriotism and dedication.

The scandal faded, largely because the Democrats collaborated with the Republicans in hushing it up. Leaders of the congressional committee investigating the affair condemned Poindexter, McFarlane, and, to a lesser extent, North, but absolved Reagan of any knowledge of the transactions. Democratic senator George Mitchell said that the country should put Iran-Contra behind us. And the Reagan administration was only too happy to do so.

The viewpoint of those involved in the scandal was perhaps best summed up by Fawn Hall, Oliver North's secretary, who had helped him conceal and destroy documents. When called before Congress to explain her actions, she said, "I believe sometimes you have to go above the written law."

BUT IT WAS IN A BOOK . . .

The fallacy that anything you read in a book is the truth goes way back to when the Church controlled literacy and books in Europe. If they said it was true, then it was. Since early books were inscribed by hand, each page took hours of labor. Perhaps because of the effort needed to create a book there really was a time when everything written was as close to the truth as possible. Then Gutenberg introduced the press to Europe and things haven't been the same since. Today every American politician has his book full of insights and caring. Does anyone really believe they write those books themselves? Do you want the men running our nation spending hundreds of hours just writing? The lie starts on the cover, just after the word "by." Books and newspapers are no less filled with lies and other deceits than any other form of communication. The difference is that books have presence. A thick leather bound book looks like it should contain the truth. Sigh.

It is reassuring in a perverse way to know that in the world of lies nothing has really changed.

THIS IS A TRUE STORY . . . NOT

Brian Thomsen

The World of Publishing from 1713 to 2006

While in the process of writing his autobiography, *The Motion of Light in Water*, science fiction writer Samuel Delany made an interesting discovery. A certain significant event in his memory could not possibly have occurred the way he seemed to remember it.

Events were compressed, the time of year was changed, and others thought to be in attendance were actually elsewhere.

Thus even the writer, the primary spectator, is capable of making mistakes in recapping his own life. More simply—sometimes our memory plays tricks and our conclusions are then based on those mistakes.

These are not lies.

Lies are intentional fabrications of untruth or fiction, and they have been ever-present in publishing since its earliest incarnations.

On April 15, 1747, a London periodical called the *General Advertiser* ran the closing statement to the bench of a young woman, Polly Baker, who had been brought up on charges of having sexual intercourse out of wedlock, a charge she had already been convicted of on several prior occasions. Each time, she said, the full blame was placed on her shoulders but not the father's. In her words of defense, she professed that "I have brought five children into the world at the risk of my own life . . . I have maintained them well by my own industry without burdening the township, and would have done it better if it had not been for the heavy fines and charges I have been forced to address."

The background story appeared initially in a pamphlet and then in numerous newspapers in "Polly's own words." A postscript was included that accented the happy ending that her eloquence and honesty yielded her—one of the magistrates fell in love with her, and they were soon married, allowing her the privilege of a legitimate relationship.

. . . but Polly never existed.

Her story was actually penned by Benjamin Franklin (himself the father of a "bastard") as a protest to the unfairness of the early judicial system charging women for having illegitimate children while not charging the fathers, a revelation he confessed in 1777, at which time he also pointed out that he himself had never reprinted the story in the newspapers that he published, preferring others to be guilty of the story's promulgation.

But Franklin was not alone in perpetrating fiction as fact.

Case 1. *Robinson Crusoe* by Daniel Defoe

"I WAS born in the year 1632, in the city of York, of a good family . . ."

Thus begins the story of Robinson Crusoe, who, as the subtitle of the book further explains, "*lived Eight and Twenty Years, all alone in an un-inhabited Island on the coast of America, near the Mouth of the Great River of Oroonoque; Having been cast on Shore by Shipwreck, wherein all the Men perished but himself . . .*"

This book by Daniel Defoe is considered retrospectively to be one of the first novels in English literature, and the classic "man against nature" survival tale.

It is also based on an intentional lie: namely, the reading public assumed it to be a true story, and Defoe did nothing to disabuse them of this notion, because back when the book was originally released, the concept of "fiction" had yet to be acknowledged. True, there were tales of fabulation and myth, romance and legend, but the oeuvre for these matters was either poetry or drama. Even the early Arthurian legend as recounted by Thomas Mallory was considered a historical chronicle.

Books, unless otherwise specified, were considered serious works, and if the title page invoked a chronicle of events as experienced by the narrator, the reader naturally assumed the events related therein to be true.

Robinson Crusoe was published in 1719 and was, for its day, an overnight bestseller. An eager audience snatched up copies as soon as they hit the book stalls, faster even than the word-of-mouth of satisfied readers. Everyone wanted to get their hands on the most exciting story of survival of their age, or, should I say, the most exciting *true* story of their age.

Fourteen years earlier, a real person by the name of Alexander Selkirk, a ne'er-do-well Scot who had gone to sea as a privateer, was marooned on a real island off the coast of Chile. Selkirk was very hard to get along with and one day, during a tantrum, he had ordered his shipmates to put him ashore on a deserted island . . . and they did. (It was rumored that as the longboat pulled away, Selkirk screamed for them to take him back; they did not, and considered themselves well rid of him.) And there he stayed until he was finally rescued by a passing British ship four years later.

Selkirk's story was published in a London magazine in 1713. Defoe read it and became "inspired." If people were willing to buy a magazine for a story about someone like Selkirk, why not a whole book? he thought . . . and given that this was during an era well prior to the imposition of such troublesome categories as fiction and nonfiction, Defoe created his story out of whole cloth, with the marketable hook of the Selkirk inspiration, for those folks who wanted to know the full story. Indeed, Defoe further stoked his audience by circulating rumors that the inspiration for Selkirk's story was actually Crusoe.

This pseudo-nonfiction worked well for Defoe. Another of his more popular titles was the so-called *A Journal of the Plague Year,* whose subtitle reads, *"Being Observations or Memorials of the most Remarkable Occurrences, as well Publick as Private, Which happened in London During the last Great Visitation in 1665. Written by a Citizen who continued all the while in London. Never made publick before"* (never mentioning the fact that Defoe was only five years old in 1665; the book was published under the initials H. F., so as not to call attention to that fact).

It proved to be many years before the reading public learned a very basic truth—sometimes the title page lies.

Case 2. *The Awful Disclosures of Maria Monk* by Maria Monk

The Awful Disclosure of Maria Monk was a scandalous memoir that fed into the anti-Catholic sentiment that pervaded the still young United States of America.

Unlike Crusoe, Maria Monk was an actual person: According to her memoir, having been seduced by a convent school, the former Protestant decided to become a nun. It was after making her vows, however, that she was forcibly introduced to her main responsibilities as a nun—namely, sating the disgusting sexual appetites of Catholic clergy.

First published in 1836, *Awful Disclosures* would sell hundreds of thousands of copies in an America barely fifty years old, eventually becoming the most famous anti-Catholic work ever written in the United States prior to *The DaVinci Code*.

The events depicted were indeed accepted as gospel, and some of Monk's allegations included that babies created by the nuns' fornications with clergy were routinely killed. (Monk claimed she had discovered a gruesome cemetery in the convent's basement where the tiny bodies were buried, along with the unfortunate young nuns who refused to take part in the perversions and, as a result, were murdered.)

Needless to say, this was quite the cause for sensation. One might say that the events depicted were more befitting a gothic thriller by Matthew Gregory Lewis than the true story of convent life—and such a skeptical reader would indeed be right. Lewis's *The Monk* (published in 1796) was one of the most popular gothic thriller-romances of the time and featured entire passages that bore a quite distinctive similarity to those in Miss Monk's memoir, which it predated by forty years.

In reality, it appears that Miss Monk had escaped from a Catholic asylum with the help of her paramour, who was the likely father of her child. In New York, she hooked up with a few Protestant clergymen who saw in her an opportunity to make an anti-Catholic statement—and a few bucks. The ministers concocted their mad and thrilling tale and approached the publishing house of Harper Brothers with Miss Monk's *true* story. (It is noteworthy that Harper set up a dummy corporation to publish the book, unwilling perhaps to have its reputation sullied with a salacious tale not for polite ears.)

Eventually Miss Monk's mother came forward and confessed that her daughter was indeed a little touched in the head and had never been a Catholic and had to be committed to the asylum due to her uncontrollable, irrational, and licentious behavior.

Case 3. *Roots: The Saga of an American Family* by Alex Haley

"Early in the spring of 1750, in the village of Juffure, four days upriver from the coast of The Gambia, West Africa, a man-child was born to Omoro and Binta Kinte. Forcing forth from Binta's strong young body, he was black as she was, and he was bawling."

Thus begins the story of Alex Haley's ancestral family, a tale cobbled together from several years of research by the award-winning interviewer and coauthor of *The Autobiography of Malcolm X*. Called *Roots: The Saga of an American Family*, and published in 1976 to coincide with the American bicentennial celebrations, the book became an instant bestseller, Pulitzer Prize winner, and the basis for two award-winning TV miniseries (which television historian Les Brown wrote "emptied theaters, filled bars, caused social events to be canceled and was the talk of the nation during the eight consecutive nights it played on ABC"). In addition to its commercial success, the book is also credited with instigating among American families a widespread faddish passion for tracing one's genealogy ("one's roots") through town hall records and interviews with grandparents whose oral histories were taken down as part of numerous school assignments. It was also responsible for a newly encouraged interest in the history of the black experience in America.

One man's family story became archetypal of the entire experience of the American people and begat numerous imitations.

. . . but it would appear that Haley was not above doing a little bit of literary imitation himself.

In 1978, Harold Courtlander filed suit against Haley on the grounds of copyright infringement and plagiarism. Courtlander charged that a part of *Roots* (set during a period prior to Haley's actual paper trail of genealogical records) was taken from his own novel *The African* (which was originally published in 1968, predating Haley's work by a decade).

Haley's response was not necessarily what one would call a firm denial of the charge. The author of *Roots* contended that the words came from "something somebody had given me," and settled out of court for $650,000, which called into question exactly how much of Haley's *Roots* was indeed real, and how much was manufactured from fiction, hearsay, and Haley's own creative juices.

Case 4. *The Education of Little Tree* by Forrest Carter

Sometimes certain titles eventually become bestsellers by word of mouth. Such was the case with the book *The Education of Little Tree.* Initially published in 1976, it was the touching memoir of a young Cherokee boy growing up in rural Tennessee who learns the ways of man and nature through the lessons of his elders and the natural world around him. The story attracted an audience both young and old. Eventually more than a million copies of Little Tree's very personal tale of his education were sold over the next decade. The author himself died in 1979, only just then becoming aware of the real success of his book.

But as the book was being prepared for paperback reprint early in its second decade of publication, a historian began to uncover some disturbing facts about the real identity of the author Forrest Carter.

Nobody disputed that he had written the book. His identity as "Forrest Carter," however, was quite another matter.

Forrest Carter turned out to be Asa Carter, a man with marginal, if any, actual connection to the Cherokee people, thus bringing into question the work's validity as a memoir. Moreover, Asa Carter's identity was fairly well documented and his real life was far from the pastoral image he portrayed as belonging to Forrest Carter. Not only was he a member of the Ku Klux Klan, he had also formerly been a speechwriter for noted segregationist politician George Wallace, only eventually to decide to run against him when he had determined that then-Governor Wallace had become too soft on blacks and Communists.

The question of how the bigot Asa Carter became bestselling egalitarian author Forrest Carter has never been answered, since no one raised it until well after the man who claimed to be Little Tree had died.

Case 5. *Sleepers* by Lorenzo Carcaterra

Lorenzo Carcaterra's first book, *A Safe Place*, was a memoir. It received nice notices but never set the world on fire in terms of sales.

His second book, however, another work of nonfiction concerning an incident from his boyhood, did indeed set the world on fire, rocketing to the top of the bestseller lists and inspiring a successful Barry Levinson film that starred both Robert DeNiro and Dustin Hoffman.

The book was called *Sleepers*, and its plot was fairly simple:

After a prank gone wrong results in a near-fatal accident, four working-class Hell's Kitchen youths are sent to a juvenile detention center, where they are physically and sexually abused by four guards. Years later, two of the boys come across the head guard in a restaurant and shoot him in cold blood. The other two boys (one of whom is allegedly Carcaterra, then a journalist, the other an up-and-coming district attorney) enlist the help of a childhood friend, a neighborhood priest, and a retired mobster to get their friends acquitted and to expose the actions of the guards and the abuses at the center.

A terrific story of old friends making good on past wrongs, the injustices of the juvenile system, young love, yadda, yadda, yadda . . .

. . . but is it a true story?

When this question was asked directly of Carcaterra, he replied, "There will be many who question this. First of all, names, dates and places were changed. Second, institutions raised questions which I have refused to answer. The bottom line is—it is a true story and it is my story. Those who chose to believe it have my heart. Those who chose not to believe it—that's for them to decide."

Yet, to accept this as a true story requires directly confronting several problematic points of contention:

- Carcaterra's school records show that between the ages of five and fourteen, he missed only three weeks of school; according to *Sleepers*, he was incarcerated in a juvenile detention center for one year when he was thirteen, so he would not have had any school records for this period.
- No murders as described in the book's closing chapters took place on the dates specified, nor do records exist for any such trial even remotely similar to the one depicted in the book.
- No records exist for any of the other three boys mentioned in the book.
- The New York Archdiocese objected to the validity of the actions of the parish priest as portrayed in the book, saying that he didn't exist and if he had, there would have been records to confirm his actions and that such records don't exist. (*Note:* the priest as portrayed is a positive character and in no way connected to the numerous abuse scandals of recent years.)

Nonetheless, Carcaterra maintains that his story was true, though names may have been changed, dates moved around, maybe even the sequence of events altered to protect certain individuals.

There is a term for such alterations. The term is "fictionalize," to make real events into fiction.

Case 6. *A Million Little Pieces* by James M. Frey

James M. Frey has always maintained, "I've never denied I've altered small details," which is understandable, given the fact that his book, *A Million Little Pieces*, labeled a memoir, is about the rehab of the author, an admitted recovering alcoholic and drug addict who has professed a firm belief in the anonymity of AA . . . but once his book was made an Oprah pick, the world changed, and it became an overnight bestseller and the author an instant celebrity.

Everyone acknowledged that the minute details weren't important—it was the intensity and inspiration of his odyssey to recovery. Who cares if a name was changed from Ann to Beth or a town's name changed to Griggsville from Jonestown or if the author had five drinks that night instead of six? No one cares about the small details. The larger details, however, turn out to be a different story.

According to the Web site the Smoking Gun, in one of the more memorable incidents in the book (an arrest) there are a few discrepancies from the facts as evidenced by the public record:

- No patrolman was struck by a car.
- No urgent call was made for backup.
- No rebuffed request was made to exit the car.
- No one said, "You want me out, then get me out."
- No one made a "fucking Pigs" taunt.
- No swings were made at cops.
- No billy club beatdown occurred.
- No kicking and screaming occurred.
- No mayhem ensued.
- No attempted riot-inciting took place.
- No thirty witnesses existed.
- No .29 blood alcohol test was performed.
- No crack was found.
- No Assault with a Deadly Weapon, Assaulting an Officer of the Law, Felony DUI, Disturbing the Peace, Resisting Arrest, Driving Without Insurance, Attempted Incite-

ment of a Riot, Possession of a Narcotic with Intent to Distribute, or Felony Mayhem charges were made.

Other than those small details, the incident may have happened exactly as described.

Soon it was apparent that Frey had embellished all over the place. Two-hour jail stays became a week, a week became months, etc. Personal agony was always intensified to a factor of five or more, and miscellaneous characters seem to have been invented for metaphoric intent. Even deaths might have been stylistic and thematic additions to the story for the sake of dramatic effect. The fact that Frey had originally proposed the book as fiction, only changing its label to nonfiction when the submission received no nibbles, is also problematic.

Finally, in January 2006, under pressure from the media and in a televised interview with Oprah Winfrey, Frey, in the presence of his editor, the legendary and esteemed Nan Talese, acknowledged that he had either embellished or outright fabricated many elements of the book.

Oprah was mad, and lambasted not just him but his editor (as the present-in-studio surrogate for the corporate publisher) more or less indicating that the publisher, too, shared in the blame for Frey's charade.

. . . and the category for *A Million Little Pieces* was quietly changed from nonfiction to fiction.

AND TO MENTION a few more: *Fragments* (published in 1998), by Benjamin Wilkomirski, a concentration camp memoir, was exposed as the work of an author who was neither Jewish nor a survivor of the camps; *I, Rigoberta Menchú: An Indian Woman in Guatemala*, a 1984 memoir by a Nobel Prize winner, recounts incidents that the author could not have witnessed; *Honor Lost*, a 2004 memoir about growing up in Jordan, was by an author who, in fact, left that country at the age of three; and of course there's *The Protocols of Zion*, the seminal anti-Semitic rant of outrageous lies and conspiracy theories, now available in graphic novel form by noted Jewish writer/artist Will Eisner.

Remember the comments in the introduction to this section about all those books by politicians being written by "ghost writers"? (To be generous, most of these politicians have at least read their own books.) Well, it seems politicians aren't the only ones . . .

THE AUTHOR OF THIS BOOK IS . . .

Brian Thomsen

As we've shown, the line between fact and fiction is sometimes intentionally blurred by the author-provocateur. Some even argue that that line is blurry at best. Who is to say what is fact and what is fiction? Simply sit back, read the book, digest its contents, and you decide.

. . . but sometimes the lie in question is simpler and more straightforward because it is as clear as the author credit on the cover of the book. In fact it *is* the author credit.

Case 1. Thomas Chatterton

ENGLAND, THE EIGHTEENTH CENTURY

Thomas Chatterton was born in England in 1752. A precocious lad, he had a penchant for medieval scholarship even before he had entered his teens. At the age of twelve, he revealed that while rooting around in an attic among some papers, he discovered the unsigned, dual-voice poem "Elinoure and Juga," by a previously undiscovered fifteenth-century poet. A few years later, Chatterton followed up that discovery with the revelation of perhaps his greatest bit of literary archeology: the works of Thomas Rowley, a monk living during the reign of Edward IV, that is, in the fifteenth century (when Master William Canynge, a wealthy local figure, ruled in Bristol's civic chair). Not just exemplary as the works of a significant newly discovered poet, Rowley's poems were considered perfectly representative of a previously undiscovered English dialect, obviously contemporary to Chaucer yet distinctive in its own right, and as a result, were perhaps just the tip of the iceberg in an entirely new canon of English literature.

At sixteen, Chatterton was quickly recognized as the authority on the Rowley materials. One of the longer works, a history of England, was sent off to Hugh Walpole for consideration for publication.

With the work's publication, the lad Chatterton was recognized as a literary prodigy of considerable merit and scholarship, despite his self-taught status. Soon there were numerous outlets for his poetry and satires, as well as ongoing Rowley scholarship, and commentary as to how the Rowley works might bring about a reevaluation of the canon of British literature thus far.

Chatterton's own young genius and his poetic muse became an icon for the soon-to-come "Romantic poets," all the more appropriate since this young genius committed suicide at the age of eighteen by ingesting arsenic. Having fallen from vogue, Chatterton found himself facing mounting debt as those who had previously praised his scholarship grew tired of his notoriety, launching unkind assaults on his literary status, while envious detractors dismissed him as a mere copyist and transcriber of the poems of Rowley. Chatterton's personal success was dismissed as the result of nothing more than a lucky discovery rather than of any real scholarship or genius. He was buried in a cemetery reserved for paupers attached to Shoe Lane Workhouse, in the parish of St. Andrew's, Holborn.

Scholarly discourse on the Rowley poems continued for many years after the lad's death . . . even after it was revealed that the works themselves were authored by Chatterton himself. Indeed, all of his "discoveries" were found to be the product of his own fertile imagination and his amazing proficiency at imitating period dialect, stylization, and syntax.

Indeed, Chatterton was not a scholar, but he was also far more than a copyist. He was a gifted poet writing in the manner of the past. There was no Thomas Rowley. Chatterton had been the author . . . and a gifted liar to boot.

OTHER WRITERS OF NOTE have also used pseudonyms to present a sense of creative authenticity to their works. Washington Irving used the monikers Geoffrey Crayon and Diedrich Knickerbocker in his fictional histories of old New York/New Amsterdam, while Charles Dickens used the moniker "Boz" for several of his literary sketches that appeared in the newspapers, as well as for the first publication of the ongoing serial that became *The Pickwick Papers*. These pseudonyms, however, were never intended as hoaxes or secrets, and were revealed to the public soon after publication.

Indeed many "working writers" fell into pseudonymous attribution to facilitate publication in a wide variety of fields. With the advent of the twentieth-century pulp era, many writers avoided becoming genre-pigeon-holed by using different names for different genres. (For example, Frederick Faust, author of the *Doctor Kildare* series, wrote Westerns under the more famous moniker of Max Brand, while Evan Hunter was identified as a serious novelist and screenwriter, while his alter ego, Ed McBain, turned out "cop novels.")

Such pen-name monikers may hide the truth (the author's real name) but they fall far short of engineering a hoax or a purposeful lie.

This, however, was not the case with several authors in the last fifty or so years.

Case 2. *Naked Came the Stranger* by Penelope Ashe

LONG ISLAND, NEW YORK, 1969

The late sixties saw the coming of the sexual revolution in the United States and the widespread promulgation of dirty books, such as John Cleland's *Fanny Hill* (a naughty vestige from the era of the picaresque) and Terry Southern's *Candy*, in the mass-market newsstand racks, as well as numerous cheap imitations in the genres of historical romance, street fiction, and mysteries. (Mickey Spillane and Richard Prather often came right up to the line of "decency" with their hardboiled yet provocative Mike Hammer and Shell Scott series, respectively.)

(Indeed within the next few years one of the longest-running bestselling hardcovers was a nonfiction title by the name of *Everything You Always Wanted to Know About Sex but Were Afraid to Ask*.)

The mass-market book buying audience was ripe for titillation and quite receptive to almost anything that hinted at sex and scandal. Ergo, it was no surprise when *Naked Came the Stranger*, by Penelope Ashe, made the *New York Times* bestseller list.

The book had everything going for it: An attractive female author from suburban Long Island who was soon the magnet for media attention. A provocative title. An evermore-provocative cover featuring a photographic rear view of an unclad young woman on her knees . . . and a plot that bordered on salacious.

A simple tale, actually: "an attractive suburban housewife named Gillian Blake becomes angry at her unfaithful husband, and plans to have sex with every married man in her Long Island neighborhood in the name of both revenge and sexual fulfillment."

Many readers thought that the fictional character Gillian Blake probably had a lot in common with the author Penelope Ashe—perhaps the book was based on her own experiences.

As it turned out, they were partially right, at least in one sense. Gillian Blake and Penelope Ashe did have something major in common: they were both fictional. Penelope Ashe didn't really exist.

The book was actually written by a columnist from *Newsday* (a Long Island newspaper) by the name of Mike McGrady and several of his associates (including John Cummings, Harvey Aaronson, Bill McIlwain, Robert Wiemer, George Vecsey, and Robert Green) in a round-robin fashion that resulted in a "can you top this" sort of sex romp full of saucy talk and rabid romance. (McGrady's sister-in-law passed herself off as "Ashe" for the author photo and in interviews, usually clad in a tight and sexy mini, espousing free-love and sexual-liberation catchphrases in order to play the role convincingly.)

Ostensibly this team of amateur pornographers had set out to demonstrate exactly how low the standards of the American reading public had fallen. Ergo the book's hodgepodge construction and semi-literate prose, which were necessary to preclude any defense of the materials on the basis of literary merit.

The fact that the book was accepted for publication more than proved their point. The fact that they all made a great deal of money on its sales (even after the hoax was revealed) was an added bonus.

Indeed one of the "silent collaborators" went on to further successful collaborations. George Vecsey co-authored, with country superstars Loretta Lynn and Barbara Mandrell, their bestselling autobiographies, *Coal Miner's Daughter* and *Get to the Heart*, though in both cases under his own name.

Case 3. *The Autobiography of Howard Hughes* by Howard Hughes (with Clifford Irving)

New York City, 1971

In the 1970s there was probably no more enigmatic a figure than billionaire recluse Howard Hughes, so when author Clifford Irving informed his publisher that Hughes had approached him about collaborating on his memoir, the New York house immediately declared their interest in the project. The McGraw-Hill board invited Irving to New York, where he showed them three forged letters, one of which stated that Hughes wished to have his biography written but that he wanted the project to remain secret for the time being. The autobiography would be based on interviews Hughes was willing to do with Irving.

McGraw-Hill was eager to preempt the deal and keep it from going to auction (thus putting them in competition with other houses) and agreed to the confidential terms that Irving presented to them on Hughes's behalf. It was understood that the contract and all payments were to be handled through Irving. McGraw-Hill offered Irving an advance of $100,000, with an additional $400,000 that would go to Hughes. Irving managed to negotiate that figure up to $765,000, with $100,000 allocated to him and the rest to Hughes.

In the autumn of 1971, Irving delivered the manuscript to McGraw-Hill. He also included notes in Hughes's handwriting that an expert graphologist declared genuine. After this, the work was vetted by Howard Hughes experts, who were convinced of its authenticity. McGraw-Hill announced their intention to publish the book that December.

Plans were immediately put in motion for the book's blockbuster-level release, with a well-promoted first-serial sale to *LIFE* magazine prior to publication . . . that is, until the reclusive Hughes partially emerged from his self-imposed exile to declare that the so-called autobiography was a fake, and through his lawyers indicated that he intended to sue all parties involved should they go through with the book's publication.

Within months of Hughes's announcement, Irving and his co-conspirator, a fellow writer by the name of Richard Suskind, confessed to their hoax and were soon indicted, tried, and convicted of fraud. They were both sentenced to prison, where they served terms of seventeen and five months, respectively. They were also forced to repay the entire amount the publisher had paid them.

Irving and Suskind had done extensive research on Hughes and had even wheedled access to unpublished materials (such as the unpublished memoirs of Hughes's right-hand man, Noah Dietrich) while also fabricating secret interviews with the reclusive millionaire in remote locations. The money that was meant, as per the publisher's contract, to flow through to Hughes was instead deposited in a Swiss bank account by Irving's wife.

The authors had banked that Hughes's intense desire for privacy would keep him from going public and exposing their hoax. They were wrong . . . and the book was withdrawn from publication.

Close to thirty years later, it was published on the Internet.

Though not an autobiography, it was nonetheless a better-than-average unauthorized biography of the mysterious billionaire, and might actually have become a bestseller had it been initially published as such.

Case 4. *The Hitler Diaries*

Berlin and London, 1983

It was billed as the find of the century, volume upon volume of the innermost thoughts of the greatest killer and tyrant of the twentieth century.

On April 25, 1983, *Stern*, a German magazine, announced they had "the journalistic scoop of the post–World War II era": all sixty-two volumes of the personal diaries of the Führer himself, Adolf Hitler. The magazine had paid a whopping $3.8 million for the newly discovered journals, which they began to serialize that day, going public with such revelations as Hitler's personal opinions of his own high command and the political situation at hand, as well as more day-to-day notes, such as gentle reminders of matters concerning his dog and Eva Braun.

The diaries had supposedly been found by farmers at a plane crash site toward the end of the war. The farmers who made the discovery did not recognize the significance of the volumes, and eventually the books made their way into the hands of *Stern*'s hard-boiled investigative reporter, Gerd "the Detective" Heidemann, through a Third Reich documents dealer named Konrad Kujau.

The *Times* of London quickly made a deal for English reprint serialization rights, and noted and revered World War II historian Hugh Trevor Roper was soon heralding the diary as the historic find of the century . . . until the entire set of bound volumes was revealed to be a hoax.

Kujau the documents dealer was more accurately Kujau the forger and, in collusion with Heidemann, had plotted a careful plan to extract millions of dollars from the coffers of the media for their forged handiwork of the Führer.

The only problem was that, though Kujau was an excellent forger, he was a lousy historian. As a result the books were riddled with the sort of errors that any high school history student should have been able to pick out on the most casual of reads (which sort of says something about the acuity of the editors at *Stern* and the *Times* of London).

The two men were convicted of fraud and sentenced to three years in prison.

Case 5. *The Heart Is Deceitful Above All Things* by JT LeRoy

San Francisco, California, 2006

In publishing, as in most entertainment media, everyone is always looking for the next hot thing. Who is the upcoming young author with a sensational story that, if handled properly, might vault them to the ranks of a Jack Kerouac or a Brett Easton Ellis of their generation—the perfect synthesis of commercial appeal and quasi-literary respectability?

For many in the New York and West Coast intelligentsia, JT LeRoy was just such a possible candidate for coronation. Despite modest sales to date, LeRoy was loaded with potential, and everyone expected him to break out at any moment.

LeRoy had been embraced by noted filmmaker Gus Van Sant and young literary lion Dave Eggers, as well as celebrities such as Winona Ryder, Courtney Love, Carrie Fisher, and Madonna—and his back story was "too real and gritty" to be ignored. A former drug addict and teen male prostitute, LeRoy had been rescued from the streets of the San Francisco Tenderloin District only to discover his true calling as a writer. Various other writers lent their support to the reclusive young talent of ambiguous sexual orientation in support of this more beneficial and reputable career choice.

LeRoy's work began to receive glowing notices, and offers of work in other milieus soon began to crop up, to be discreetly handled by LeRoy's agent, as the author had become very private, preferring to bare his/her soul on the printed page instead.

The Heart Is Deceitful Above All Things was published in 2001. In early 2006, however, more than LeRoy's heart's deceit was exposed to the public—his/her real identity was revealed, too.

JT LeRoy had never actually existed. His/her whole life story was fabricated by writer Laura Albert and her ex-partner Geoffrey Knoop as a means to get Albert's writing noticed, and indeed the charade worked, complete with JT LeRoy sightings and rumors—

even the opportunity for "LeRoy/Albert" to do a script for HBO's critically acclaimed series *Deadwood.* But eventually the pressure of the facade became too much for the couple, and they split—and JT LeRoy was outed as a fortysomething woman lacking the drug habit, ambiguous sexuality, and prostitute past he/she had claimed.

The fourth estate has prided itself on its constant vigilance in seeking the truth. Through the years, though, it has shot itself in the foot when stories were revealed to be less than truthful. One of the blackest days came in 1981, when the prestigious Pulitzer Prize had to be returned.

THE JANET COOKE PULITZER FIASCO

WASHINGTON, D.C., 1981

Robert Greenberger

Jimmy was only eight years old, but ask him what he wanted to be when he grew up and the answer came back: "drug dealer." Jimmy was also a heroin addict, a third-generation drug user living in the shadow of the nation's capital, in the rundown, poverty-stricken neighborhoods people never talk about.

When Jimmy's sad tale was printed in the September 29, 1980, edition of the *Washington Post*, people were shocked. Shock led to calls for action as politicians and law enforcement officers asked the reporter, Janet Cooke, for details so they could find Jimmy. Cooke refused, claiming her need not only to protect her source but also that her life would be endangered by drug dealers if she revealed her notes. Undaunted, the search for Jimmy proceeded without her, and ultimately proved futile, despite Mayor Marion Barry's actually saying at one point that Jimmy was known to his administration and was receiving treatment.

The *Washington Post*'s assistant managing editor, Bob Woodward, famous for his role in breaking the Watergate conspiracy and an icon of dogged reporting, thought Cooke's story truly important and so nominated it for the Pulitzer Prize. The reporter, recently arrived at the *Post*'s "Weeklies" section, had terrific credentials, starting with her Vassar College degree and then her time at the fabled Sorbonne. She had even won an award at the *Toledo Blade*, so the twenty-six-year old, who also said she spoke four languages, showed a lot of promise.

By then, though, people were wondering about Cooke's story and the fate of Jimmy. Did he even exist? When questioned by *Post* executives, Cooke defended her story. So they went public, standing behind both their story and their reporter.

On April 13, 1981, Cooke was notified that she had won the Pulitzer, with many expecting it to be just the first of numerous accolades due her. As word spread of her award, Cooke's credentials were made public—and that's when both Vassar and the *Toledo Blade* spoke up, indicating that Cooke's claims weren't quite accurate. Benjamin C. Bradlee, managing editor of the *Washington Post*, even questioned Cooke in French to test her supposed fluency. Further investigation proved that much of her résumé had been fraudulent. When questioned again, she admitted the fabrication.

Two days after the Pulitzer was announced, Bradlee admitted the truth and shamefacedly returned the prize to the Pulitzer committee. Cooke offered the *Post* her resignation, which was accepted.

At the time of the incident, Woodward stated:

> I believed it, we published it. Official questions had been raised, but we stood by the story and her. Internal questions had been raised, but none about her other work. The reports were about the story not sounding right, being based on anonymous

> sources, and primarily about purported lies [about] her personal life—[told by men reporters], two she had dated and one who felt in close competition with her. I think that the decision to nominate the story for a Pulitzer is of minimal consequence. I also think that the fact that it won is of little consequence. It is a brilliant story—fake and fraud that it is. It would be absurd for me or any other editor to review the authenticity or accuracy of stories that are nominated for prizes.

Janet Cooke faded from sight almost immediately and, since she couldn't work as a journalist, took a minimum-wage store clerk's job, married a lawyer, moved to Paris, divorced, returned to America, and was a mere afterthought until 1996. By then, Bradlee had retired and written his bestselling memoir. He devoted a chapter to the Cooke affair and called it a dark incident that would haunt him into retirement. To be fair, Bradlee contacted Cooke for a conversation, which Cooke refused. Instead, she told her story to a writer for *GQ*, while working as a sales clerk in Kalamazoo, Michigan.

In the profile by Mike Sager, Cooke explained that her assignment, to locate information on a new type of heroin, had proven difficult. She heard tales of children like Jimmy but couldn't actually find any such children or even information on the new heroin. Feeling the pressure from her editor, Vivian Aplin-Brownlee, and the other executives, Cooke felt she had little choice but to write her story and create Jimmy as an amalgam of the victims she had heard about. She had earlier touched on these themes when, in 1982, she appeared on the *Phil Donahue* show to defend herself.

Cooke tried to rehabilitate her image, starting with the magazine profile and following with appearances on *Nightline* and *Today*. Subsequently, she sold her life story to TriStar Pictures and hoped to use her cut of the $1.5 million option to get her life in order and back to writing. The movie never got made and she never returned to writing. In 2001, though, Tracey Scott mixed Cooke's story—along with *The New Republic*'s disgraced Stephen Glass—to frame his play *The Story*.

In the aftermath of her hoax, attention was deflected from Cooke's story—the growing problem of drug abuse and poverty in Washington, D.C.—which was only exacerbated when Mayor Barry himself was arrested for drug use. Cooke not only failed her assignment but failed the city her newspaper served.

As a result, her 1996 return to the public eye was greeted with a mixed reaction. Many debated the reasons for her actions, starting with the corporate culture at the *Washington Post* and the state of investigative journalism in the years following Watergate. Rosemary Armao, the executive director of Investigative Reporters and Editors, wrote to GQ attacking Sagar's sympathetic article and contending that Cooke has done little "to win back trust."

Some claims sound too good to be true, and invariably they are. Here's the story of one writer who gave the Church of Jesus Christ of Latter-day Saints everything they could possibly imagine.

MARK HOFFMAN'S FORGERIES AND MURDERS

SALT LAKE CITY, 1985

Robert Greenberger

Nothing is sacred to deceivers, and the sacred are fair game for all sorts of deceptions. In the Near East, holy artifacts, even such items as Jesus's brother's casket, have been forged. Many lies have been calumnies against religions and their followers, some of them efforts to extort from the faithful. Knuckle bones of St. Elvis, anyone?

I take Joseph aside & he says it is true I found it 4 years ago with my stone but only just got it because of the enchantment the old spirit come to me 3 times in the same dream & says dig up the gold but when I take it up the next morning the spirit transfigured himself from a white salamander in the bottom of the hole & struck me 3 times & held the treasure & would not let me have it because I lay it down to cover over the hole when the spirit says do not lay it down."

The Joseph referred to is Joseph Smith, founder of the Church of Jesus Christ Latter-day Saints. According to a letter from Martin Harris to W. W. Phelps, dated October 23, 1830, Smith had an encounter with a white salamander that transformed into an angel.

When presented to the Church's president, the letter caused quite the stir. Handwriting specialists examined the letter and agreed that it was authentic, and the church acquired it from the man who said he'd found it.

It was some time before the president and the Church learned that they had purchased a forgery. The letter and subsequent documents purchased by the church were the work of Mark W. Hofmann, a first-class forger with a grudge against the Church.

Born in 1954, Hofmann was raised in the Mormon Church, his family devout followers of the Church's teachings. His grandmother, for example, was the wife of a polygamist despite the Church's having outlawed the practice a century earlier. Given some of the perceived hypocrisy within his family and the Church, Hofmann grew disenchanted. By his teen years, the Eagle Scout claimed to be an atheist but did the required two years of missionary work. During these years, he read up on the church's history and was thus assured in his belief that the Church had not been forthcoming as to its origins. He sensed that the Church would willingly buy works embarrassing to them in order to keep them secret.

In 1979, he married Doralee Olds at the Salt Lake Temple and they had four children, before divorcing in 1988.

Once done being a missionary, Hofmann set upon his first career as an antiques dealer. It was during this time he perfected his art of forgery, changing books and coins to his whim. With time and practice, he got to be terrific, and almost as good at coming up with plausible histories behind each item. Along the way, he schemed to exact a form of revenge against a Church he felt had lied to him and its followers.

In April 1980, Hofmann "discovered" the Anthon Transcript, purportedly an 1828 report from Smith's amanuensis Martin Harris to Columbia University's Charles Anthon. Hofmann explained he had discovered the document secreted inside a 1668 Bible, with signatures from Smith's ancestors. Anthon, a classics scholar, was concerned that the translation differed from what he recalled from the transcript possessed by the sect called the Community of Christ. Hofmann had seen to it that the document matched Anthon's expectations, eliciting his support. Dean Jessee, an expert on Smith, declared the handwriting and signature were real. The Church purchased the document from Hofmann on October 13 for twenty-five thousand dollars' worth of artifacts, which included a five-dollar gold Mormon coin, Deseret banknotes, and a first edition of the Book of Mormon.

Having hoodwinked them once and establishing his bonafides along the way, Hofmann was emboldened to "discover" more such works. Less than a year later, on September 4, 1981, Hofmann turned up with another document. This one was said to have been written by Thomas Bullock along with a blessing from Joseph Smith III, that implied it was he and not Brigham Young who was the legitimate leader of the Church. The letter, dated January 27, 1865, has Bullock attack Young for destroying copies of the blessing. Elder Gordon B. Hinckley, the Church's president, was given the letter and insisted that its contents be kept private, for fear of dividing the Church.

While he continued to "find" letters and sell them to the Church, it was the Church's willingness to buy them that confirmed to Hofmann that the Church was a political creature, seeking to obfuscate the perceived truth to maintain the "official story." He continued to sell documents to the Church and then expanded his circle to other collectors.

Another letter arrived circuitously, from Hofmann to documents collector Brent F. Ashworth and on to the Church. Hofmann and Ashworth announced the letter's discovery on August 23, 1982, with Jessee once more on hand to confirm the authenticity.

A month later, on October 5, Ashworth announced with the Church a letter from Martin Harris to Walter Conrad, Young's brother-in-law. Soon after, Hofmann sold the Church a letter from David Whitmer, one of the witnesses to Smith's discoveries. The Church felt that the collection of documents they had been accumulating further legitimized itself.

Hofmann made a nice living from the believers, but he also traded in other fake works, including efforts from Abraham Lincoln, Emily Dickinson (a poetic forgery sold as late as 1997 for twenty-four thousand dollars), and Mark Twain.

The infamous Salamander Letter was revealed in early 1984 when Steven F. Christensen paid forty thousand dollars to obtain it. Not only did the document purport to tell of the gold plate–protecting salamander that became an angel, it also showed Smith to practice folk magic and that the origins of the Church differed from the accepted version.

Flush with success, but needing more money, Hofmann announced in 1985 that he had uncovered two copies of the long-lost seventeenth-century document Oath of a Freeman. He wanted to put these up for auction, and had submitted them for authentication. While that was happening, Hofmann was in default of an $185,000 loan. Miraculously, he found a series of documents written by William McLellin, a Mormon apostle who left the Church in 1838 and spoke against the new faith. Hofmann found buyers for the letter, but couldn't complete the forgeries in time to make delivery. He needed a stalling tactic.

So he resorted to planting bombs in Salt Lake City, with the first going off on October 15, 1985, killing Steven Christensen. A second bomb went off the same day, killing Kathleen B. Sheets.

A day later, Hofmann almost became his own victim as a bomb, probably intended for Brent Ashworth, went off in his own empty car. During the following police investigation, Hofmann's equipment for forgeries was discovered and the truth came out. He was finally arrested in February 1986 and charged with murder and forgery. Hofmann pled guilty to reduced charges and was given life in prison. While there, he attempted suicide twice but failed both times.

Hofmann's efforts at blemishing the Church worked to a degree as critics wondered at the complete lack of skepticism that had accompanied each amazing discovery. The Church further embarrassed itself when the quorum of Twelve Apostles studied their archives to check every document Hofmann had handled and discovered that the Church in fact owned the actual McLellin documents, and had since 1908.

Ironically, Hofmann's forgeries have now become collectibles themselves.

Writers have been fabricating the facts and passing them off as truth going back to the first stone tablets. With time, though, the repercussions of these untruths have grown in strength. While some have never been forgotten, others, and their lessons, have, including this one.

THE *NEW YORK TIMES*'S KHMER ROUGE STORY

NEW YORK CITY, 1981

Robert Greenberger

Christopher Jones had been to Cambodia in 1980, covering the Khmer Rouge for the Asian edition of *Time* magazine. The twenty-four-year-old had written for the publication in the past, and this was just another assignment. But former prime minister Pol Pot's guerilla battles must have captured his imagination and he desired a chance to return.

Jones pitched such a story to Cambodian officials and received written approval for a return trip. He had just one problem: no ready cash for the travel expenses. So, instead of journeying to East Asia, he spent the summer of 1981 sitting in his parents' villa in Calpe, Spain, writing the story. He shared the villa with Eva Fitzek, a German physiotherapist, who aided and abetted the writer. "I wanted to do the job, but I couldn't. I had to do my best from what I had, and consequently reconstructed it," Jones would later explain.

He pulled together his best research, including notes from his two trips to the region in 1980 and maps, and cherry-picked Khmer names from the notes, turning them into new characters. One example had a woman from the Khmer Rouge's Paris office suddenly become Comrade Kanika, patriot.

When the article was complete, he and Fitzek drove together from the Mediterranean villa to Locarno, Switzerland, in an effort to convince Jones's editor in New York that he had just flown there from Asia.

The *New York Times* loved the report, which was filled with delightful details about the freedom fighters and the first sighting of Pol Pot in two years. They rushed it through the editing and fact-checking process, and on December 20, 1981, the *New York Times Magazine* splashed "In the Land of the Khmer Rouge" over nine pages. Jones was also given a second assignment as a reward.

The article recounted his supposed one-month visit with the guerillas fighting for freedom against the Vietnamese, who had controlled the country for three years. He quoted Premier Khieu Samphan and Foreign Minister Leng Sary, and described firefights with the Vietnamese. It was vivid and dramatic reporting—if only it were true.

On January 13, 1982, Alexander Cockburn at the *Village Voice* wrote about the article, asking some pointed questions. Skeptically, he questioned how Jones could casually have scanned the night with binoculars and just happen to spot the elusive Pol Pot, a man sought by trained soldiers for years. He then noted that one paragraph describing an "old blind man chanting the Ramayana, a part of Cambodia's cultural heritage, as he twanged a primitive guitar" was lifted almost verbatim from the novel *La Voie Royale* (*The Royal Way*), by André Malraux. Written nearly sixty years earlier, Malraux's novel was based on his visits to the region in 1923 and 1924, prompting Cockburn to note, "If he was old when Malraux heard him . . . the singer must be quite marvelously venerable by now."

Not one to miss tweaking a competitor, the *Washington Post* joined the skeptics by pointing out quotes in the *New York Times Magazine* story that were identical to Jones's earlier report for *Time*. On February 18, 1982, they then quoted Cambodian officials who said Jones had not been in the country during 1981. That was more than enough for A. M. Rosenthal, executive editor of the *Times*, who ordered a thorough investigation.

In the meantime, that same week, *Time* magazine covered the story, since, after all, they were also involved. Using experts on Cambodia, they combed Jones's article and found other factual errors. They noted that the capital city of Democratic Kampuchea had been misnamed, and that the Khmer Rouge did not tip their *punji* sticks with poison.

A day later, the paper of record printed a story indicating that they, and their readers, might have been duped. While the *Times* tried to contact Jones, he was nowhere to be found. They also received conflicting statements from the U.S. State Department and Thiounn Prasith, the Cambodian ambassador to the United Nations as to whether Jones had been in the country.

That same day, Jones was found—hiding in the villa. Frustrated at not being able to speak to their writer, the newspaper dispatched a team consisting of the magazine's editor, Edward Klein, Madrid bureau chief James M. Markham, and correspondent Henry Kamm. They approached the villa, and the fifty-two-year-old Fitzek first told them that Jones was not there. When they pressured her for his location, she finally led them inside to where Jones was hiding.

Without money to finance the trip to Cambodia, he told his inquisitors, "It was a gamble—that was it. Unfortunately, the gamble was too big, and wasn't sufficiently researched, or tied down. The gamble was a mistake."

Jones was clearly distraught under scrutiny and, according to witnesses, rambled and had trouble recalling even his own biographical details. They noted that he hadn't fully grasped the severity of his deception, quoting him as saying, "Maybe it's too early to tell. Maybe it's fair to say that I'm still in a state of shock." He even defended lifting the passage from the Malraux novel by saying, "I needed a piece of color."

The writer had gone so far as to submit fraudulent bills from Bangkok's Peninsula Hotel, using blanks he lifted in 1980, as part of his expense report.

The *Times* was embarrassed, with Rosenthal saying,

> We checked his reputation and were informed by a publication for which he had worked in Asia that he was a reliable journalist. After his piece came in, it was put through checking procedures—scrutiny by editors, researchers and telephone conversations with the author on many points.
>
> We do not feel that the fact the writer was a liar and hoaxer removes our responsibility. It is our job to uncover any falsehood or errors.
>
> The major mistake we made is in not following our customary procedures in showing an article in a specialized subject by any writer without outstanding credentials in the field to one of our own specialists.
>
> I regret this whole sad episode and the lapse in our procedures that made it possible.

Jones vanished from the annals of journalism.

Have you lost faith in the New York Times*? Feel the* Wall Street Journal *is a tool of the robber barons? Newspapers have long been accused of making up their news or stretching the truth. In 1835, people were more amused than outraged when a struggling newspaper pulled off a journalistic hoax heard around the world and beyond.*

THE *NEW YORK SUN*'S SIX-PART STORY ON LIFE ON THE MOON

NEW YORK CITY, 1835

Robert Greenberger

The *New York Sun* was one of many newspapers struggling to build circulation in the relatively sleepy days of the 1830s. At four pages for a penny, it was a bargain. But each day, they could count on maybe ten thousand copies being sold. During a particular hot summer, the writer/editor Richard Adams Locke, decided to run a series to build circulation, carefully doling out fascinating revelations throughout the last week of August. The series was about science, but not just any discovery . . . this was the first newspaper to report about life on the moon.

It was also all fiction.

Locke took advantage of the summer doldrums to lampoon a certain Dr. Thomas Dick. Dick had authored several science books that were very popular (numbering among his fans was Ralph Waldo

Emerson), more for Dick's fanciful theories and moral preaching than for the books' truthful content. He had even gone so far as to write one volume about life on the moon, proposing ways of communicating with our celestial neighbors.

Using Dick's work as inspiration, Locke figured to have some fun and possibly increase his paper's circulation. Like his muse, Locke mixed fact with fiction, stirred in some printer's ink, and went to press.

Sir John Herschel was a noted astronomer, son of the famous scientist Sir William Herschel, known for discovering Uranus. Sir William, accompanied by his sister Caroline, studied and catalogued the stars and planetary bodies in Earth's solar system, but was also known for mixing in fanciful interpretation along with stolid science. According to the *Sun*'s report, Herschel had used a super-sophisticated telescope to magnify images of Earth's nearest celestial object some forty-two thousand times. After a period of observation, Herschel first published his findings in the respected *Edinburgh Journal of Science*, before it was supposedly purchased for reprint by the enterprising *Sun* in 1835. While observing the moon from the Cape of Good Hope two years earlier, Herschel wrote that he had catalogued sixteen species of animals (similar to Earth animals but with additional horns or appendages), thirty-eight species of trees, and seventy-six species of plants. After several days came the biggest revelation of all: humanoid-shaped creatures, part-man, part-bat! Had the *Weekly World News* been right all along, over a century later, with their reports of the mysterious Bat Boy?

Covering his bases, Locke noted that the sun's intense light traveled through the telescope and, magnified by its lenses, burned out the device and created a fifteen-foot wide area of destruction.

On August 25, the first day of the series adapted from Herschel's scholarly reports by Herschel's companion and secretary, Dr. Andrew Grant, sales leapt to 15,000 copies. By the final installment, sales had topped 19,360, allowing the paper to boast of having the largest circulation in the world. Few in New York knew of the *Edinburgh Journal of Science* let alone the fact that it ceased publication in 1833, the year Herschel was still "studying" life on the moon.

Locke, the Cambridge-educated reporter of record, was suddenly a celebrity. That is, until the day two professors from Yale University came to the *Sun*'s offices asking to see the *Edinburgh Journal of Science* issues. They had scoured the Yale Library and couldn't find the specific volumes, so they wanted to see the actual science of Herschel for themselves.

The reporter apologized for not being able to accommodate them, but the journals had been sent to a printer. The professors were happy to visit the printer, so Locke went ahead to notify the printer of their need. Instead, he bribed the printer to lie and so began a series of hand-offs. One printer after another indicated that the journal-printing assignment had been subcontracted to one shop after another. On a hot August day, two Yale professors traversed Manhattan's dusty streets in vain. They returned to Yale without having seen the journals for themselves.

Other questions of the reports' veracity came up, including an article in the *Sun* itself. Then the *Journal of Commerce* approached Locke about collecting the series in a pamphlet, and finally Locke thought enough was enough. On September 16 the *Sun* carried two astonishing stories: the first story reported Locke's resignation and the second addressed the veracity of the series by writing, "Certain correspondents have been urging us to come out and confess the whole to be a hoax; but this we can by no means do, until we have the testimony of the English or Scotch papers to corroborate such a declaration."

People from all over were affected by the story and the revelation of its being a work of fiction. It's said that Edgar Allan Poe paused in writing his story "The Unparalleled Adventures of One Hans Pfall" for having been outdone by Locke. A Springfield, Massachusetts, missionary society wanted to find a way for missionaries to find the Bat-Men and convert them. *The Sun*'s readers were quick to forgive, and the high circulation remained in place, keeping the paper afloat. It survived intact until it merged with the *New York Herald* in 1920, then with the *World-Telegram* in 1950, then faded away for good in 1967.

Herschel himself finally heard about his name being associated with life on the moon by year's end. He denied any responsibility for the hoax but retained British civility about the incident, saying, "It is too bad my real discoveries here won't be that exciting." Sometime later, when the story refused to fade away, he was said to have complained, "I have been pestered from all quarters with that ridiculous hoax about the Moon—in English, French, Italian, and German!"

As for who actually wrote the stories credited to Herschel and Dr. Grant, Locke is generally considered to be the sole author. Others, though, suspect he was aided by the French astronomer Jean-Nicolas Nicollet despite Nicollet's being in Mississippi at the time. Some think *Knickerbocker Magazine* editor Lewis Gaylord Clark might have had a hand in the hoax, but no proof of this exists. Locke himself never said who, if anyone, contributed to the fiction, and he remained amazed at how his story caught the peoples' imagination and how long it lasted.

TRUST ME, I CAN CURE YOU

There are some things no one would lie about. These are, uh, well, duh, no? then maybe . . . okay maybe not. But you would think there has to be something so important that no one would lie about it. Nothing is more important than life itself. So how about your health? Actually health rates as one of the most lied about topics we researched. From outright frauds, fatal deceptions, and hidden ailments, the area of medicine has traditionally been one of the lushest fields for lies. Yes, Virginia, there is no Marcus Welby.

Leaders used to not be elected. But they still needed to have everyone accept their authority. Everyone has to believe that the king had to be something more than just a man. Which was often quite a stretch. Here is one way they did it, with a lie that lived for centuries.

THE ROYAL TOUCH THAT HEALED

E. J. Neiburger

Since the early days of civilization, tribal chieftains invoked supernatural powers as a way of impressing the lowly citizens and keeping the common folk in check. Possession of unusual and wondrous powers was part and parcel of being a king, queen, empress, priest, or other royalty. Not only did the king have a military force to impose his will but he also claimed the goodwill and aid of the gods, whose infinite powers made the king more powerful and politically secure.

Of course some of these royal powers worked simply because the king was present or governed wisely. Other powers emanated from the king himself, or from his royal subcontractors (e.g., priests and barons), who many believed could cure the ill. In ancient civilizations, a commonly held theory about the cause of disease involved an angry god/spirit or an imbalance in body elements. Ancients believed they needed supernatural intercession to heal illness by driving off the demon spirit, or medicinally restoring the "natural" balance. Unlike today, most ancient people were psychologically immersed in spirits, angels, and gods, which were mythologized to the degree of explaining every observed event, from birth to death. It was the gods' fighting that created thunder or a spirit weeping that caused the rain or a punishing god who brought a plague to the sinners. Believing that the king or other royalty had some of this supernatural power was not a stretch, and through preaching, mythology, and folktales, this belief was greatly encouraged.

Expectations

In ancient Mesopotamia, Egypt, Greece, China, and other areas, the concept that the royal touch possessed curative powers was accepted and encouraged. The king had it; the people wanted it, and when they received it, it was a blessing of great worth.

The superstitious population believed in the power of the royal touch, and through the placebo effect alone, one third of those receiving this "treatment" benefited. Of course, the emotional effect of the royal touch would, in a way, constitute a form of waking hypnosis, with subconscious suggestions of good health and well-being thus increasing the expected curative effect.

TO BE ONE of the rare individuals approached and touched by a king was awesome in its social implications. Such people became celebrities in their own right, and thus knowingly or subconsciously would spread the word of their "cure" and their increased sense of well-being. Being a "celebrity" helped the sick individual by increasing the community's attention on him. The ill could get many gifts from neighbors, who often visit, bringing food or drink. Imagine what would happen today if your sick neighbor was visited by the queen of England. Who would later come over for a visit and a talk? Wouldn't they bring food, medicine, gifts?

Many cases of the royal touch included some alms or other payment (a touchpiece) that could be used as a talisman or for food and especially protein. In ancient times, most people were in a state of relative poverty and protein deficiency. Using the alms to buy a duck for food gave the patient's protein-dependent immune system an incredible boost. This substantially increased the rate of healing and recovery. In some cases, people paid the "blessed" for the privilege of touching the spot that the king had touched, thus receiving a secondary royal touch benefit. Of course the king had to be discriminating. His touch was not a complete cure-all, and even though most monarchs actually believed in their own powers, they had to be selective in what they attempted to cure. Too many failures would call into question their own mortality and the quality of God's support of them.

A History

For about eight hundred years (circa A.D. 1000 to 1800) European royalty actively practiced the royal touch. One of the most common ills so treated was the neck lesion scrofula, an open, pus-filled, malodorous lymph node eruption caused by tuberculosis. These ugly wounds, termed "the king's evil," would appear and spontaneously heal; an ideal malady for the royal touch. After being touched by a king, these lesions would often heal on their own, thus proving the power the royal hand.

In England, Queen Elizabeth I healed many people with her touch. Charles II healed a hundred sick subjects at a church service in 1633. During his reign, he touched a total of about a hundred thousand people (not counting pretty women). On Easter Sunday in 1686, French king Louis XIV touched sixteen hundred subjects. Of course, few royals knew modern germ theory and thus happily contaminated their hands and the wounds of hundreds of people with infectious TB bacilli. They would touch one person and then spread his germs to the next in line, and to themselves. This practice may have greatly influenced many of the wars of succession as well as the civil rebellions that plagued Europe over the last millennium, where great numbers of royalty died from this terrible and very contagious disease.

The 1800s, with its emphasis on modern science and medicine, saw the reduction of the popularity of the royal touch ceremony. Even though we know better, the touch of kings and queens is still popular and newsworthy; if not for healing, then as a statement that touching a patient is safe. A few years after her coronation, Queen Elizabeth II held the hand of a leper patient in Nigeria. Princess Diana frequently held and touched HIV/AIDS patients. The royal touch is still with us.

In some cases, what a president doesn't say can be significant. Such was the case toward the end of the nineteenth century.

GROVER CLEVELAND'S SECRET DENTAL SURGERY

NEW YORK CITY, 1893

Robert Greenberger

Most people remember Grover Cleveland today as a rotund man who had the distinction of being the only person to serve two nonconsecutive terms as president of the United States. Historians today look back at Cleveland as a fairly undistinguished president, but he was not without colorful incidents. Among them were the circumstances of his secret dental surgery, hidden not only from the public but also from the media and fellow members of the federal government.

A Democrat at a time of Republican power, Cleveland was ushered into office for the second time thanks to an unusual combination of Democratic and Republican supporters, dubbed the Mugwumps. As a result, he won the 1892 election, besting Benjamin Harrison, and returned to the White House. Shortly after the second term began, on Saturday, May 27, 1893, Cleveland noticed something wrong inside his mouth while brushing his teeth. Describing it as a rough patch, he had Dr. R. M. O'Reilly, take a look. Dr. O'Reilly, later surgeon-general of the United States Army, took several looks and, on June 18, found an ulcerated sore inside Cleveland's mouth. Dr. O'Reilly had the White House dentist also take a look, and he confirmed this was beyond a dental issue. Later, Dr. William Keen, Jr., wrote of it as an "ulcer as large as a quarter of a dollar, extending from the molar teeth to within one-third of an inch of the middle line and encroaching slightly on the soft palate, and some diseased bone." Keen had examined the president at the time of his March inauguration and the sore was not there, so it had developed quickly. Samples were taken, and Dr. William H. Welch, a pathologist at nearby Johns Hopkins Medical School, confirmed that it was cancer and spreading. To be cautious, the samples were also shown to the pathologist at the Army Medical Museum, who also labeled it cancerous, without knowing the name of the patient.

Cleveland was presented with the news and asked O'Reilly what he should do. The doctor suggested the president discuss options with Dr. Joseph Bryant, his close friend and personal physician. Bryant had already been summoned from New York by O'Reilly and had been examining the president's mouth over ten days. Bryant said, were it him, he'd have it removed, which was good enough for the president.

When Cleveland returned to office, America was suffering through a horrible economic depression. The last thing he wanted to do was add fuel to the fire and announce he was ill and needed surgery. "We cannot risk any leak that would touch off a panic," he said at the time. "If a rumor gets around that I'm 'dying,' then the country is dead, too." Instead, he determined what was best for the country was to keep the entire thing quiet. Checking the calendar, he and the doctors picked the summer to allow him to recover while Congress was enjoying its recess.

Cleveland announced that he, too, was taking a vacation, and left for New York on July 1. On June 30, as part of the plan, he declared that he was calling Congress into special session on August 7, determined to stop financial danger by the repeal of the silver clause of the Sherman Act. Cleveland needed to be healthy enough to address Congress at that time.

He did not disclose to his vice president, Adlai E. Stevenson, his Cabinet, or senior members of Congress the truth behind the vacation. The sole administrator he told was his secretary of war, Col. Daniel S. Lamont, who suggested that the surgery take place on Commodore E. C. Benedict's yacht. Cleveland boarded the *Oneida*, where the surgery was performed. The surgical team was headed by Dr. Bryant and assisted by Dr. John F. Erdmann, Dr. Keen, Dr. Ferdinand Hasbrouck, and Dr. Edward Gamaliel Janeway (an expert in the newfangled field of anesthesiology).

The start of the surgery was a performance worthy of *Mission: Impossible* as the various doctors boarded the yacht separately, each bringing some of the necessary tools. Janeway had the toughest part, sneaking aboard with tanks of nitrous oxide, which was in its infancy as a surgical tool. Hasbrouck was recruited for the dentistry aspect but felt that the oxide would hold the president for only the beginning of the surgery, so ether would need to be administered later. To Janeway, everything had to be carefully controlled, since, at that time, the mortality rate from being put under anesthesia was 14 percent.

The president was anesthetized using nitrous oxide, and as the yacht cruised up the East River, the doctors worked from inside the mouth to avoid disfiguring his face any more than was absolutely necessary. In the end, they needed to remove his upper left jaw and portions of the hard palate. Dr. Keen wrote why this was necessary, saying, "This extensive operation was decided upon because we found that the antrum—the large hollow cavity in the upper jaw—was partly filled by a gelatinous mass, evidently a sarcoma."

By the end of July 2, Cleveland was able to get up and move around, his body adjusting to the surgery quite readily.

Dr. Bryant examined the president and was not pleased with what he saw, feeling that there was more sarcoma to remove. A second surgery was required and scheduled, once more in secret. On July 17, the medical team and the president met in Greenwich, Connecticut, and once more boarded the *Oneida*. During the surgery Dr. Bryant cleaned out the remaining sarcoma. Then, Dr. Kasson C. Gibson fitted Cleveland with a hard rubber prosthesis to ensure that his speech and the shape of his mouth would be restored.

Speculation about Cleveland's health occurred regardless of the steps taken to protect the secret. On July 7, a press conference was held where it was disclosed that he had had several teeth removed. The *New York Times* wrote, "Dr. Bryant said the President is absolutely free from cancer or malignant growth of any description. No operation has been performed except that a bad tooth was extracted." Still, The *Philadelphia Press* did print the truth on August 29, including details of the procedure—leaked by Dr. Hasbrouck—although the participating doctors downplayed the severity.

Finally, in 1917, long after Cleveland was dead, one of the doctors, Keen, wrote of the surgery in *The Saturday Evening Post*, with the permission of the Cleveland family. The detailed account was subsequently published as a book.

The cancerous lump from the president was preserved and is on display, for those interested, at Philadelphia's Mütter Museum.

Medical breakthroughs have a way of galvanizing people on one side or the other. Few theories were as polarizing as the notion of radionics and its proponent, the greatest quack of the twentieth century.

DR. ALBERT ABRAMS AND THE ERA

SAN FRANCISCO, 1916

Robert Greenberger

The traveling medicine show, with supposed doctors hawking their serums and cures, went the way of the buggy whip as the twentieth century dawned. This did not mean, though, that quacks and frauds had vanished. They just got more sophisticated, as witnessed by the fame and fortune earned by Albert Abrams and his ERA system.

Abrams was born in San Francisco in 1863 and was educated in medicine at the University of Heidelberg. Among his professors was Herman Von Helmholts, one of the foremost scientists in Europe in the latter half of the nineteenth century. Abrams returned to America as professor of pathology at San Francisco's Cooper College from 1893 to 1898. The doctor was elected vice president of the California State Medical Society in 1889 and president of the San Francisco Medico Churgical Society in 1893. He was a respected expert in neurology.

In 1904, Abrams began thinking outside the box, as witnessed by the series of books he wrote, starting with *The Blues: Splanchnic Neurasthenia*, followed in 1909 by *Spinal Therapeutics*, and in 1910, *Spondylotherapy*. He borrowed from the budding chiropractic theories and osteopathy. He subsequently developed the notion of "electricity therapy," based on the idea that electrons could be stimulated to cure diseases. Abrams wrote *New Concepts in Diagnosis and Treatment* in 1916 to discuss this new medical theory.

As he refined his sales patter, Abrams took to calling his work the Electronic Reactions of Abrams (ERA) or Radionics. Recall, electricity was still a novelty in those early years, so the common folk didn't understand what it could or could not do. Basically, Abrams said everything normal vibrates at one rate, and abnormalities vibrate at different rates. He had managed to isolate these vibrational rates, he said, identifying which rate matched which disease. Abrams sounded convincing enough to gain supporters from coast to coast.

Encouraged, he developed several machines that used the ERA principles, and began using them for a fee. The first and best-known machine was his Dynomizer, which he claimed could analyze a single drop of blood—wet or dry—or even a photograph or sample of handwriting, and offer an accurate diagnosis. He later expanded his claims to being able to perform a diagnosis, complete with personality review, over that other newfangled device, the telephone.

By 1918, as the country was gripped by the Great War, Abrams distracted Americans with his next device, the Oscilloclast, which would then treat the diagnosed problems. Once again playing with electronics, he provided a series of charts that would determine what frequency of radio waves would work over the course of repeated treatments. In some ways, this was not dissimilar to Professor J. W. Keely's vibrational efforts to unlock "ether" from matter just decades earlier.

Abrams, or his trained followers, would use the Dynomizer to perform a diagnosis, often coming up with frightening conclusions, such as cancer or syphilis. In fact, Abrams coined the term "bovine syphilis," to make matters sound even more dire. Then, of course, his Oscilloclast would be up to the challenge of defeating the disease. No fool he, Abrams made certain never to guarantee a 100 percent success rate.

As his fame spread, Abrams branched out, teaching others how to use his devices. He opened a clinic and taught courses that fetched two hundred dollars per student—a significant sum in those days. Upon completing the course, the students would lease a machine from Abrams (for two hundred dollars plus five dollars per month) and implored them never to open the devices, for fear of disturbing the delicate mechanisms within.

Within three years, Abrams said there were 3,500 graduates practicing ERA around America. Such claims proved alarming to the medical community, especially since the work had never been independently verified.

That would change in 1923, when a patient at the Mayo Clinic was diagnosed with stomach cancer. The elderly man didn't like the word "inoperable" and went to an ERA man, who used the machine and declared him cured. A month later he died, and the public noticed. This finally spurred into action the American Medical Association, which began a war of words between skeptics and believers. In their publications, *Journal of the American Medical Association* and *Hygeia* (known now as *Today's Health*), they were vocal in their concern. Abrams was gratified to have the likes of Sir Arthur Conan Doyle and Sir James Barr, a past president of the British Medical Association, write in support of his work. And in June of 1923, noted novelist Upton Sinclair wrote "The House of Wonders" (which appeared in *Pearson's Magazine*) in Abrams's defense.

During all this controversy, the *California State Journal of Medicine* asked Abrams to work with them to scientifically evaluate his methods. The good doctor adamantly refused.

It was determined that an impartial third party should be brought in to study ERA and render an educated opinion. The noted *Scientific American*, which had also helped cast a jaundiced eye on Professor Keely's efforts, stepped forward, spending twenty thousand dollars over the course of a year studying the machines. The magazine's editors were spurred into action based on the number of readers who had written asking the magazine to cover this remarkable scientific theory.

Abrams's colleague, known as Doctor X, worked with *Scientific American*, analyzing samples provided by the magazine. They started with six vials of blood with unidentified pathogens that needed analysis. Doctor X went 0 for 6, and then said the problem was that each vial was labeled in red ink, which had caused vibrations that confused the machine. Provided with fresh samples with appropriate labels, Doctor X failed again. These initial results were published, igniting a war in the magazine's letter columns, and research continued.

When Abrams himself was asked to cooperate, he agreed, but then always found a reason not to be available.

"The adventures of Alice in Wonderland are tame in comparison of those of an investigator in the land of ERA," *Scientific American* wrote in April 1924. In their final report, the conclusion read, "This committee finds that the claims advanced on behalf of the electronic reactions of Abrams, and of electronic practice in general, are not substantiated; and it is our belief that they have no basis in fact. In our opinion the so-called electronic treatments are without value."

The AMA decided to do its own research and sent a sample to one of Abrams's followers. While the report came back indicating that the blood showed malaria, diabetes, cancer, and syphilis, the AMA revealed the blood was not even human but that of a Rock rooster. Samples were sent out to other practitioners, showing due diligence on the AMA's part—and sure enough, they were all wrong.

This led to several court cases in which ERA men were charged with fraud. Abrams was called to be a witness in a Jonesboro, Arkansas, case but wisely died of pneumonia in January 1924. Interestingly, he tested his own sample sometime before his death and the results indicated that he would die that year.

Without Abrams around to complain, the AMA finally decided to open one of the Dynomizers and found, to no one's surprise, lights, wires, and buzzers.

In the years following, Abrams's believers kept his work alive and even today Web sites proclaim that he was a genius ahead of his time, as many of his theories about electrons, electricity, and curing people with vibrational therapy all got developed and accepted by medical science.

People with health problems want to be cured. They want it very badly. This makes them vulnerable, and there is a long tradition of exploiting vulnerable people. The first emperor of China died from taking every potion anyone told him would make him immortal. Some potions included arsenic, and the people proffering them were paid in gold. That was three thousand years ago. Nothing has changed.

THE HIGH-VOLTAGE CURE-ALL

E. J. Neiburger

New technology has always attracted the needy and opportunists. The new technology of the later nineteenth century was electricity. This new, mysterious source of energy was billed, just like nuclear energy eighty years later, as a cure-all for the needs of the world. Electricity could light homes and cities, power factories, transport people, cook food, execute criminals, and cure all that ailed you. It was wonderful, and many claimed it was God's gift to mankind.

Life in the late 1800s was much different from how it is today. The majority of people were overworked, poorer, and poorly housed. Lack of nutritious food was a serious problem, and vitamin deficiencies were common and often fatal. In the rural areas of the United States, half of the children born died before the age of five. In cities, death rates were higher due primarily to bad water and sanitation. An average citizen who lived long enough to become an adult could only expect to live to the ripe old age of forty-three.

In that Victorian society, people were uptight, obsessive, and easily influenced. It was the heyday of hypnosis, snake oil, heroin cough drops, and parlor mysticism.

Visiting a doctor was a fifty-fifty adventure in which you had as great a chance of being harmed as being helped by a marginally trained doc. In the polluted, smoke filled cities, you had a one-in-four chance of dying of tuberculosis; that's if food poisoning, typhus, cholera, or the flu didn't get you first. Cancer and heart disease (today's biggest killers) weren't a problem. You rarely lived long enough to die from either. There wasn't a family who was untouched by an early death. With minimal, and questionable, medical care, poor living conditions, and people dying like flies, the terrified populace searched for answers and help. Religion and hygiene (clean the home and save your family from disease) were old, but limited, solutions. Then came electricity!

Electricity was new. It was strange. It was "modern"—and thus became many folks' true salvation. There was a big demand for it. Many grew wealthy meeting the medical needs of the people with quack, worthless electric devices long on show and short on effectiveness.

One electric device that became very popular was the battery-powered electric "Buzz Box." Forms of this device were sold from the middle 1800s until 1950, when the FDA banned their general use. These devices began an evolution in sophistication, starting with a simple tube containing a dry-cell battery with an electrode at one end (+) and a wire with a second electrode at the other (-). The patient would hold or clip the electrodes to himself or have a friend do it. The electricity emanating from the 1.5–3.0-volt machine would be applied to the body part needing treatment. Often the electrodes were rollers, plates, or rods that could be rubbed on, rolled over, inserted into, or passed over the ailing torso. If your back hurt, you would rub you back with the electrode. If you were losing your hair, you would rub the "rake" electrode on your head (assuming that was the place you were losing your hair). If you had a hemorrhoid, you would insert the appropriate electrode into your anus, and deafness would be helped with a rod electrode in the offending ear. At the turn of the century, sexual problems were seldom discussed; sex was repressed but often bubbled up in private. The Buzz Boxes were used to increase sexual desire, fertility, cure frigidity, and strengthen "libido." Guess where they stuck those electrodes!

The Buzz Boxes were so popular that more than a hundred companies manufactured them, and they even retailed through mail-order giants such as Sears and Montgomery Ward. Their appeal was not only the use of a new power. They also were inexpensive (four dollars), could be used by the individual (no expensive third parties such as doctors), were private (remember, it was a Victorian society, where undressing for someone was shunned), and claimed to cure all ills from asthma to zinc deficiency. The sick, superstitious, and fickle populace was easily duped by Buzz Box vendors, who promised everything but had no scientific data to support their claims.

Some people were actually helped by coincidence or the placebo effect. Occasionally, the required cleaning of the body before the Buzz Box's application or accidentally scraping and thus relieving the pressure of an abscess actually helped the patient. Most nonfatal illnesses of the day were transitory and thus, with time, would heal themselves. The makers of the Buzz Box took full advantage of this fact and increased their claims.

Physicians, dentists, and other healers of the day saw the popularity of the device and jumped on the bandwagon. If the patients felt better with their little Buzz Boxes, think of what big, fancy Buzz Boxes would do? The placebo effect would be magnified. You could charge for treatments. The manufactures met this demand with bigger, fancier, more expensive (i.e., fifty dollars) "professional Buzz Boxes."

The Buzz Box Race

Since so many manufacturers were making Buzz Boxes and people were buying them, competition became fierce. Bigger and better, lower-cost and more efficient boxes were turned out by the tens of thousands. The simple battery tube Buzz Box, which did little but apply electricity (which was not of sufficient strength to enter the body) was replaced by a true buzzing device. Low-voltage batteries were connected to two nested wire coils with an electric vibrator. This vibrator turned the electrical current on and off rapidly, causing the magnetic fields in the coils to generate high-voltage electricity (twenty thousand volts) at low amperage. The vibrator made a loud buzz (thus the name "Buzz Box") and could be adjusted with a set screw.

First invented by Nikola Tesla in 1888, these Tesla coils gave the patient a high-voltage boost. (The low amperage kept the patient from electrocuting himself.) The high-voltage electricity tingled, shocked, and otherwise made weird sensations as it was applied to the skin, vagina, or teeth. The patient really knew something was happening and thus inferred that this was strong medicine. As the vibrator noisily vibrated, it gave off an ozone smell and electric arcing. Now that was very strong medicine. Early high-voltage Buzz Boxes were usually made with all sorts of chrome, dials, switches, and knobs so as to suggest "sophistication." To the Victorian mind (and the manufacturer), fancy was better than plain. Ornate Buzz Boxes in fine wooden cabinets of all sizes flooded the market. Some later machines even used household current (110 VAC) as increasingly more homes were electrified.

Finally the market was saturated, and World War I economies ended the days of expensive boxes and fancy gilt findings. The market turned its focus to the "average" American, the poor and rural worker who needed the healing of a less expensive Buzz Box. Cardboard units were produced and sold for a few dollars. Some were for both household use and battery-powered.

Around 1920, demand began to wane. Modern medicine and sanitation were becoming more effective in treating people's ills. Modern germ theory (germs cause disease, so wash your hands, doctor), better medicines, and improved health equipment (e.g., X-ray machines, anesthesia) became the norm and fewer people died. The manufactures needed a new gimmick for their old Buzz Boxes.

The Wonders of Gas Electrodes

The emphasis of Buzz Box treatment now focused on chronic diseases, not the ones modern medicine could successfully treat. Aching backs and feet, hair loss, bad complexion, breast and penis augmentation, spider veins, and so on became the target of new ads. The Buzz Boxes could not possibly treat these conditions, as every doctor and manufacturer knew, but people were desperate, the government weak, and there was money to be made.

By placing a Geissler tube to the electrode of the Tesla coil, you had a real miracle machine. The Geissler tube was a vacuum tube with a little argon or neon gas. When a high voltage was applied, the tube glowed. The usual color was violet, and thus the "Buzz Box" became the "Violet Ray." With the Violet Ray you got not only the high-voltage tingle upon application but also cosmic glowing colors and a very strong ozone smell due to the electrical discharge. At first these were machines were in box form with separate electrodes, but later the popular torpedo-shaped instrument was developed. The Violet Ray was generally a Bakelite (plastic) tube three inches in diameter and eight to ten inches long. At one end was an electric switch and control knob that operated the vibrator; thus high voltage was generated. At the other end was a socket in which you could insert a wide variety of different Geissler tubes.

These tubes (termed electrodes) came in all shapes and sizes, usually costing between four and twenty dollars each. There were anal electrodes, hair (rake-shaped) electrodes, back electrodes, eye electrodes, tongue electrodes, right side of the mouth electrodes, vaginal electrodes, complexion electrodes, and so on. Manufacturers found that the more different the electrode, the more people would buy. The electrodes were also made of glass and would often break, necessitating their replacement.

Now the public could have a relatively cheap medical device that they could use for every type of malady, real or imagined. It glowed, it buzzed, it sparked, it reeked of medicinal ozone, and it tingled. This was *electricity* in its utmost form. "Our prayers are answered, our ills will be cured!"

The "Buzz Boxes" lasted from 1888 to 1950, when they were banned by the FDA as being ineffective. Sears, Montgomery Ward, and other retailers stopped selling them. The days of the Buzz Box were over. But this is not true. There is resurgence in Buzz Box sales. If you look on the Internet under "Violet Ray" you will see numerous ads and electrodes on new units. It seems that the S&M sex crowd has adopted these devices for not-too painful sexual stimulation practices.

I GUESS THIS proves you can't keep a good product down.

In medicine what you don't know can kill you. What you don't tell the patient can be fatal, and has been. Here is the story of one of the cruelest and embarrassing medical deceits in American history.

BAD BLOOD

TUSKEGEE, ALABAMA, 1932–1972

Brian Thomsen

"LIE: 'You're just suffering from *bad blood* and we can treat that if you sign up for the program. We'll give you free medicine, insurance, transport to and from our medical center, and even a hot meal with each visit. We're here to help you.'"

—NURSE EUNICE EVERS (AKA "MISS EVERS")

Such was the bill of goods sold to the men enrolled in the Tuskegee Syphilis Study. The only problem was that they were never told that they had syphilis nor were they ever given the treatment that was eventually available to save their lives.

The Tuskegee Syphilis Study was conducted at a medical facility near Tuskegee, Alabama, where four hundred poor, mostly illiterate and borderline indigent African American sharecroppers were recruited for a short-term study on the treatment history of syphilis. The study was spearheaded by Dr. Taliaferro Clark, whose idea was to observe untreated syphilis in a group of black men for a period of six to eight months and then follow up with a treatment phase. Clark, however, retired during the first year, and even prior to that point the study began to change its parameters.

Though the men had all signed an agreement to be part of the program, none of them was informed of the life-and-death consequences of his decision. What we now refer to as "informed consent" did not then exist, and indeed information about their condition and the risks that existed for their proximate loved ones was purposely withheld from them.

The program was originally devised as an exploratory project of short duration to benefit the overall "public health" by the advancement of the knowledge of syphilis symptoms under controlled observational conditions. The protocol for the study was established and approved, and a test population was chosen. The study recruited four hundred syphilitic black men and two hundred healthy black men as controls.

Unfortunately the foundation that was supposed to fund the treatment phase of the study backed out due to a change in its financial status. The limited data that would be compiled was no longer considered worth the expense in time and funding. Rather than terminating the entire project, however, in order to obtain long-term control data previously unavailable from human subjects, the study was redirected to continue its observations without a treatment phase, even after a cure for the disease (penicillin) was widely adopted in the late 1940s. The study evolved into "the longest nontherapeutic experiment on human beings in medical history" and one of the greatest shames in America's lifetime.

It was not just that these men were not being treated. They were also kept unaware that they could pass their "bad blood" onto their wives and children, even though the simplest prophylactic measures could have cut the risk of contamination drastically.

Moreover, none of the men was told that his disease was fatal. In fact, the entire tenor of the study suggested to the subjects that there really was nothing major to be done and that they would be more than compensated for their time and inconvenience (e.g., free meals, transportation). If the men balked at any of the necessary procedures (such as an exploratory lumbar puncture) that might be added to the regimen to help further flesh out the scientists' data, they were threatened with the withdrawal of those benefits. Even noncurative treatments that might have eased their suffering were withheld so as not to mask any of the symptoms of the disease that was allowed free rein over its hosts' bodies.

Even when several U.S. government medical programs were implemented to form so-called "rapid treatment centers" to check the spread of the disease, or when several nationwide campaigns to eradicate venereal disease came to Macon County, the Tuskegee experimenters prevented their study's subjects from participating. (During World War II, 250 of the subjects registered for the draft as required by law and were consequently diagnosed and scheduled to obtain treatment for syphilis prior to basic training, only to have those orders redirected, resulting in their being exempted from treatment without their knowledge.)

The men in the study trusted their doctors. "These educated men are looking out for our best interests," the subjects thought. They all considered themselves fortunate to have such professional medical attention made available to them, especially compared with many of their fellow sharecropper friends and neighbors, for whom medical care was an unobtainable luxury. They did not realize that those educated men were killing them.

Eventually, though not until 1972 (forty years into a study originally planned to last less than one), a public health official leaked the program's existence to the media via the *Washington Star*, and as a result the full story was made public. On July 25, 1972, the headline on page one of the paper read, "Syphilis Patients Died Untreated." The story by Associated Press reporter Jean Heller stated: "For 40 years, the U.S. Public Health Service has conducted a study in which human guinea pigs, not given proper treatment, have died of syphilis and its side effects . . . The study was conducted to determine from autopsies what the disease does to the human body."

The public outcry was immediate. Comparisons invoked the inhuman studies by such mad, sadistic Nazi scientists as Dr. Josef Mengele, and the still-developing civil rights movement quickly and correctly cast the Tuskegee experiment as a racist issue as well as an extreme breach of medical ethics.

As a result, the research program was soon terminated and the study shut down.

By the time of the study's final abortion in 1972, only seventy-four of the test subjects were still alive. Twenty-six of the men had died directly of syphilis, while one hundred more were dead from what was categorized as syphilis-related complications. Moreover, forty of their wives, who had not signed up to be part of the study, had also been diagnosed with syphilis, and nineteen of their children with congenital syphilis.

In restitution, a nine-million-dollar settlement was divided among the study's participants and free health care was given to the men who were still living and to their infected wives, widows, and children.

No one dared to invoke the early arguments of "the public good" that would be derived from the study, and new parameters for all future human studies were put in place requiring both informed consent and oversight by an impartial body. Any good intentions of the initial study design had obviously been perverted by virtue of the withholding of treatment from these suffering individuals, especially after, in the name of the same "public good," that selfsame treatment was legislated as mandatory for every other syphilis victim.

In the eyes of the study's scientists, the Tuskegee men ceased to be patients, let alone U.S. citizens. They became nothing more than test subjects, no different from the lab rats the doctors had dissected back in medical school.

The only thing these poor individuals had done wrong (exempting contracting syphilis in the first place) was to trust these well-educated doctors to look out for their best interests as they said they would.

The doctors lied.

It used to be that presidents were treated with respect and granted a certain amount of privacy. It wasn't until after Franklin Delano Roosevelt died that the American people were let in on a little secret: he had been wheelchair-bound after contracting polio.

FDR'S LEGS

WASHINGTON, D.C., 1933–1945

Robert Greenberger

Much was expected of the Roosevelts. After all, they came from money, had a large extended family, and one of their own opened the new twentieth century as president of the United States. In fact, Theodore Roosevelt's example proved inspirational to distant cousin Franklin. However, the younger Roosevelt may have seemed a ne'er-do-well, but he aspired to more than the family thought him capable.

By the time Franklin was readying himself for public service, he had already married his other distant cousin Eleanor, and they had had five children. In August 1921, while vacationing at Campobello Island, New Brunswick, Franklin and two of his sons helped clear firebreaks when a forest fire ignited near their camp. To refresh himself, he took a dip in the Bay of Fundy and then, while still wet, sat down to read his mail. Finally, he took to his bed with what he at first thought was a cold. His symptoms—fever, protracted symmetric ascending paralysis of the upper and lower extremities, facial paralysis, bladder and bowel dysfunction, numbness, and dysesthesia—led doctors to assume he was suffering from a blood clot. It took four weeks before a physician examined Franklin and determined that he had paralytic poliomyelitis, and by then his body was too ravaged for a complete recovery.

One reason the polio took so long to diagnose was that, despite its being an epidemic in the northeastern United States at the time, Franklin was thirty-nine and not a likely candidate for the disease. In fact, in 2003, a medical review of the records led a group of doctors to conclude that he was more likely struck by the similar Guillain-Barré syndrome.

The future president was racked with pain each day, could not sleep, and fretted over Eleanor's having to play nursemaid while single-handedly raising their children. Once the diagnosis was handed down, Franklin's mother begged him to drop out of public life, but he wouldn't hear of it. In fact, combating the disease that ravaged his body proved he had an inner well of strength that had finally been tapped. "I know that he had real fear when he was first taken ill, but he learned to surmount it. After that I never heard him say he was afraid of anything," said Eleanor. Franklin himself observed, "Once I spent two years in bed trying to move my big toe. After that job, anything seems easy."

Thus began a painful and arduous process of rehabilitation. Apparently a six-week treatment at Warm Springs, Georgia, did more for him than any other regimen in the preceding three years. The waters there were considered curative, and he invested a sizeable percentage of his personal wealth in building up the facilities, which were eventually renamed the Roosevelt Warm Springs Institute for Rehabilitation. (When he returned in subsequent years, the institute earned the nickname "Little White House.")

Even though Franklin poured some two hundred thousand dollars into buying Warm Springs in 1926, the facility needed more money for operations, and so a new tradition was created. January 30 became cause for celebration with the introduction of Birthday Balls, commemorating FDR's birth and doubling as a fund-raising party for polio research. The Birthday Balls lasted from 1934 through 1945 and were brought back starting in 2003.

With time, Franklin regained strength but was never again able to walk. He used heavy iron braces to stand erect and then developed a swivel-hipped movement to simulate walking, but there was always someone at his side for this. When seated, usually in his wheelchair, blankets covered his legs and the wheels looked more like a rich man's affectation than covering up a medical condition. At most, people saw him use crutches in public, something forgivable considering what he had endured.

The family closed around Franklin so only they and a few close friends knew of his true condition. It was that shroud of secrecy that would be a subplot for the rest of his life. Franklin was determined to return to the public eye despite the wisdom of the day that anyone with a handicap could not perform as well as a healthy individual.

His work ethic and carefully placed comments led fellow politicos and then the general populace to believe that he had dramatically recovered, allowing him the opportunity to seek office. By 1924, Franklin was ready for the public. First he opened a law firm in Manhattan and then attended the Democratic Convention, where he nominated Alfred E. Smith for the office of president. His "happy warrior" speech returned Franklin to the spotlight and put his political career back on track.

For the rest of his life and career, Franklin deceived the public as to his general health and well-being. Holding the lectern with both hands, he seemed forceful and confident, letting audiences focus on his expression and his words.

When Franklin was elected president in 1933, he became the first man unable to walk ever placed in a leadership position around the world. As president, he created the National Foundation for Infantile Paralysis. Franklin encouraged friends and business associates to support his efforts, and the notion of Birthday Balls spread across the country, with proceeds split between the hosting community and Warm Springs. To support the National Foundation, Eddie Cantor, the great radio star, told listeners to send their spare change to the president to help wage this most personal of battles. He described it as "a march of dimes to reach all the way to the White House." The phrase stuck in the public consciousness, and soon the White House was inundated with change. In 1945 alone, the March of Dimes raised $18.9 million while Americans were also supporting war bonds, scrap paper drives, and rationing. Roosevelt's various efforts are credited with one of the chief reasons a vaccine was eventually found for polio, and for steering researchers to the field of molecular biology.

While he refused to let his condition slow down his ability to govern or even campaign, Franklin did insist that trains he traveled on never exceed thirty-five miles per hour, to minimize the vibrations. When Thomas E. Dewey competed against FDR, going for his fourth term, he dared to publicly accuse him of being an invalid, confined to Washington. To prove otherwise, Franklin toured New York City's five boroughs. However, the disease had taken its toll on his overall health, so when he earned his fourth term, he delivered his shortest address, a mere 557 words, allowing him to speak while standing at the microphone.

As president, FDR enjoyed relaxed relations with the press. As a result, no official photographs were ever taken with him obviously in a wheelchair. A handful of candid pictures did survive the era and provided the inspiration for the statue that was unveiled at Washington, D.C.'s FDR Memorial in 2005. Apparently, Franklin never grew comfortable in the wheelchair, detesting the device. He probably would have hated the statue.

Medical deceit is not limited to doctors or patent medicine salesmen. With the highly personal interest each person takes in his own health, many companies have and do use that concern to encourage people to buy their products. This can be good when trans fats disappear from chips or low-calorie meals appear at fast food places. But when the benefit is a lie, and the product can kill you, it has to rate way up there with those from Nazis and bigots on the most-evil-lies list.

SMOKING IS GOOD FOR YOU

E. J. Neiburger

Tobacco use (mostly smoking cigarettes) is the cause of one in six deaths in the United States. The number is higher in the rest of the world, where the rate of cigarette smoking is increasing. The 5 trillion cigarettes produced each year can be directly linked to the 2.5 million deaths worldwide per year due to bronchiogenic cancer. The associated mortality from other tobacco-related diseases, such as emphysema, pneumonia, and asthma, swell the numbers many times over.

Smoking, sniffing, and chewing tobacco is an old, time-honored custom that increased alertness, concentration, and attention, and reduced appetite. Modern developed societies coveted these "benefits" and, due to tobacco manufacturer marketing, added the qualities of sex appeal, sophistication, and longevity. What few people discussed was that the tar and nicotine in tobacco became very addictive so that most smokers could not stop using the product.

Today, though 25 percent of all Americans smoke, few would regard the habit as good, healthy, or clean. Most scientific evidence links smoking to the aforementioned diseases and to a miserably shortened life span. Even the great Philip Morris Corporation, badgered by lawsuits and government regulation, now advertises on TV that "there is no safe cigarette." This wasn't always the case. There was a time when tobacco executives knew the deleterious effects of smoking, even advertised these effects, and then maintained that smoking was good.

Tobacco was first used by natives in the New World and then exported to Europe and Asia a year after Columbus's first voyage. By the 1550s, tobacco was big business and imported in multi-ton lots. Many nations banned the evil weed, but governments learned (and embraced) its value as a tax source due to its popularity with the public. The people used tobacco as a magical medicine and smoked, sniffed, and chewed it with abandon. But there were problems. Even as early as 1775, physicians such as Sir Percival Pott were publishing medical reports linking tars and other smoking products to cancer.

In 1826, nicotine was extracted from tobacco and actually was used as a contact poison. At that time, tobacco consumption was severely limited due to its expense. Those people who could afford the luxury either smoked pipes or chewed or snorted tobacco. In an age when life spans were very short (compared to today) and multiple deadly diseases were rampant and poorly understood, the ill effects of a little tobacco habit, especially when compared with typhus, malaria, dysentery, syphilis, and cholera, were seldom noted. It was rare to meet a person who had managed to live into his sixties, the age at which a smoker's lung cancer would normally kill him.

By the late 1850s, however, cigarette factories had perfected the production of cheap, easy-to-smoke nicotine-delivery systems, which made smoking affordable for the masses. At the same time, the medical journals (e.g., *The Lancet, British Medical Journal*) published a stream of articles on the clear association between tobacco use and cancer and lung disease, but the articles did little to slow the growing fascination with cigarettes. A hundred years later, in 1964, the U.S. Surgeon General published the famous "Smoking Causes Cancer" statement.

Now everyone knew smoking was bad, but 50 percent of America was already addicted. To calm consumer fears, the cigarette companies pursued a campaign of misinformation and false remedies that eventually cost the nation millions of lives and trillions of dollars. A look at old cigarette ads tells the story of these lies and deceptions.

Since the turn of the century, cigarette manufacturers promised sophistication, sex appeal, health, and general coolness through smoking. Cigarettes caused problems that the cigarette companies tried to downplay, like the painful, dry, scratchy throat that told smokers they were not doing something healthy. The cigarette filter was one gimmick used to mislead the public into believing that smoking was safe. Pall Mall cigarettes advertised that their product, with its newly developed filter, "Guard against throat scratch" and "reaches you cooler." If your throat was hot, then a cool smoke (like Kools) was needed, and filters would make it safe and smooth.

In the 1950s there was even an ad on a Pall Mall box that read, "Throat scratch, yes. Pain in the neck, old aggressive malignant growths, no." Of course the "throat scratch" was, in reality, the act of chronically irritated bronchial cells becoming cancerous. Filters did little good except to help rationalize tobacco addicts' and cigarette manufacturer execs' worries that smoking was harmful. Some cigarettes advertised "cooler smoking" (Chesterfields), "extra mild" (Camels), "as mild as May" (Marlboro), and "gentle for modern tastes" (Philip Morris).

Cigarillos advertised that "they cut down chain smoking" referring to the recognition that chain-smoking was not healthy. Julips, a

1940s-vintage brand, stated that their cigarette was so mild and safe that customers could "switch to Juleps and smoke all you want."

Aggressive lobbying and advertising by the Tobacco Institute, which had supported research since 1954, produced "scientific verification" that smoking was, if not entirely safe, sort of okay. This muddied the scientific debate about the severity of smoking dangers. In the 1950s, concern over smoking hazards initiated the move toward "safe" cigarettes. Filtered cigarettes appeared in the 1950s, including those with the famous Micronite filter, which contained asbestos. Menthol cigarettes provided a "cooler" and thus "healthier" smoke. Low-tar brands were next, but they omitted consideration of nicotine and the fact that low-tar cigarettes still contained cancer-promoting tar. In 1941, Camel cigarettes, advertised as "slower burning," boasted "28% less nicotine," and Smokeless cigarettes such as Premier (R. J. Reynolds) and low-side-stream smoke Passport (1985) came and went, while ads about this study or that study scientifically proving that smoking was safe, abounded. In the 1950s Chesterfields advertised on every pack, "A responsible consulting organization reports a study by a competent medical specialist and staff on the effects of smoking Chesterfields . . . subjects were not adversely affected."

The main effect of these ads was to quiet criticism and confuse the public by questioning the opponents of smoking. The reductions in nicotine and tars in cigarettes caused the population actually to smoke more because their ever-increasing nicotine addictions required more and more of the drug, and each cigarette had less nicotine to offer; smoke more and you will get your fix. Added to this problem were mixtures of differently genetically selected tobaccos and processing methods that added saccharine, ammonia, sugar, and other ingredients to alter taste, drug delivery rates, and comfort.

For hundreds of years, most people knew or suspected that long-term tobacco use was bad. Yet its use is still a protected right in our society. The fact that its toxic effects are not generally felt until the person is old and relatively less useful in society (such as the aged in China and elsewhere), makes it a perfect drug and a fabulous moneymaker. The cigarettes you smoke for forty or so years support governments, farmers, retailers, distributors, and on and on. They're good for business. Later, as you finally sicken, the medical and pharmaceutical establishments will make money caring for your last days. And to think, nobody forced you to do it! Smoking is good for you.

There are some lies we want to believe. Like Roosevelt's legs, some lies are to conceal a problem. In this era of tell-all tabloids, with the once-prestigious New York Times *regularly descending into one of them, the type of lie of omission here probably could not work today. But, then, if it did, we wouldn't know it.*

A-OK JFK

The Presidential Campaign Trail, 1960

Brian Thomsen

"I'm forty-three years old, and I'm the healthiest candidate for president of the United States."

—John F. Kennedy

A handsome war hero, John F. Kennedy appeared to be the perfect candidate for the U.S. presidency.

Though a member of the politically prominent Kennedy family and an Ivy League graduate, he nonetheless had served his country in the military during World War II , taking part in active and hazardous duty. As commander of the PT109, he was cited for exceptional bravery for rescuing fellow sailors in the South Pacific. He received the Navy and Marine Corps Medal under the following citation:

> For heroism the rescue of 3 men following the ramming and sinking of his motor torpedo boat while attempting a torpedo

> attack on a Japanese destroyer in the Solomon Islands area on the night of Aug 1–2, 1943. Lt. KENNEDY, Capt. of the boat, directed the rescue of the crew and personally rescued 3 men, one of whom was seriously injured. During the following 6 days, he succeeded in getting his crew ashore, and after swimming many hours attempting to secure aid and food, finally effected the rescue of the men. His courage, endurance and excellent leadership contributed to the saving of several lives and was in keeping with the highest traditions of the United States Naval Service.

His other decorations from the Second World War included the Purple Heart, the Asiatic-Pacific Campaign Medal, and the World War II Victory Medal. It has been noted by his detractors (who have included Douglas MacArthur) that a close reading of the citation could be: "received numerous medals for actions resulting from failing to accomplish a meeting, losing one's ship of command, and as a result causing one's self bodily harm."

This "war hero" (an image the Kennedy camp fostered first through an interview in *The New Yorker* entitled "Survival," and then in an article about the PT109 episode printed in *Reader's Digest* just before Kennedy's first congressional run, offprints of which were included in campaign materials) was elected to Congress in 1946, and then to the Senate in 1952, conveying both the tough-as-nails, hawkish attitude one would expect from a "war hero" and the compassionate and altruistic sensitivity one would expect from a New England liberal.

Kennedy's wife was young and beautiful, and theirs was the picture of a perfect upper-crust marriage. At the youthful age of forty-three, he was on track to be not only the face of the new generation of the Democratic Party, but also the youngest man ever to be elected president of the United States. (*Note:* Theodore Roosevelt was indeed the youngest-serving president of the United States when he succeeded McKinley, but he was actually older than Kennedy when he subsequently ran for office for his next, elected term.)

Young, vibrant, and heroic—the perfect candidate.

Kennedy even won a Pulitzer Prize for his tribute to senatorial integrity *Profiles in Courage*.

When confronted with the possibility that his Catholic faith might be an obstacle to his electability he met the issue head on with the statement: "I am not the Catholic candidate for President. I am the Democratic Party's candidate for President who happens also to be a Catholic. I do not speak for my Church on public matters—and the Church does not speak for me," once again exhibiting the sort of integrity that he had written of about senators in the past.

From a public point of view, there was nothing that should have stood in the way of his becoming president of the United States—that is, until certain of his detractors started whispering concerns about his health.

It was widely known that Kennedy was wounded in the war, and underwent several spinal operations during his congressional tenure, but such was the price for heroism, and it would have seemed unseemly to hold against him injuries suffered in the line of duty.

. . . but these were not the only "health matters" people were whispering about. There was some talk that Kennedy's war wounds might have been more debilitating than the public was told. There were whispers of Addison's disease, and a few of his detractors even spoke about the possibility of treatment for a venereal disease.

As with the Catholic issue, Kennedy confronted these rumors directly, declaring, "I'm forty-three years old, and I'm the healthiest candidate for President of the United States," thus putting the matter to rest.

He was also lying.

Award-winning investigative journalist Seymour Hersh has gone so far as to claim that "He was probably one of the unhealthiest men ever to sit in the Oval Office"—which is obviously a bit hyperbolic given such predecessors as William Henry Harrison, Woodrow Wilson, and Franklin Delano Roosevelt, but nonetheless refutes the candidate's claim to good health.

The insiders happened to be right about the Addison's disease. John F. Kennedy did suffer from it.

It is estimated that Addison's affects about 1 to 2 in 100,000 people. It occurs when the adrenal glands fail to produce enough cortical and/or aldosterone. This kidney area–based syndrome results in symptoms that include weakness, abdominal distress, twitching, emotional instability, and, under crisis circumstances, the possibility of death. Moreover, it can exacerbate other biological disorders, and itself be exacerbated by toxic conditions.

This, however, was not the only medical problem Kennedy was hiding from the public. Indeed, according to Robert Dallek's insightfully researched volume *An Unfinished Life: John F. Kennedy, 1917–1963*, Kennedy suffered from and was treated for numerous related and unrelated maladies and disorders, including chronic diarrhea, osteoporosis, spastic colitis, Crohn's disease, arthritis, prostatitis, and urethritis, as well as chronic pain related to his back injury. There were also numerous, if not necessarily substantiated, reports of recurrent venereal diseases.

Moreover, the prescribed treatments for these many maladies often resulted in equally debilitating side effects. The pain medications alone could have sidelined a lesser man, making him incapable of meeting the demands of any job, let alone that of the president of the United States.

Such matters were not the subject of press investigations the way they are today, and indeed candidate Kennedy was given a pass on medical matters (not to mention on his claims to being "happily and dutifully married"), so America elected a president who looked the picture of health, and only years later discovered that the picture itself had been doctored.

If ever there is a lie that just drips irony, it is the phrase "We are from the governments, and we are here to help you." It should be true. Government is supposed to serve the people, not deceive them for its own purposes. These are a few cautionary tales of what happens when those who define the truth are those telling the lie.

KILLING BY BUREAUCRACY

E. J. Neiburger

Most mass deaths of people, other than from disease and natural disasters, have been caused by political leaders who have established bureaucracies to deal with human problems. People such as Attila the Hun, Stalin, Hitler, Mao, Saddam Hussein, and many others laid down the ground rules, and the bureaucracies they created did the killings. The most egregious were the deliberate attempts to destroy people, as in the Nazi death camps or Stalinist gulags. But thousands have died, often just as horribly, from inadvertent, unintentional consequences of devised bureaucracies and systems that have knowingly been created and allowed to continue operating for a variety of assumed, "beneficial" reasons. Take, for example, the Food and Drug Administration of the U.S. government.

The FDA

The U.S. Food and Drug Administration, known by the acronym FDA, is a scientific, regulatory, and public health agency responsible for "protecting" the health and safety of the American public. It oversees the manufacture, safety, testing, effectiveness, and "healthfulness" of a wide variety of commonly consumed products. Most food (except meat and poultry), drugs, medical devices, biological agents, cosmetics, and health items are monitored by or covered by FDA regulations. These include the development, manufacture, testing, use, storage, shipping, and labeling of the products.

Begun in 1906 by the Federal Food and Drugs Act, the agency looked for fraud, adulterants, mislabeling, and outright poisoning by regulated products. This was quite beneficial in the early twentieth century, when there were no controls and no penalties for the defective or harmful products that filled store shelves. In those days, poisonous chromium was added to foods to color them an appetizing green, cocaine and opium were freely available in patent medicines, and unsanitary food processing sickened millions throughout the nation.

As time went on and the agency grew, increasingly more items and classifications were added to the FDA's regulatory list, which, in bureaucratic fashion, grew exponentially as armies of lawyers and politicians had their way. From a few people in 1906, the agency has grown in recent times to more than ten thousand employees, with many more contract personnel and advisers. The agency's budget has also grown, from a few thousand dollars to more than two billion dollars annually.

Within a decade the FDA began to develop a regulatory culture that encouraged painfully slow approval of new technologies and products under the bureaucratic, reflexive belief that risks generally outweighed benefits and it was better to deny than to approve. The bureaucracy was rewarded for its caution and the slowness in product approvals and severely penalized if something went wrong. The result was the snail-slow speed of new drug and device approvals, made infinitely more expensive by the regulatory morass and delay placed in the way of developers and manufacturers. Quoting its "successes" for having been cautious, such as in the thalidomide and DES drug disasters, the FDA developed a culture of caution that increased the price of drug and device manufacture, restricted the U.S. availability of safe, life-saving drugs commonly used in other countries, and garnered the support of generations of bureaucrats and politicians who could not or would not consider the actual costs (in life and money) of delaying approval of important medicines.

This system of bureaucratic over-caution exploded in the FDA's overreaction by stopping production of or banning products such as saccharin, silicone breast implants, ephedra, flu and tetanus vaccines, baby formula, and myriad badly needed cancer drugs that were essentially safe but that ran afoul of some minor and often inconsequential regulation (i.e., absolute proof of efficacy). To add insult to injury, the FDA began to exact huge payments from manufacturers for pre-market approvals and device user fees (e.g., two hundred thousand dollars per application), which drove the small, innovative manufacturer out of the drug business, leaving only the large manufacturers able to produce new products. This boosted the cost of drugs to the public, often pricing life-saving drugs out of citizens' budgets and thus impoverishing and shortening many lives. When frustrated poor and elderly patients turned to sources outside the United States, the FDA attempted to halt importation of less expensive drugs from Mexico and Canada by U.S. citizens.

FDA regulations require good scientific investigation and evaluation as the basis for approval of drugs and devices, but politics often get in the way of science. The banning of non-sugar sweeteners such as cyclamates, saccharin (reversed by congressional act), silicone breast implants, and, recently, the morning-after pill, are some of the scandals in which the FDA administrators ignored both science and their advisory groups to follow political agendas instead. This created increased hardship and the unavailability of new, badly needed drugs and other products. Knowing that many products used in other countries were safe and effective but were stalled in the glacial FDA approval process, the bureaucrats focused on power trips and lockstep compliance to their regulations, leaving thousands of Americans to sicken or die.

The t-PA Story

In 1981, Tissue Plasminogen Activator (t-PA) production was first discovered by the cutting-edge drug manufacturer Genentech. This was a naturally occurring compound that, in suitable quantities, could dissolve blood clots in heart attack victims. By "clot busting," this drug, if given quickly in a single dose after a heart attack, could prevent the eventual heart damage and death that claimed the lives of 768,000 Americans per year. Being genetically engineered, the compound was safer and more effective that the other clot-buster drug, Streptokinase, then in use. Though t-PA was produced in 1981, FDA regulations prevented its marketing or use in the United States until early 1988. Other countries were less obstructive and quickly approved t-PA's use for their citizens, while in the United States, the drug languished in the FDA's bureaucratic ether for seven years. The FDA knew about the successes of t-PA in Canada, Japan, and Europe but disregarded its benefits until the drug crept through the regulatory process.

During that time, Streptokinase, having been previously approved, remained in use by emergency room physicians but it did not save as many lives as t-PA could have.

The Numbers Killed

In a number of epidemiological studies of heart attack victims, Streptokinase was found to reduce heart attack mortality (deaths) to 7.3 percent. In other words, of every 1000 heart attack victims arriving at the hospital and receiving Streptokinase clot busters, 73 would die (927 would survive). If the patients had been given t-PA instead of Streptokinase, the heart attack mortality rate would have been 6.3 percent; 63 would have died, 937 would have lived. This 1 percent (10 individuals) difference seems statistically insignificant until considered in the context of the FDA's (1987) estimate of 768,000 annual U.S. deaths from heart attacks . . . pre-t-PA availability.

If t-PA had been approved and used by ER physicians in 1981, 7,680 more people (1 percent of the total) would have survived than with Streptokinase alone that year. If you multiply this annual number of deaths by the seven years the FDA delayed the drug's approval and distribution, you may note a total of 53,760 Americans who would have been saved by the drug had it been available. These people did not have to die. They could have been saved by early FDA approval of t-PA.

The FDA knew this and yet continued the slow pace of t-PA's approval for seven years. The FDA culture required agency managers to comply with the impractical regulations, not save lives. In a press release issued on November 13, 1987, the FDA finally announced the approval of t-PA and the fact that the drug could significantly curtail the nation's 768,000 annual heart attack deaths.

When questioned about this mass killing of Americans, an FDA apologist stated, "They [the heart attack victims] would have eventually died anyways." That is true. But remember, *everyone* eventually dies anyway. What matters is how much time you live, and why the FDA isn't following its mandate to improve the health and life of U.S. citizens. It's the bureaucracy. They have become mass killers.

This story is about just one drug. There are many other such stories. Maybe one day you'll need a drug or medical device that could improve or save your life or the life of a loved one. Hopefully the

FDA will have approved its use. Otherwise they will indirectly kill you or your loved one. Over the years, politicians have claimed to be working to "speed up" the FDA approval process. Not much has happened.

STAY HEALTHY.

WHAT LIES AHEAD?

"He who permits himself to tell a lie once, finds it much easier to do it a second time, and third time, till at length it becomes habitual; he tells lies without attending to them and truths without the world's believing him. This falsehood of the tongue leads to that of the heart, and in time depraves all its good dispositions."

—Thomas Jefferson, August 1785

Following is a selection of other fun lies. And several that can only be described as tragic. The real theme is probably that nothing has changed and we have to wonder why. On another level, this entire volume is definitive proof that people have been lying about very important things for a very long time. Before that time we hadn't developed language yet. Yet we are here, and civilization marches on despite them all. So maybe there is hope for the future despite the New York Times.

This lie involves money, religion, and politics. Well, being the Knights Templar, they did leave out lying about sex, but it seems to cover about all of the other bases.

"WE ARE HERE TO SAVE THE HOLY LAND, MAKING A PROFIT IS JUST INCIDENTAL!"

MEDITERRANEAN SEA, MIDDLE AGES

Paul A. Thomsen

Best known for the accusations of heresy levied against them in 1312, and the later fanciful tales that portrayed them as guardians of the Holy Grail, the Poor-Fellow Knights of Christ and the Temple of Solomon (also remembered as the Knights Templar), were really just papal policemen who wouldn't temper their zeal or their business savvy.

When Pope Urban II declared a crusade to reclaim the Holy Land (the eastern portion of the modern Middle East) from the region's Muslim rulers in 1096, like most of history's leaders, he likely gave little consideration to the logistics involved in taking or holding that piece of real estate. At the time, such a consideration wasn't immediately necessary. While the first few military forays into the region were disorganized and made few initial gains (for example, the 1096–1097 slaughtering of Peter the Hermit's peasant army at the hands of a veteran Turk fighting force outside the city of Constantinople), the knights of the First Crusade met with little resistance upon entering the area the Christians collectively referred to as Outremer. (French for "overseas," Outremer encompassed portions of the modern nation-states of Israel, Palestine, Syria, Jordan, and Lebanon.) Religious rivalries and uncoordinated attacks among the Muslim defenders assured the Crusaders a quick victory, and in 1099 the combined Christian might of Europe liberated the city of Jerusalem.

In their taking of the city, however, the Crusaders had sown the seeds of future conflicts. Upon entering Jerusalem's walls, the Christian force looted the city, desecrated their adversaries' sacred places, and slaughtered a multitude of the city's largely Jewish and Muslim population. As one can imagine, the region's surviving Jewish and Muslim populace did not react positively to this news. As many of the crusading armies returned to Europe with cleansed souls and pride in having completed their appointed holy mission, the region's newly installed leaders faced a new dilemma: security. With the departure of the Muslim powers, long-dormant radical and criminal elements were rising to challenge the new authority and appropriate the valuables of Christian pilgrims rushing into the new and unprotected Christian kingdoms.

For a brief period, it seemed as if Outremer would fall faster than it was taken, but then, in 1119, a new order of knights arose to subdue the troublemakers, the Knights Templar. Comprised of a handful of French nobles and veteran Crusaders, these individuals, sworn to protect the Holy Land and beholden only to the Pope, rapidly assessed the military needs of the situation, and used the influence of their old military and regal contacts for support to stabilize the region. The response to the group of avowed self-impoverished knights was overwhelming. In fewer than fifty years, their frugal use of donations and recruited men suppressed dissent in Outremer, severely curtailed the actions of highwaymen throughout the region, and improved the influx of pilgrims into the Middle East through their growing fleet of transport ships. In fact, while other orders in the region were undergoing a peacetime retrenchment, the Knights Templar saw an unprecedented growth in new recruits, fiscal assets, political power, and prestige.

This newfound boom only multiplied with the advent of the Second and Third Crusades. As history often shows, wars have always been costly endeavors, and holy wars have been little different. It was one thing to secure one's place in the afterlife by killing an ideological or religious competitor. It was entirely another to feed, clothe, and support tens of thousands of soldiers. The costs incurred in the First Crusade had had a negative impact on the treasuries of many European powers. The foresight of the Knights Templar, however, had changed matters, perhaps a bit too well.

While the warrior monks had taken personal vows of poverty and only had their swords and red-cross-marked white mantel to call their own, the order's founding knights had made certain investments that would provide for a potentially indefinite occupation of the Holy Land. Rather than renting ships to meet the region's needs, or pay a heavy transport fee as their preceding crusaders had done in the pursuit of Christian regional stability during the interwar period, the Knights Templar bought and managed their own fleet of ships. And instead of paying others to facilitate their supply needs, the order developed its own, more cost effective supply network. In Outremer, they rebuilt castles in strategic military locations and garrisoned themselves in quarters atop Jerusalem's ancient ruins of the Temple of Solomon. This simultaneously established them as the preeminent symbol of the new Christian rule while allowing them to curry favor with visiting Muslim dignitaries as quasi-protectors of the Temple Mount's other holy site, the Dome of the Rock. By the time war once more erupted in the region, the Knights Templar had their managerial system in place and had made certain inroads with the indigenous populace, leaving them well prepared to service the needs of Europe's armies looking to be placed within striking distance of the enemy.

When things went badly for the Crusaders, many sought to blame someone other than the "inferior" Saracen warriors for their losses. As religious idealists, the Crusaders did not question their leaders or battlefield commanders. Furthermore, to have blamed corrupt papal authorities or the decisions of the absent ruling nobility would have gone against the Crusaders' beliefs.

So, as a wealthy and largely autonomous order, the Knights Templar became easy victims in the ensuing blame game. Their fortresses, technically community property, had frequently sheltered fleeing armies and refugees, but in the wake of frustration and failure, they became symbols of the order's perfidy. Their facility with regional dialects and Muslim customs was talked about by some as de facto proof of the Templars' covert allegiance to the enemies of Christ. While their dissension against failing military strategies likewise became synonymous with a lack of faith and battlefield will, many of the order's gestures of heroism were largely overlooked, including their sheltering and safely removing refugees from the war zone and their periodic suicidal charges against enemy positions to buy other Crusaders time to reverse poor military encounters. Still, before long, even the most basic actions by the Knights Templar were unquestioningly taken as further indication of the order's infirmity. For example, during the 1291 siege of the Knights Templar fortress at Acre, Grand Master William de Beaujeu was hit in the armpit by a Saracen's arrow. Refusing to yield to the wound, he rode into battle, and as he died, his mount began to move erratically. Onlooking Christian warriors, who had not seen the arrow strike, dismissed his behavior as simple cowardice.

By the end of the Third Crusade, however, the order's vital assistance to the campaign of British king Richard the Lionheart against Saladin gave a few participants reason to reevaluate their opinion of the knightly order as a collective of greedy autocrats, but with the negotiated forfeiture of control of Jerusalem, the poor knights had become an order bereft of all purpose but making money.

In more than a century of fighting to protect the Holy Land, the Knights Templar had periodically accepted small parcels of land from faithful European nobles in lieu of donations of hard currency. While some of the land was designated as order prefectures and supply depots, much of it was developed to grow crops the order could use or sell to finance their goals. Similarly, over time the very same infrastructure the knights had employed to move currency from the westernmost provinces of Europe for use in their eastern war-torn outposts, was, likewise, transformed into a network of banks and lending houses to protect the fiscal assets of European pilgrims and cash-strapped rulers, as with their other services, at a below-market value. The increased frequency of wartime transactions and their acquired loans as a fiscal lender began to net the Knights Templar both a tidy profit and an increasing retinue of enemies. While many excused such practices as essential to the securing of the Holy Land for a Christian Europe, without Outremer, their increased wealth became a presumed sinful weight about the order's neck.

As the liquid assets of Europe's great powers continued to dwindle with the identification of new threats to stability and Christian rule, the Knights Templar continued to sign over to the regional nobility large sums of money, financed through their now likewise lucrative farming and trading services. Soon much of Europe was buried in debt to the order. With the papacy protecting them, however, no noble or king dared challenge the order's new fiscal purview. But pontiffs live only so long. In 1305 French king Philip IV saw his opportunity to end his debts to the Knights Templar in Bertrand de Goth's succession to Pope Benedict XI as Pope Clement V. Clement V had come to power through the machinations of the Vatican's French cardinals, and King Philip wasted little time forging a close friendship with the new pontiff. On Friday, October 13,

1307, the French king ordered the arrest of every Knight Templar within the kingdom of France on charges of heresy and satanic worship. Several hundred members of the order were promptly rounded up and turned over to the Holy Inquisitors for interrogation under pain of torture. In time, some members gave the French king exactly what he needed: confessions. In 1312, Pope Clement V officially disbanded the Knights Templar and ordered the arrest of the remaining membership. In 1314, the last Grand Master of the Poor-Fellow Knights of Christ and the Temple of Solomon, James de Molay, and his adjutant, Geoffrey of Charney, were burned alive, and the recovered assets of the order were split between the Church and the French king.

In less than two hundred years, the order, which had employed as their seal the image of two knights sharing a mount in poverty, had amassed such power and standing that they became the bane of both Christian and Muslim leaders. Whether or not they failed to protect the Holy Land, the Knights Templar's mortal sin was in making a profit.

Science is about truth and discovery. Okay, I'm lying. For a very long time prestige and, lately, grants tend to be as important. There are many dedicated scientists working for many worthy goals. But even two hundred years ago there were also men who yearned for the fame and wealth that a "breakthrough" would gain them. In England the carrot was membership in the Royal Society. Here is the story of just how far one man would go to achieve this goal.

THE FAKE OF A FAKE

CARDIFF, NEW YORK, 1869

Peter Archer

On October 16, 1869, workmen digging a well on the property of William C. Newell of Cardiff, New York, reported finding the stone body of a man ten feet tall. Word spread rapidly, and people began to gather, begging for a glimpse of the "petrified giant," as the discovery became known. Newell, ever alert to make a buck, started charging ten cents a head. He then increased the charge to twenty-five cents, then fifty cents. And still people came—nearly five hundred daily for weeks to come. Newell's farm became known as "Giantville."

In his autobiography, Andrew Dickson White, founder of Cornell University, gives a breathless account of the scene:

> The roads were crowded with buggies, carriages, and even omnibuses from the city, and with lumber-wagons from the

> farms—all laden with passengers . . . [We] found a gathering which at first sight seemed like a country fair. In the midst was a tent and a crowd was pressing for admission. Entering, we saw a large pit, or grave, and, at the bottom of it . . . an enormous figure . . . It had a color as if it had lain long in the earth, and over its surface were minute punctures, like pores . . . Lying in its grave, with the subdued light from the roof of the tent falling upon it, and with the limbs contorted as if in a death struggle, it produced a most weird effect. An air of great solemnity pervaded the place. Visitors hardly spoke above a whisper.

In Genesis 6:4, the King James Bible says, "There were giants on the Earth in those days." Excited spectators wondered if the workmen had at last uncovered the remains of one of those giants.

More sober observers believed the work to be a statue, though they could not imagine who had carved it or why. One thought it had been shaped by a Jesuit missionary in the seventeenth century, perhaps as an attempt to impress local Native American tribes.

Newell sold three quarters of his interest in the giant figure to a syndicate in Syracuse for $37,500, an immense sum in that period. What he didn't tell them was that he knew where the Cardiff Giant had come from and who had carved it.

The craftsman was a distant relative of his, George Hull. Hull was a cigar manufacturer and a convinced atheist. He decided to perpetrate the fake, he said later, after arguing all evening with a fundamentalist minister. Hull wondered if people could really be convinced that his creation was a giant dating back to biblical times. He had some evidence to believe they would, because there had been debates in newspapers during the previous decade suggesting that humans could be petrified.

He soon found out. The hoax was far more successful than he had imagined. Hull hired workmen to carve a block of gypsum in

Iowa. He had the stone shipped to Chicago, where he hired a stonemason to carve it into the required likeness. He used himself as a model and carefully treated the stone figure with sulfuric acid to give it the appearance of age. The entire project cost Hull $2,600. He buried it, he said, in 1868, but it took a year for reliable witnesses to discover it.

Once the giant had been purchased by the Syracuse syndicate, it was moved to Syracuse. There, under closer scrutiny, its true nature became quickly apparent. One inspector pointed out that chisel marks in the stone were obvious. Dickson White had already expressed the opinion that the thing was a fake, pointing out that the workman who "found" it must have been part of the scheme, since there was no good reason to dig a well in that particular spot, so far from the main house.

Hull confessed and said that he and Newell had agreed to split the money, but crowds kept coming to the see the giant, referring to it as "Old Hoaxey."

The giant attracted the attention of the great showman P. T. Barnum, who asked the syndicate to rent him the statue for three months so he could exhibit it. When the syndicate refused, Barnum had a novel solution: He hired a craftsman to make a plaster cast of the giant, creating a fake of a fake. With complete confidence in his powers of persuasion, Barnum put his fake on display in New York and declared the original Cardiff Giant to be a fake.

Barnum was no stranger to hoaxes. In 1842 he exhibited the Fiji Mermaid in his museum, a grotesque creature that seemed to be half human and half fish. In fact, it was the creation of an Indonesian, who had sewn together a fish's tail, the torso of a baby orangutan, and the head of a monkey. In 1850, Barnum publicized the existence of a weed that would transform African Americans into Caucasians. Needless to say, no such weed existed.

Lawsuits flew back and forth between the syndicate and Barnum.

Finally, in 1870, a court ruled that both giants were frauds and that Barnum could not be sued for calling a fake a fake, even though his fake was fake as well.

Mark Twain, an amused observer of such human follies, made the Cardiff Giant's ghost a character in "A Ghost Story." The ghost haunts the New York hotel room of the narrator, who confronts it and demands to know what it wants. The ghost replies that it has been haunting the museum across the street, where its remains are displayed but without success. "Then it occurred to me to come over the way and haunt this place a little."

The narrator explodes in amazement. "This transcends everything! Everything that ever did occur! Why you poor blundering old fossil, you have had all your trouble for nothing—you have been haunting a *plaster cast* of yourself—the real Cardiff Giant is in Albany! Confound it, don't you know your own remains?"

After the furor over the hoax, Barnum's fraud, and the lawsuits died down, so, too, did interest in the giant. It was sold several times and moved around the country. Today the Cardiff Giant is on display at the Farmers' Museum in Cooperstown, New York, where it competes with the Baseball Hall of Fame for tourist dollars.

Barnum is said to have remarked that no one ever got poor underestimating the intelligence of the American people. The Cardiff Giant is a sad confirmation of that cynical judgment.

If royalty encourages a mythos to separate themselves from the masses, then the places of kings also have those who have an interest in weaving tales around those places. Here is one such building that has been painted dark and dangerous. Well . . . it does attract the tourists.

TOWER OF LONDON

Not Really Where You Get a Head

James M. Ward

William Shakespeare constantly referred to the Tower in his plays as a terrible place. From *The Tragedy of Richard the Third,* Richard says, "Three times to-day my foot-clothed horse did stumble, And started when he look'd upon the Tower (the Tower of London), As loath to bear me to the slaughter-house." And in act V, scene 1 of *The Tragedy of King Richard the Second,* the Queen says, "This way the king will come. This is the way of Julius Caesar's ill-erected tower. To whose flint bosom my condemned lord is doom'd a prisoner by proud Bullingbrooke."

Thomas B. Bacaulay, an early English historian said of the Tower, "In truth there is no sadder spot on earth." Ask the man on the street in England and in America about the Tower of London and you'll probably hear the same thing: "Ah, isn't that the big dungeon where they chopped off heads? I know that place, English kings tossed people they didn't like into the dungeons there, didn't they?"

To most of us, the Tower of London inspires dark images of dungeons, the headsman's ax, and the end of hopes and dreams. With just a moment's digging, it appears as if William the Conqueror, who was interested in presenting a terrifying aspect to the rebellious citizens of London in 1066, started the bad press on this place. He did such a good job with his Middle Ages marketing effort that almost a thousand years have gone by with people still thinking the Tower is a nasty place.

American impressions of the Tower are inspired by the English kings of old, and even ancient playwrights such as Shakespeare and other writer types sought to increase the prison-like reputation of the Tower by purposely instilling fear and terror of the Bloody Tower into the hearts and minds of the theatergoing populace. It took hundreds of years of history to layer on the reputation of the dungeon and the headsman and his ax, but it has worked for the royalty of England, and today that image inspires thousands of people a year to visit the Tower looking for the chopping block.

William the Conqueror conceived plans for the Tower in 1066. He wanted an intimidating structure in London that would bring awe and fear into the hearts of rebellious people living in and around London. He'd just invaded and wasn't the most popular man in the city at that time. However, the structure was never just a single tower. Even in those days, it was a complex of towers, chapels, stables, and walls. For hundreds of years, people looked at the tower thinking the Romans had built it, but the Romans were good at building walls and other nasty things. The Roman emperor Hadrian wasn't very popular with the populace of Scotland or England in the day. In truth, a Roman was part of the complex, but the invading William, who masterminded the last successful invasion of Britain, in 1066, gave the Tower its reputation as the best prison in the world.

Murders and executions did happen within the confines of the Tower, but most of the official executions happened on Tower Hill and not inside the Tower of London at all. Only the most royal of people received the honor of death inside the Tower.

Far from a tower of death filled with dungeon cells and torture chambers, the Tower of London complex was the comfortable residence for many kings and queens. In 1078, the Tower foundations were laid, and twenty years later, the entire complex was finished. Great kings and queens were constantly adding to the complex in an effort to make it even more luxurious and not a dank dungeon at all. When done, the main tower rose one hundred feet high, with walls fifteen feet thick. Inside it was a chapel, extensive sets of royal apartments, guardrooms, and crypts. From its earliest days, the Tower was falsely rumored to be the perfect, inescapable dungeon.

In 1189, the rule of England passed to Chancellor William Longchamp while Richard the Lionheart went on crusade. Longchamp worked to expand the Tower complex, doubling its size and giving it a new and deeper moat. Richard's brother, John, put those new defenses to a terrible test as he challenged Longchamp's authority and forced him to surrender the Tower. More plush, royal apartments were added to the Tower complex in 1216, creating a great hall and huge kitchen.

Kings were constantly fleeing behind the protection of the Tower walls. It wasn't much of a hardship for royals to go to the Tower, as it was kept stocked with the best food and wine of the age. In 1236 and 1238, King Henry III fled to the Tower, fleeing the rioting populace. Not a dungeon or death spire at all, the Tower served as a powerful citadel where kings and queens could retire in complete safety, enjoying quiet time as commoners battered the walls with pitchforks and shovels to no effect.

During his reign, Edward I made the Tower a royal mint (the coin kind, not the julip kind) and started using it for storing the royal records of the country.

One of the most famous royal murders happened in the Tower,

to Edward V and his brother, Richard, in 1483. The two young boys were sent to the Tower by their uncle Richard, the Duke of Gloucester. The Duke was crowned king when his two royal wards mysteriously disappeared from the Tower. The boys were killed and buried in a stairwell of the structure. Their bodies lay hidden there for almost two hundred years until a repairman discovered them in 1674.

One of the first royal prisoners of the Tower was the Bishop of Durham. A fat, greedy man, he was sent to prison by his brother for very un-priestly acts. Along with him, for his comfort, went a host of servants and cooks (yes, it seems he needed more than one), as well as many satchels of gold the bishop had managed to collect over the years. Fearing torture and death in the Tower, the good bishop instead was amazed to find luxurious apartments, where his servants took care of his needs with the only provision being he couldn't leave the rooms of his apartment until his case was decided. (The Crown was in no hurry to decide the case.) On a night in February of 1101, the bishop was unusually generous and gave a lavish banquet with huge amounts of food and liquor for everyone in the Tower complex. Unwatered-down wine was an unusual luxury in those days, and everyone drank himself into unconsciousness—and the bishop, and his gold, escaped the Tower through a large, unbarred window.

In 1240, King Henry III made the Tower of London complex his home, whitewashing the Tower; indeed, for hundreds of years it was called the White Tower and known not for its beheadings but as the home of kings. Henry III built the Lion Tower and erected the first zoo in England inside the walls of the Tower of London. All the while, the public was still made to fear being sent to the Tower as the place for executions and a quick end.

In 1471, Henry VI was murdered while praying in the Tower complex. In that same section of the Tower, the Crown Jewels were stored from 1879 to 1967.

Kings and queens enjoyed living in the Tower of London complex until the death of Henry VII. The only reason they stopped staying there was that other castles were built that were even more luxurious in nature.

The Tower of London was also the site of many royal pageants. The marriage of King Henry VIII to his second wife, Anne Boleyn, took place in the Tower on May 19, 1533. The complex hosted a huge wedding party lasting eleven days, finishing in one of the most enormous feasts anyone had ever seen. Anne was one of the few people thought royal enough to be ordered executed in the Tower.

In 1530, the Queen's House was built, the site of the Council Chamber, where the famous Guy Fawkes stood alone to be interrogated, and, in later years, of the chamber where William Penn, founder of Pennsylvania, was once a prisoner. Allowed servants and sleeping in a chamber once used by kings of England, Penn was later to remark that the Tower was one of his favorite places to be held prisoner.

In 1534, Sir Thomas Moore spent some quality prison time in the Tower for refusing to acknowledge the validity of Henry VIII's divorce from Catherine of Aragon. He was executed in July of 1535 for daring to say that the king was wrong. Moore clearly wasn't the most diplomatic of men in his thoughts and deeds. Throughout the time of the Tudors, many royal and politically powerful prisoners spent a year or two in the many towers of the Tower complex. Most often, prisoners of all types were allowed servants, given the normal living conditions of the wealthy of the day, and fed better than most of the people of the countryside.

During the two world wars, German spies were executed in the courtyard of the Tower. Hitler's deputy, Rudolph Hess, found himself imprisoned in the Tower.

Until recently, the Jewel House held the Crown Jewels and one of the world's largest collections of jewels and royal regalia.

The Tower complex also holds the roost for the royal ravens. An ancient superstition suggests that if the Tower ravens ever left the Tower, the power of the Tower of London and indeed all of England would fail. To this day, bird keepers clip the wings of the ravens and take excellent care of the birds in all other respects.

Far from an evil dungeon, the Tower complex holds a community of a little over 150 people who live happily within the walls. The yeoman warders (Beefeaters) and their families live on the royal Tower grounds. Early in the history of the Tower, the guards of the gates came to live in the Tower during the reign of Henry VIII. Their blue undress uniform was introduced in 1858. The Duke of Wellington was constable of the Tower for twenty-six years. He brought a more military flavor to the guards of the Tower.

For more than a thousand years, the Tower has been an ever-changing building project for the kings and queens of England. Walls and towers (thirteen inner and six outer) and a huge moat were built over the centuries.

History now records that if you wanted to book a wedding, the Tower would be the best place. If you wanted to take some time off and write a book in hotel-style accommodation, the Tower would be just the place. However, if you had to get your head chopped off, it would be a good bet, as they sent you to the Tower, that you'd be having it done on a foggy, wet morning, outside in the rain, and not by a nice warm fire. In modern times, the Tower is officially called "Her Majesty's Royal Palace and Fortress the Tower of London."

When I write a book about traveling to the moon, it is a fictional novel. But it wasn't that long ago when the masses, entranced by the real miracles scientists were providing, believed just about any lie told in the name of science.

ARE MY ARMS TIRED!

Brian Thomsen

Seventeenth-Century France . . . and the Moon

"I've just flown back from the moon."

Though travel literature has always been popular, it slightly boggles the mind that not one but two legendary storytellers wrote of their lunar exploits prior to the dawn of the nineteenth century.

. . . and indeed both of these famous individuals are probably guilty of more than a bit of résumé padding on their own part, and as a result, may be remembered more as fictional characters than as themselves.

The real Cyrano de Bergerac (1619–1655) had very little in common with the character who entered the public consciousness.

He did not have a large proboscis.

He was not a Gascon soldier (a group known for their swashbuckling skills), and indeed had a less than auspicious military service due to his pacifist beliefs and nonconformist manner.

. . . and, most important, especially for the fans of the Rostand play, purportedly based on Cyrano's life, there was never any great unrequited love named Roxanne, as Cyrano was most probably, given the evidence at hand, a homosexual.

But just because Rostand took great liberties with the facts of Cyrano's life, this in no way balances out the amount of misinformation that Cyrano himself promulgated about his life and exploits.

The myth that he was a Gascon soldier was probably promoted by Cyrano and/or his patrons to bring greater attention to his fine swordsmanship, and once he retired from the military, his embrace of a more libertine philosophy of life did indeed set him against the standard mores of the time. As a result he became more vicious yet subtle in his criticisms of society, masking his views in works such as *Other Worlds: The Comical History of the States and the Empires of the Moon and the Sun*, which includes his travelogue description of how he managed to travel back and forth to the moon (which noted science fiction authors Arthur C. Clarke and Brian Aldiss credit as the origin of the use of rocket propulsion for space travel).

The "fantastic" nature of this travelogue helped to immunize Cyrano from the more pointed arguments of his detractors, who would have liked to see him tried for treason and blasphemy.

Eighteenth-Century Germany . . . and the Moon

The exploits of another lunar traveler took place in the following century. Karl Friedrich Hieronymus, or as he is better known, Baron von Munchausen (1720–1797) was a German nobleman who served in the Russian military, taking part in two different campaigns against the Ottoman Empire.

After his service, he returned home to Bodenwerder, where he felt free to expand his reputation with numerous tales of his "actual" exploits to pretty much anyone who would listen to him.

(These stories were collected and published in English in London in 1785 by Rudolf Erich Raspe as *Baron Munchhausen's Narrative of His Marvellous Travels and Campaigns in Russia*; after his death, the tales were retitled *The Surprising Adventures of Baron Munchhausen.*).

Munchausen has gone down in history as a self-aggrandizing teller of tall tales and personal exaggerations (though there is substantial evidence that his "legacy" continued to be further embellished unto absurdity even after his death). His exploits included:

- journeys to locations all over the world (including both poles and North America) by numerous incredulous means of transport (including riding on a cannonball) within spans of time that boggle the mind even by today's standards;
- not one but two different trips to the moon;
- numerous captures and escapes from slavery;
- accomplishments of technical expertise and proficiency, such as the killing of fifty brace of ducks and other fowl with a single shot; and
- numerous other exploits (such as those alluded to in chapter 10 of his story "Pays a visit during the siege of Gibraltar to his old friend General Elliot — Single handedly sinks a Spanish man-of-war—Wakes an old woman on the African coast—Destroys all the enemy's cannon; frightens the Count d'Artois, and sends him to Paris—Saves the lives of two English spies with the identical sling that killed the Great Philistine Goliath; and raises the siege flag."

. . . and despite all of his fantastic claims, if any of his readers feared that the narrative in any way strayed from credibility (including the lunar trips), the Baron continually took great pains to assuage these fears and certify his assertions:

> Amazement stood in every countenance; their congratulations on my returning in safety were repeated with an unaffected degree of pleasure, and we passed the evening as we are doing now, every person present paying the highest compliments to my COURAGE and VERACITY . . . All that I have related before, said the Baron, is gospel; and if there be any one so hardy as to deny it, I am ready to fight him with any weapon he pleases . . . Yes, cried he, in a more elevated tone, as he started from his seat, I will condemn him to swallow this decanter, glass and all perhaps, and filled with kerren-wasser [a kind of ardent spirit distilled from cherries, and much used in some parts of Germany]. Therefore, my dear friends and companions, have confidence in what I say, and pay honour to the tales of Munchausen (From Chapters 20–21 of *Baron Munchhausen's Narrative of His Marvellous Travels and Campaigns in Russia*).

Whether either Cyrano or the Baron was a man of true veracity in his tale telling is probably not important. Given the fact that the modern reader is more aware of Cyrano (Rostand's Dr. Phil with a big nose and a sword), who never existed, than the real person, and of a psychotic syndrome (Munchausen syndrome) than the actual war hero and baron of the eighteenth century, either man's assertion that they were literally "the first man on the moon" is probably a trivial concern at best.

Snake oil salesmen, used car salesmen, politicians—they all tell lies. But here is how the real professionals do it.

NO SPEAK ENGLISH

Brian Thomsen

LIE No. 1: "We're Chinese," said the Russian sub.

On or about April 11, 1968, a Golf II–class diesel-electric K-129 submarine armed with ballistic missiles floundered and sank while on patrol in the Pacific Ocean. The American SOSUS (Sound Surveillance System) hydrophone network detected an accidental explosion and surmised by their data that it must have occurred aboard a Soviet submarine. Explosion-related observations were also recorded by a U.S. satellite and a civilian marine research vessel. (The cause of the submarine's failure remains unknown, though most speculation suggests a missile malfunction of some kind.)

The Soviets, despite mounting a considerable effort, apparently failed in their attempts to locate the submarine. No one could determine its final resting place for salvage, nor were the Soviets truly forthcoming in providing any details on the submarine's orders/mission.

The United States figuratively threw its hands up in the air, ascertaining that as a result there was nothing to be done about the matter (even after the Soviets suggested that it might have collided with a U.S. sub on a secret mission).

. . . and so the story would have died then and there if not for more than a few lies on the part of all parties concerned.

IN THEIR BOOK *Red Star Rogue*, Kenneth Sewell, a nuclear engineer and a veteran of intelligence operations with the U.S. Navy's submarine branch, and Clint Richmond, a veteran journalist, assert that the K-129 was on a top-secret mission to provoke a war between China and the United States, as such a war would undoubtedly have destroyed China and opened it to Soviet occupation and future dominance while also distracting the American military and weakening its ability to stand up to world communism.

The Soviet Golf II–class (of which the K-129 was a member) was not a particularly technologically advanced submarine, even by 1968 standards. It was also not nuclear powered, although it carried nuclear warheads (three R-13 ballistic missiles and two nuclear-tipped torpedoes). Moreover, it wasn't a top-of-the-line model for the Soviets, either, as it was the same type of ship they had sold to China when the two nations were on friendlier terms (and the Soviets always withheld their own top-of-line technology, even from allies).

The K-129's mission was to pass itself off as a Chinese sub (probably one of the ones the Soviets had sold them) and then, from a short range, hurl a missile at Pearl Harbor (well within the capacity of China's limited missile technology rather than the larger capabilities of the Soviets). The Soviet planners surmised that U.S. surveillance technology would quickly discern that the parameters of the attack were far below those available to Soviet technology, and by examining the available data (missile range, surveillance detail on the sub) would conclude that the Chinese were responsible for the attack.

The only problem was the less-than-cutting-edge technology that they were relying on for their deception failed them. The missile went off in its tube, mortally wounding the K-129 and its crew before it had the chance to execute its orders.

LIE No. 2: "We can't find it, let alone salvage it, so what are you worried about."

The Soviet's acknowledged that they had lost a sub, and the first thing they did was to try to blame an American sub, perhaps from an underwater collision that occurred when both subs deviated from their routine patrol routes. The Americans denied that such an altercation was possible, but nonetheless offered to help recover the missing submarine. The Soviet's responded with a curt "no, thank you," and eventually had to give up any hopes of salvage, resting comfortably that evidence of their deceitful plan was now safely buried beneath the sea far from the risks of possible exposure.

The Americans had to agree—such a recovery would be impossible given present technology, and besides, how could they possible know where the sub had gone down?

Washington knew that the now-sunk Soviet submarine carried something they really wanted to get their hands on: cryptographic gear for transmitting and receiving encoded, secure communications (as the British did during World War II when they recovered the Enigma decoding machine from a captured Nazi sub), and an opportunity to study and deconstruct Soviet technology through reverse engineering.

It was therefore well worth their time and effort to recover the sub.

Thus project code name Jennifer was undertaken. Jennifer's objective was to locate and recover the K-129, and do it as surreptitiously as possible.

The U.S. Navy Oceanic Research team on the USNS *Mizar* pinpointed the position of the K129 with assistance from a pair of submarines, USS *Halibut* and USS *Seawolf*. Locating the submarine took three naval crews weeks working with the available surveillance data they had from the moment of the explosion. Unfortunately, the K-129 had plunged to an unreachable depth of nearly 17,000 feet (5,200 meter, or 3.2 miles), far beyond the reach of contemporary recovery efforts.

As dictated by the situation, a recovery ship was designed to effect the salvage. This was the *Glomar Explorer*, built by Howard Hughes at the Sun Shipbuilding and Dry Dock Company. Ostensibly funded by Hughes as part of his Deep Ocean Mining Project (DOMP), with the dubious purpose of mining magnesium from the ocean bottom, *Glomar Explorer*'s two-hundred-million-dollar price tag was almost certainly funded at least in part as a black budget item of the CIA's. (It is worth noting that Howard Hughes's favorite film, which he allegedly watched nonstop for days at a time, was *Ice Station Zebra*, a submarine thriller that involved a race to recover crashed Soviet technology.)

The *Glomar Explorer* was specially designed to remain in one place through the use of global positioning so that a single directed effort below could be maintained with minimal drifting (anchoring the vessel was quite impossible with the sea floor seventeen thousand feet below). With robotically controlled salvage claws, the *Explorer* was eventually able to grip the submarine's hull (possibly in pieces) and drag it to a more secure location for salvage.

Obviously the entire operation did not occur overnight, but the wait was well worth it with the Soviet sub and its contents safely and surreptitiously in secure American hands, complete with all of its clandestine secrets ready for study.

Of course none of this was made public.

. . . so when the United States authorities maintained years later that there were no American submarines within three hundred miles of the K-129 (the excuse they used to dismiss the charges that the sub had been bumped by a clandestine U.S. spy sub), they weren't lying. There were, in fact, many U.S. submarines within 350 miles of the K-129's final resting place, as that was the distance it was from Pearl Harbor, a detail the U.S. authorities would only be able to assert if they had concrete knowledge of the sub's actual location.

Thc final disposition of K-129's salvage remains unknown.

One source claims that the United States succeeded in lifting the whole submarine from its initial resting spot but that during the long journey to the surface some of the claws gave way and a large portion of the sub fell back to the ocean floor, where it probably still rests today.

Another source claims that the United States retrieved the entire sub in pieces over a prolonged period of time.

The United States government has never officially acknowledged the salvage operation of K-129, and the Soviet government has never acknowledged its loss. Yet in August of 1993, at a summit meeting, the American ambassador presented his Russian counterpart with the brass bell of the K-129, which could only have been recovered if the entire sub had been salvaged, since the bell would have been permanently affixed to the sub's bridge deep within the sub itself.

Lies about law, lies about people, lies in defense of the nation—we had to have one about someone who lied about love.

ERIC CLAPTON'S UNDYING BUT TEMPORARY PASSION FOR PATTI BOYD-HARRISON

HURTWOOD EDGE, ENGLAND, 1970

Brian M. Thomsen

"If I could choose a place to die it would be in your arms."

—Eric Clapton

The gut-wrenching pain and ecstasy of unattainable love is a recurrent theme of all passionate music, and for the post-Beatles rock 'n' roll generation there is no harder driving anthem of passionate pain than "Layla," by Derek and the Dominos.

Derek and the Dominos (the band's name was supposed to be either "Eric and the Dominos" or "Eric and the Dynamos," depending on the source cited, but a flub by the announcer during their debut stuck, leaving them known as Derek and the Dominos) was a blues rock supergroup formed in the spring of 1970 by guitarist and singer Eric Clapton, keyboardist and singer Bobby Whitlock, bassist Carl Radle, and drummer Jim Gordon (who all were previously members of Delaney & Bonnie and Friends). Slide guitarist Duane Allman of the Allman Brothers Band was also present at the beginning of the recording of their first and only studio album.

Though initially greeted by mediocre sales and reviews (and numerous offstage personal tragedies, including the death by overdose of Duane Allman), the album has been dubbed a classic, and the song "Layla," one of the top ten all-time love songs of rock 'n' roll. No less than CNN has gone on record saying, "The 1970 *Layla* album—considered Clapton's greatest by most critics—is a seventy-five-minute tale of wrenching emotion, complete with a cover of Billy Myles's 'Have You Ever Loved a Woman,' a song about being in love with your best friend's wife."

Music album archeologists have determined that "Layla" is obviously directly inspired by the classic Persian love story *Layla and Majnun*, or *Leyli and Madjnun*. It is supposedly based on the real story of a young man called Qays ibn al-Muwallah in the Umayyad era, who upon seeing Layla fell in most passionate love with her, and went mad when her father prevented him from marrying her; for that reason, he came to be called Majnun Layla, literally "Crazy for Layla."

. . . and the "Layla" of the Clapton power ballad is Patti Boyd, who just happened to be married to Clapton's good friend, former Beatle and benefactor of the "Concert for Bangladesh," George Harrison. The supreme frustration of the situation drove the master guitarist to self-destructive depths, including drug abuse, heroin addiction, and alcoholism.

Patti Boyd was no stranger to being adored by rock musicians.

George Harrison (who wrote the tender love song "Something" about her) met her during the filming of *A Hard Day's Night*. They married in 1966, and from that point on she was a permanent fixture of the Beatles scene, even singing backup vocals on such classics as "Yellow Submarine," "Birthday," and "All You Need Is Love."

As master musicians of their generation, Harrison and Clapton met and soon became fast friends. Their admiration for each other's talent was without bounds . . . but so was the obsessive love/infatuation that grew within Clapton toward his friend's wife.

The Harrisons often week-ended for music and decadent debauchery with Clapton and whoever his current romantic "companion" happened to be (including, for a time, Patti's kid sister Paula). According to *Survivor: The Authorized Biography of Eric Clapton*, by Ray Coleman (published in the United Kingdom in 1985), Clapton and Harrison even held a guitar duel over Patti at Clapton's Hurtwood Edge mansion during one such weekend (Clapton won).

Clapton privately proclaimed his passion for her (if one disregards his thrashings of longing expressed on stage), and she reciprocated, the two of them snatching moments together while still partnered with other people.

Finally, in 1977, Harrison granted her a divorce, publicly commenting, "I'd rather she be with him than some dope." Patti was immediately received into Clapton's waiting arms.

She and Clapton married two years later in a ceremony attended by Harrison, and unlike the tragic love stories of the past such as those of Romeo and Juliet and Othello and Desdemona, one of rock 'n' roll's greatest love stories was allowed to come to a happy ending . . . for a time.

Though Clapton kicked heroin, he continued to drink very heavily throughout this time, without the justification of the torturous frustration of his longing for the previously unattainable Patti. Moreover, even though he was now wed to his greatest love and passion, "the woman in whose arms he would contentedly die," he continued to seek sexual gratification with numerous other partners, fathering illegitimate children with both Yvonne Khan Kelley and Italian model Lory Del Santo.

It would appear that Patti was not his everything but more likely just "everything that is unobtainable for the moment, and therefore most desirous."

In the words of Bobby Whitlock, Eric's bandmate from Derek and the Dominos, who happened to be good friends with both Harrison and Clapton, "He was all hot on Patti and I was dating her sister. They had this thing going on that supposedly was behind George's back. Well, George didn't really care. He said, 'You can have her.' That kind of defuses it when Eric says, 'I'm taking your wife' and he says, 'Take her.' They got married and evidently, she wasn't what he wanted after all. The hunt was better than the kill. That happens, but apparently Patti is real happy now with some guy who's not a guitar player. Good for her and good for Eric for moving on with his life. George got on with his life, that's for sure."

Clapton and Boyd were divorced in 1988.

Boyd married a non-rock superstar thereafter, and Clapton, no doubt, became "Crazy for Layla" for someone else, at least until she, too, became attainable.

Dick Tracy's classic villain Mumbles had nothing on his real-life counterpart, a Mafia boss who perfected an act and took it on the road from the streets of New York to the Federal Courts.

VINCENT "THE CHIN" GIGANTE

NEW YORK CITY, 1928–2005

Robert Greenberger

In 2003 the curtain rang down on the longest running show in town as Vincent Gigante admitted to Brooklyn Federal Court judge I. Leo Glasser that he had been feigning insanity for the previous thirty years.

Gigante (March 29, 1928–December 19, 2005), known to tabloid readers in five boroughs and beyond as The Chin, was a legendary crime boss for the Genovese Family, one of the five Mafia families that controlled New York City's underworld. The son of a watchmaker and seamstress, both from Naples, he attended Manhattan's Textile High School but dropped out in ninth grade. Gigante excelled as a boxer, with a 21–4 heavyweight record by the time he turned nineteen. He was at one time managed by Genovese boss Thomas (Nicholas Pasciuto) Eboli, establishing his family ties.

He began his life of crime as a protégé of Vito Genovese, with seven arrests by the age of twenty-five. Gigante, called "Cinzenzo" by his mother and shortened to "the Chin" by his pals, received only one sixty-day sentence for his misdeeds. He quickly became an assassin and first gained attention beyond the family in 1957, when he tried to whack Frank Costello, known as the Prime Minister of Organized Crime. The hit failed, and even though he was ID'd by Costello's doorman, Gigante was acquitted in 1958. Justice caught up with him, though, a year later when he was jailed on charges of dealing heroin. He was paroled and returned to the streets in 1964.

Five years later, the Chin beat charges of bribing police officers in Old Tappan, New Jersey, by parading a series of psychiatrists into court to attest to his legal insanity. They claimed the mobster displayed signs of insanity, psychosis, schizophrenia, and infantilism—all deteriorating and irreversible conditions. Satisfied with the victory, Gigante decided to play this card at every opportunity. His fellow crime lords and even his family knew of the ruse and supported his efforts.

Law enforcement agents spent years trying to track evidence that Gigante was faking it—without success. They came close, though, when Vincent "Fish" Cafaro testified that Gigante had assumed leadership of the Genovese Family in 1981. The Chin seized power from boss Anthony "Fat Tony" Salerno after he suffered a stroke, keeping Salerno around as a front. Cafaro spoke about this at Salerno's trial, which resulted in Fat Tony being sentenced to one hundred years in prison.

In a subsequent trial, "Little Al" D'Arco, former acting boss of the Lucchese Family described how Gigante helped maintain his ruse. Seated at his headquarters under a World War II poster that proclaimed "The Enemy Is Listening," Gigante would whisper his instructions in people's ears, avoiding eavesdropping.

Throughout the years, Gigante would become a successful street performer, heading out for unscheduled performances. As a result, the New York tabloids, which frequently ran photos from these matinees, dubbed him the "Oddfather." The *New York Times* observed,

"In the 1980s Vincent 'Chin' Gigante was a familiar sight on Sullivan Street in Greenwich Village, where he lived with his mother. The large middle-aged man was often seen wandering around in his pajamas, robe, and slippers with a cap pulled down over his head. Usually he showed a few days' growth of beard on his sagging, expressionless face. His downcast eyes were dull and vacant, allegedly the result of his daily medications, which included Valium and Thorazine." Whatever he mumbled never made sense to those passing by. To reinforce his crazed reputation, between 1969 and 1990 Gigante checked himself in to St. Vincent's Psychiatric Hospital in Harrison, New York, twenty-two times.

The prosecutors tried again in 1990, when Gigante was arrested and charged with racketeering and committing murder. As happens with such cases, the legal proceedings dragged out for seven years, and all during this time, Gigante appeared mentally unstable. Attempts to dismiss the charges failed. This occurred during a decade when one "made man" after another eschewed his promise of *omertà* (staying loyal to the family) by cutting a deal to save his own neck. When Gigante was finally tried, a parade of Mafia witnesses, led by Salvatore "Sammy the Bull" Gravano, spoke about how lucid the Chin appeared during meetings. Philadelphia's Bruno Family was represented by Phil Leonetti, who said Gigante ordered a series of slayings in the 1980s. The Lucchese Family of New York admitted they were recruited by Gigante to help murder rival mob boss John "the Dapper Don" Gotti.

Finally, in 1996, the Chin was arraigned. In September, Gigante appeared before Judge Eugene Nickerson for a twelve-minute performance. One reporter noted, "He twitched and he trembled. His lips quivered and his arms shook. He played with his ear; he rubbed his chest. He shook his head, stroked his chin, and scratched himself. And as the judge and opposing lawyers spoke to each other, Gigante talked to himself." He was convincing enough that the federal prosecutors, Andrew Weissmann and George Stamboulidis, never got around to asking that his one-million-dollar bail be revoked. The trial was postponed to allow Gigante to undergo heart surgery that December. After his hospital release in January 1997, the Chin finally went to trial that summer. This time, despite his appearing unstable, he was convicted and began a twelve-year sentence in December 1997. The jury did acquit him of ordering six mob hits, while the statute of limitations got him off the hook for conspiring to murder Gotti. His bid for appeal was rejected in 1999 and he was subsequently accused of hiring a sexy woman to find material to influence the jurors during his original trial.

Despite being in jail, Gigante's family influence remained. As a result, on January 23, 2002, his son Andrew, acting boss Liborio (Barney) Bellomo, and The Chin were accused of masterminding extortion rackets in New York, New Jersey, and Miami. With the dock scheme exposed, federal prosecutors let Gigante know they finally had their smoking gun: audiotape of a phone tap revealing a lucid and caring Gigante checking in with his family in the aftermath of the September 11, 2001, attack on the World Trade Center.

Finally, this trial led the Chin to admit his act in open court as part of a plea bargain that resulted in three more years being added to his existing sentence. the Chin died at seventy-seven from heart disease in a Springfield, Missouri, prison in 2005, five years before he was due to be released. With the Chin gone, stories have emerged from fellow mobsters regarding the lengths to which he went to protect his freedom, one of the longest running acts on record.

EPILOGUE

Color Him Red-Faced

Bill Fawcett

Doing a book on lies, it is irresistible to try to name the greatest liar of them all. After looking at a very, very large number of candidates, here is our choice for the worst liar in history.

There are so many candidates for the greatest liar in history that we almost didn't do this section. For happy liars you have to pick P. T. Barnum as king. Politicians as a group have an unfair advantage. People actually come to hear them, and we have all been conditioned to think it is somehow okay for them to lie. But when you can designate only one Greatest Liar, then you have to look at other factors. When you look only at recent history, the list has to include Goebbels, Hitler, Baghdad Bob, several major fraudsters, more than a few of those American politicians, plagiarists, cult leaders, and an array of talented deceivers from Madison Avenue.

To decide among this field it was necessary to set the criteria for what constitutes being the worst, and therefore greatest, liar. To begin, the lies have to be multiple, major, and public. They have to be clearly shown as lies by the record. The lies of our winner were also judged by the impact the lies had on others; how many people were affected and how significantly. With false prophets, ad agencies, and politicians in the running, the final result was a bit of a surprise to the authors.

Our candidate for the greatest liar in recorded history is Joseph Stalin. As we researched the man, we found that nothing published, said, or filmed about or written at the behest of him was actually true. To begin, his very position as the head of the Communist Party was based on the lie of the "worker's paradise." In plain fact, it is now apparent that among the Communist leadership until very recently, there was little concern for the worker and a lot of concern for maintaining power. Perhaps the only part of the Communist philosophy that most of Russia's leaders lived up to was the belief that "the end justified the means" in their "workers' crusade." But on a personal level, as absolute ruler of Russia for almost three decades, Joseph Stalin outshone with deception and hypocrisy even the most entrenched Russian bureaucrat or self-serving congressman.

And how was just about everything about Joseph Stalin a lie?

In hundreds of books, pictures, movies, and even poems, Stalin was shown as an equal partner to Lenin in leading the Bolshevik revolution. The reality, which was never told, is that during the revolution, he was a fairly minor official known for being efficient if not imaginative. Virtually every single statement, movie, poster, and book about what he did before becoming the dictator of Russia was a carefully crafted lie. Everything printed earlier was banned and destroyed to ensure that the party line was all anyone could read.

One of the most offensive lies was Stalin as the protector of the

Russian people. His quote that "of all the treasures the state can possess the lives of its citizens are for us the most precious" was constantly published on posters, in books, even on banners. The reality is that Stalin was the greatest butcher in the history of Russia. He has to rival Hitler and Genghis Khan as the cause of mass murder. Under his rule, often inspired by his personal and blatant paranoia, the liquidation of whole ethnic groups happened more than once. He ordered the murder or exile of every independent farmer in Russia, the Kulaks. He also ordered the deportation to Siberia, itself a death sentence most of the time, of nearly all Soviet Jews, virtually all Cossacks, several Islamic groups, all professionals in every field, and everyone who had held any important job before Stalin took power. When opposed by some Ukrainians, he deported or killed everyone in the eastern half of that nation and settled "loyal" Russians there. That nation remains politically and ethnically split to this day. Anyone and everyone that might be a threat was simply killed. On the off chance that the army might someday revolt, in 1937, Stalin ordered the death of more than forty thousand of its officers. Any soldier with any initiative might someday be a threat to Stalin, so he killed them all. Rather than caring for the Russian people, the truth was that Stalin was directly responsible for millions of ordinary Russians being executed, starved, or frozen to death.

Stalin liked to portray himself as the "little father" of the Russians. His propaganda machine constantly depicted him as the protector of children. Again, this was a constantly repeated lie. Statues and pictures of Stalin surrounded by well-fed, happy children were everywhere. The reality was that he had no regard for the children of anyone or any group he chose to dislike. And his dislike was often fatal. Newborn babies were exiled with their parents. He had no concern at all for children in general, either. Orphans were often left on the street, as they had no part in his five-year plans to industrialize Russia. Child labor was endemic in the system. Perhaps the best demonstration of his deceit is a picture of him with one young girl. She has chubby cheeks and a beaming smile. Millions of copies of the picture were made, and the image was reproduced on posters and in statues. In reality, Stalin later had the same girl's father executed a few years later, likely dooming the child. Stalin's own wife committed suicide, and his son tried to and failed.

Since Joseph Stalin was in charge of everything, and his every economic and industrial plan failed miserably, he had to find someone else to blame. The big lie here was that the last survivors of the old regime had become "wreckers" who thwarted his every brilliant effort. Then, to make sure everyone knew that things were not his fault, the secret police constantly found new "wreckers" and executed them. Tens of thousands of innocent people were tortured into confessing, and then killed. All this just to support the lie that Stalin was perfect.

Finally, we have the lie that Stalin led the Soviet Union to victory over Hitler. What was left out was Stalin's behavior at the start of the German invasion. First, the dictator refused to believe the spies who warned him the invasion was coming. Then he refused to believe his own generals—the ones he hadn't executed yet, anyhow—that the Germans were massing for an attack. Finally, when Operation Barbarossa began, he not only panicked, but for over a week, he disappeared. It appears now that he retreated into a bunker in the lower levels of the Kremlin and did nothing while millions of Russian soldiers died or were captured. At the start of the war, rather than guide his nation, Stalin left it leaderless. Moreso, because he had just a few years before executed all of his competent officers. Once he emerged from hiding, the fate of the generals who lost battles, even hopeless ones, was again execution. So Stalin, far from being the savior of Russia in World War II, was one of the main reasons the Russian army, leaderless at the top, collapsed when Hitler attacked. Two million soldiers were killed or captured in the first months of the invasion. Twenty million more Russians died in the war.

So, here is our choice. The greatest liar in history, using all the resources of a vicious dictatorship to spread his lies, is the man whose lies and paranoia caused at least thirty million deaths. Joseph Stalin has to get the nod as the biggest, worst, and most deadly liar in history.

BOOKS BY BILL FAWCETT

HUNTERS & SHOOTERS

An Oral History of the U.S. Navy SEALs in Vietnam

ISBN 978-0-06-137566-8 (paperback)

Fifteen former SEALs share their vivid, first-person remembrances of action in Vietnam—brutal, honest and thrilling stories revealing astonishing truths that will only add strength to the SEAL legend.

OVAL OFFICE ODDITIES

An Irreverent Collection of Presidential Facts, Follies, and Foibles

ISBN 978-0-06-134617-0 (paperback)

Featuring hundreds of strange and wonderful facts about past American presidents, first ladies, and veeps, readers will learn all about presidential gaffes, love lives, and odd habits.

YOU SAID WHAT?

Lies and Propaganda Throughout History

ISBN 978-0-06-113050-2 (paperback)

From the dawn of man to the War on Terror, Fawcett chronicles the vast history of frauds, deceptions, propaganda, and trickery from governments, corporations, historians, and everyone in between.

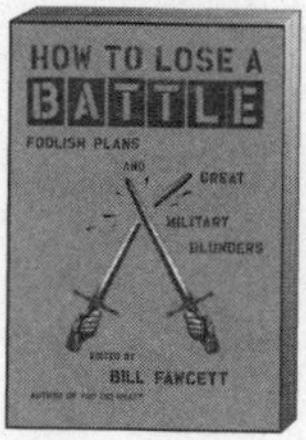

HOW TO LOSE A BATTLE

Foolish Plans and Great Military Blunders

ISBN 978-0-06-076024-3 (paperback)

Whether a result of lack of planning, miscalculation, a leader's ego, or spy infiltration, this compendium chronicles the worst military defeats and looks at what caused each battlefield blunder.

YOU DID WHAT?

Mad Plans and Great Historical Disasters

ISBN 978-0-06-053250-5 (paperback)

History has never been more fun than it is in this fact-filled compendium of historical catastrophes and embarrassingly bad ideas.

PRAISE FOR
BLOO

"Witty, fast-paced, and fabulous, *Bloodshot* is a refreshing addition to the urban fantasy genre. Priest's darkly hilarious tale will leave readers anxious for more adventures with the charmingly neurotic Raylene and her unlikely entourage. A vastly entertaining read!"
— JEANIENE FROST,
New York Times bestselling author of *This Side of the Grave*

"With *Bloodshot*, Priest catapults the kick-ass urban fantasy heroine into the realm of the truly bad-ass. Raylene's fascinating mix of the old ultra-violence with snark and self-deprecation had me riveted. The combination of such an interesting character with a plot that continually out-thunk me makes *Bloodshot* one of my favorite reads this year." — NICOLE PEELER, author of *Tempest's Legacy*

"Cherie Priest's urban fantasy debut is a fun, fast-paced adventure with a dash of romance and a heaping scoop of conspiracy. I'm looking forward to more, especially if Sister Rose is onstage."
— LUCY A. SNYDER, author of *Shotgun Sorceress*

"*Bloodshot* is, hands down, my favorite urban fantasy book of 2010. By turns frightening, funny, and fabulous, it was a joy to read and damn near impossible to put down. It's a ton of fun, brim-full of Cherie's wonderful, quirky voice and deliciously twisted imagination. More, please!" — KAT RICHARDSON, author of *Labyrinth*

"Cherie Priest delivers a fantastic urban fantasy that takes us back to the genre's noir roots and proves there's still new blood to be found in old tropes. The engrossing, complex mystery and smart, refreshing heroine makes this one a must-read for genre fans!"
— KELLY MEDING, author of *Another Kind of Dead*

And for her previous novels

DREADNOUGHT

"An intimate, well-crafted portrait of a nurse on a mission adds depth to this exceptional Civil War steampunk thriller. . . . The battles and intrigue are entertaining, but the real draw is Priest's latest no-nonsense heroine, who comes equipped with a full measure of sharp judgment and brutal competence as well as a nurse's kind (but not saintly) heart." — *Publishers Weekly,* starred reivew

CLEMENTINE

"The moral complexity of the novel elevates it above pure escapism, and adds depth to the chase adventure. . . . Priest has once again constructed a fascinating and fun-as-hell narrative, a worthy addition to her Clockwork Century." — SF Site

"An intriguing yarn that is excellently paced . . . strong and compelling . . . *Clementine* will certainly appeal to fans of steampunk and alternate history, and the interesting characters might also attract casual readers." — *San Francisco Book Review*

"Piracy meets politics head-on in this steampunk thriller. . . . Explosive battle scenes, riveting action, and a sharp-eyed examination of the mistrust between Croggon's all-black crew and very white, very Southern Maria play out in a desperate race against the clock."
— *Publishers Weekly*

"An over-the-top romp driven by pirates, aerial battles, revenge, conspiracies, secret weapons, and a forced alliance between deadly enemies . . . There are cliffhangers aplenty, and the world Priest has set up is a promising one, but the book's real attraction is the well-realized portrayal of [Maria Isabelle] Boyd, who is as resourceful, charming, and dangerous as she was in real life." — *Scifi Magazine*

"Effective on all counts, smart and strong and written at a breakneck pace, *Clementine* is the best kind of fun reading. Priest [also] gives readers . . . two memorable characters who are so incredibly above average and unique from standard tropes that one wonders why it has taken so long for anyone to write this kind of book." — *Bookslut*

"Manages to pack in all the steampunk goodness you could ask for. In its 200 action-packed pages it manages to cram in airships, pirates, Gatling guns, and an improbable super weapon. It's fast moving and fun, with a fast-paced plot and endearing characters." — *SFRevu*

BONESHAKER

"Maternal love faces formidable challenges in this stellar steampunk tale. . . . Intelligent, exceptionally well written and showcasing a phenomenal strong female protagonist who embodies the complexities inherent in motherhood, this yarn is a must-read for the discerning steampunk fan." — *Publishers Weekly,* starred review

"Priest has a knack for instantly creating quirky, likable, memorable characters that keep the goings-on interesting even when no one's under fire or in danger of being eaten. . . . And setting the steampunk technology at the fringe of the American frontier gives a refreshing spin to a concept now being mined commercially for every possible nugget of bookstore gold." — *The Roanoke Times*

"Zombies, steam-powered technology, airships, pirates, and mad scientists—what more could you want? How about great storytelling, compelling characters, and an interesting plot? Priest combines all of these things and somehow even more." — *Library Journal*

"[*Boneshaker* gives] richly defined characters a real world to inhabit, no matter how fantastic the story. Add excellent characterization and a concept second to none, and *Boneshaker* proves to be one of 2009's best novels and is not to be missed." — *Fantasy Magazine*

"The fast pace of the narrative with its memorable battle scenes and snappy, clever dialogue will keep you hooked and not wanting to put the book down, and once you have finished it you will certainly be left wanting more." — The Book Zone (for Boys)

"Cherie Priest's *Boneshaker* is a veritable grab bag of subgenre tropes. But, fortunately, it's far less about clockwork and brass than it is about human adaptability and the shifting nature of the American Dream."
— i09.com

"*Boneshaker* is a cross-genre book that should be sought out by readers of fantasy and horror alike. It's consistently inventive and entertaining. It's also well written and a hell of a lot of fun to read."
— *Chiaroscuro*

"A mash-up of action, history and science that is everything good about steampunk while maintaining a decidedly original Pacific Northwest twist. If you like the genre, you'll love this and if you've been worried that it's getting stale or trendy then you will be thrilled with Priest's way of taking the formula and turning it inside out. . . . Give Cherie Priest fifteen minutes of your time, trust me—you won't look back." — *Bookslut*

"A fast-moving story filled with cool steampunk technology and scary zombies. Fans of science fiction will find much to enjoy here. An impressive and auspicious genre-hopping adventure."
— *Kirkus Reviews*

"Riveting adventure story; great characters; perfectly captures the flavors of the steampunk and zombie subgenres. [It's got] a great hook; a steampunk/zombie mash-up is instantly appealing. The question is whether it can last the length of a novel. In short: absolutely. *Boneshaker* simply pulls you in and doesn't let go."
— SF Signal

"Think *The Wild Wild West* meets Fallout (a videogame series) meets George Romero. . . . The story was a lot of fun, the setting was creative, and I cared about the characters. . . . In short, I immensely enjoyed *Boneshaker* and can't wait to read more books in the Clockwork Century series." — Fantasy Book Critic

"There are plenty of alternate Civil War novels, but none quite like Cherie Priest's *Boneshaker*. . . . A fantastic whirlwind tour of an alternate history and a steampunk version of *The Lord of the Flies*."
— *BookPage*

"If anyone can force steampunk into the mainstream reader's consciousness, it is Cherie Priest. . . . This world's texture is luscious and deep—and it will be interesting to see what happens in it next."
— *Locus*

FATHOM

"Equal parts horror, contemporary fantasy and apocalyptic thriller . . . Priest's haunting lyricism and graceful narrative are complemented by the solemn, cynical thematic undercurrents with a tangible gravity and depth. This is arguably her most ambitious—and accomplished—work to date." — *Publishers Weekly,* starred review

"Priest masterfully weaves a complex tapestry of interlocking plots, motivations, quests, character arcs and background stories to produce an exquisitely written novel with a rich and lush atmosphere."

— *Montreal Gazette*

"*Fathom* is an odd gumbo of disparate ingredients, containing elements reminiscent of the Pirates of the Caribbean movies, Alan Moore's *Swamp Thing* comic and Stephen King's most recent novel, *Duma Key*. It is, however, its own unique thing, an atmospheric war between elemental beings. Priest does a good job of coordinating the action sequences, making dangerously unstable Bernice and down-to-earth Nia a formidable set of antagonists."

— *San Francisco Chronicle*

"[Priest's] creative vision is unlike anything else in contemporary fantasy." — *Booklist*

"[Priest] again demonstrates her keen eye for detail and ambiance as she re-creates an enchanting part of America as the setting for a tale of horror of biblical proportions." — *Library Journal*

"Pleasantly offbeat, with plenty of vivid, compelling action sequences." — *Kirkus Reviews*

THOSE WHO WENT REMAIN THERE STILL

"Priest's tightly constructed novel qualifies as a 'weird Western,' in the tradition of Joe R. Lansdale's early work, Nancy Collins' *Walking Wolf*, George R.R. Martin's *Fevre Dream* and Emma Bull's *Territory*. . . . According to her introduction, the author's mother refused to read this book because it was too strange and scary. That's a good enough recommendation for me." — *Rocky Mountain News*

"Cherie Priest continues her exploration of place and America's ghostly history. Her stories and novels are exquisite in the way they tap into our national consciousness. . . . Priest is not to be missed and this is certainly one of her best pieces of work to date." — *Bookslut*

DREADFUL SKIN

"*Dreadful Skin*'s design is carefully crafted to evoke the penny dreadfuls and melodramas so popular in the nineteenth century, [but] Priest is tackling classic genre questions that feature prominently in such nineteenth-century speculative works as Mary Shelley's *Frankenstein*, or *The Modern Prometheus* and Bram Stoker's *Dracula*: What separates humans from monsters? How well can we control our beastly instincts? Like her genre forebears, Priest doesn't offer any easy answers, and her work is all the more memorable as a result." — Strange Horizons

"While there is still no archetypal werewolf novel in the way *Dracula* serves for vampires, *Dreadful Skin* comes closer in my opinion to demonstrating just how seductive and soul-destroying lycanthropy could be." — *Weird Tales*

"[Priest] is already a strong voice in dark fantasy and could, with care, be a potent antidote for much of what is lacking elsewhere in the genre this decade." — *Rambles*

"A smash bang of a story; a tale that draws readers in from the very beginning and keeps you turning pages long into the night . . . This one crosses all the genre lines and soundly delivers on the promise of good storytelling. A reader could not ask for anything more from a fiction writer, and Cherie Priest, thankfully, has given us her best."

— *Bookslut*

"A werewolf-hunting nun, characters portrayed with empathy and skill, Gorey-esque illustrations, high adventure, and pathos—there's nothing to dislike about *Dreadful Skin*. Absolutely nothing."

— JESS NEVINS, author of *The Encyclopedia of Fantastic Victoriana*

"When one must become a monster in order to kill a monster, can the hunt still be justified? This book raises tantalizing philosophical questions about good and evil as well as the roles of hunter and prey."

— *Publishers Weekly*

FOUR AND TWENTY BLACKBIRDS

"Southern Gothic at its best. An absorbing mystery told with humour and bite."

— KELLEY ARMSTRONG,
bestselling author of the Women of the Otherworld series

"Cherie Priest has created a chilling page-turner in her debut novel. Her voice is rich, earthy, soulful, and deliciously southern as she weaves a disturbing yarn like a master! Awesome—gives you goosebumps!"

— L.A. BANKS,

bestselling author of the Vampire Huntress Legend series

"Breathlessly readable, palpably atmospheric, and compellingly suspenseful, *Four and Twenty Blackbirds* is a considerable debut. It's written with great control and fluency, and it looks like the start of quite a career." — RAMSEY CAMPBELL, World Horror Grand Master

"Spooky and engrossing, this revenge play is as sticky as a salmagundi made from blood and swamp dirt. Priest can write scenes that are jump-out-of-your-skin scary. This is the first installment in what I can only hope will be a long and terrifying friendship."

— CORY DOCTOROW, author of *Makers*

"Fine writing, humor, thrills, real scares, the touch of the occult . . . had me from the first page. I read straight through. An absolutely wonderful debut, and a book not to be missed."

— HEATHER GRAHAM,

New York Times bestselling author of the Bone Island trilogy

"Wonderful. Enchanting. Amazing and original fiction that will satisfy that buttery Southern taste, as well as that biting aftertaste of the dark side. I loved it."

— JOE R. LANSDALE,

Stoker and Edgar award-winning author of *The Bottoms*

"Cherie Priest kicks ass! *Four and Twenty Blackbirds* is lush, rich, intense, and as dark and dangerous as a gator-ridden swamp."
— MAGGIE SHAYNE,
New York Times bestselling author of *Kiss me, Kill Me*

"A remarkably assured debut, a creepy modern-day Southern gothic that doesn't rely on cliché but delivers an emotional, powerful tale of self-discovery and the supernatural." — *San Francisco Chronicle*

"Ghost stories are a dime a dozen, so it's especially satisfying when one comes along that makes you forget all the others you've read, and sucks you into the narrative so completely that you'll stay up all night finishing it because you can't wait to find out what happens next—and because you're too creeped out to go to sleep. . . . A stunning debut novel, one that displays the finely-honed prose and tightly-drawn characterizations of a master craftsman."
— *Orson Scott Card's Intergalactic Medicine Show*

"What do you get when you weave together a ghost story, a voodoo mystery, a family curse, a sharp-tongued protective aunt, a murderous young man intent on doing 'God's Will,' and a bullheaded young woman determined to learn her origins? The answer: *Four and Twenty Blackbirds*, a fantastic debut novel by Cherie Priest that leads the reader on a merry chase down a not-so-primrose path from her home in Tennessee to the desolation of a condemned insane asylum, and finally to a fetid swamp in Florida. . . . Close the doors, turn off the phone, get a glass of sweet tea and settle into your favorite reading chair. This is one you're not going to want to put down."
— *Black Gate* magazine

"Priest kills as a stylist. Debut novel? You could have fooled me. *Four and Twenty Blackbirds* feels like it was written by an author with the assurance and experience of already having many books under her belt. . . . The narrator's voice is pitch-perfect, the cast wonderfully eccentric and realized, the plot suitably puzzling and steeped in mystery, and that setting. . . . In other words, the book has everything going for it and you should definitely pick up a copy to see for yourself." — CHARLES DE LINT, *Fantasy and Science Fiction*

"The classic Southern gothic gets an edgy modern makeover in Priest's debut novel [and] Eden is a heroine for the aging Buffy crowd." — *Publishers Weekly*

WINGS TO THE KINGDOM

"This is an excellent work, rich in local flavor, nicely steeped in goosebumps, and filled with characters you want to know more about. Well done." — *Bookgasm*

"The plot, which begins slowly by setting the stage, builds a roiling crescendo and climaxes in an explosive scene at the top of the tower at the battlefield's edge. The flamboyant mix of ghosts, the preternatural Old Green Eyes, and murder keeps one on edge." — *Booklist*

"A consummately crafted novel that is neither fish nor fowl, but simply a wonderfully written tale of imagination, the supernatural all wrapped up in a deep south family saga . . . These Eden Moore books, put simply, rock" — *The Agony Column*

"I'm more than ecstatic to have discovered Cherie Priest so early on. Ten years down the line when she's got a handful of books out and everyone is tossing her name around like she's Stephen King's holy granddaughter, I'll gladly smile and nod, maybe throw out a 'I knew her when.'" — Fantasy Book Spot

NOT FLESH NOR FEATHERS

"Chock-full of chilling details and soaked to the bone with suspense."
— *Southern Living*

"This one has all the elements of a good ghost story: family secrets, mysterious disappearances and Tennessee River zombies attacking the town. Well-written, quick paced and detailed, every page is a shivering delight." — *BookPage*

"Priest's tale crackles with action and occult thrills, especially in the scenes of the inundated city reeling under the double assault of Mother Nature and the supernatural. Fans will find this her most assured outing yet." — *Publishers Weekly*